Gateway
B1+
Student's Book
David Spencer
MACMILLAN

Contents

B1+

Listening	Writing	Speaking	Exam success/Study skills
Describing personality Describing pets and personalities Song: *She's leaving home* Meetings and introductions	Describing a famous person Describing appearance with look Making notes An informal email	Describing yourself Pair interviews Asking for personal information	Reading: True/false activities Grammar: Form, use and meaning Listening: Identifying the speaker Studying: Taking responsibility
Describing accommodation Hurricanes – radio programme Marco Polo Buying a train ticket	Past habits Making notes Giving emphasis – a holiday postcard	Giving opinions Talking about a special journey Planning a film Talking about extreme weather Role-play: At a ticket office	Writing: Checking your work Vocabulary: Learning new words Speaking: Having a conversation / Everyday expressions
Describing places and buildings in a city The Erasmus project Describing photos – personal opinions	Making notes An informal letter describing a place	Describing places and buildings Describing photos Preferences and personal opinions	Reading: Missing sentences / Prediction Use of English: Multiple-choice cloze activities Writing: Steps in the writing process
Food qualities The US Fast Food Industry Life in the year 2050 – predictions	Making notes A poem of apology Explanations of words and phrases in context Invitations and replies – formal and informal	Describing food Making predictions Presenting a project Making plans Pronunciation: Intonation in suggestions and offers Role-play: An invitation to a meal	Grammar: Knowing which structure to use Speaking: Negotiating Writing: Transactional tasks Vocabulary: Prefixes and suffixes
Instructions University life Extra-curricular activities Describing photos	Descriptions and opinions Making notes Formal letter of application	Pair interviews – school Giving advice and comparing ideas Talking about university courses Making hypotheses Describing photos Role-play: An interview	Use of English: Cloze activities Speaking: Spoken and written language Reading: Reading for general and specific information Writing: Following the instructions

1 Identity Match

Grammar ‣ Present simple and present continuous
‣ State and action verbs

Vocabulary ‣ Appearance ‣ Personality
‣ Synonyms and partial synonyms

Speaking ‣ Asking for and giving personal information

Writing ‣ An informal email describing people

‣ Vocabulary

Appearance

1 **Work with a partner. Put these words in the correct column.**

bald blonde curly dark fair good-looking
~~handsome~~ long medium-height overweight plain
pretty ~~short~~ straight tall ~~thin~~ ugly well-built

Build	Height	Hair	General
thin	*short*	*short*	*handsome*

2 1.01 **Listen, check and repeat.**

3a PRONUNCIATION 1.02 **Listen to these words. Do we pronounce *gh* in these words?**

height straight weight

3b **We only pronounce *gh* in two of these words. Which ones? How do we pronounce *gh* in each of these two words?**

although bought caught daughter enough ghost through

4 SPEAKING **Work with a partner. Take it in turns to describe the people in the photos.**

He's short and a little overweight. He's got long, dark hair.

Personality

5 **Match the personality adjectives with their opposites.**

1 serious a untidy
2 lazy b unfriendly
3 tidy c talkative
4 quiet d cheerful, funny
5 patient e hard-working
6 friendly f impatient

6 **Match these personality adjectives with their definitions.**

arrogant bossy clever nice
reliable selfish shy

1 When you think you are better or more important than other people.
2 When you only think about yourself and you don't care about other people.
3 Good, friendly, kind.
4 Good at learning and understanding things.
5 When you are not very confident or comfortable with other people.
6 When people can depend on you or count on you to do something.
7 When you are always telling other people what to do.

7 LISTENING 1.03 **Listen to four people talking about themselves. What adjective of personality best describes each person?**

1 Rose ....
2 William ....
3 Jessica ....
4 Brandon ....

8a SPEAKING **Choose five adjectives from 5 and 6 which describe you. Tell your partner your adjectives and say why you chose them.**

I'm quite shy because I feel a bit nervous when I meet new people.

8b **Now tell the class about your partner.**

Maria chose the adjective 'shy' because she feels a bit nervous when she meets new people.

1 Work with a partner. Discuss these questions.

1 What is an avatar?
2 Do you or your partner have an avatar? If you do, describe their appearance.
3 Why do you think avatars are popular?

2 Read the text. Complete the table with information about the people and their avatars.

	Real life	Online
Jason Rowe		
Kim Nyvang		
Elizabeth Brown		
April Hatch		

Avatars and their Creators

1 In Hindu mythology the word 'avatar' described the descent of a god into a physical form on Earth. Nowadays, an avatar is a visual representation of a person on the Internet. At this very moment, millions of people around the world are chatting and interacting in online games and most of them use avatars to do this.

2 So, how do people create their avatars? A photographer and journalist called Robbie Cooper is very interested in the connection between avatars and the real people behind them. His book *Alter Ego: Avatars and their Creators* looks at particular examples in the world of online computer games. Generally, people do things in different ways. For example, some people make their avatars very similar to their real identity, either in appearance or personality. Other people use their avatars to express a different side of their personality. And occasionally people decide to make an avatar that is almost completely opposite to their real identity, showing them not as they are, but as they would like to be.

3 Take the example of Jason Rowe. He has severe muscular dystrophy in real life. He needs a special machine to live and breathe. But when he plays online he is a tall, strong, well-built, futuristic soldier. Jason plays online 80 hours a week and he enjoys it because other people treat him totally normally. When people meet him in real life, he finds that they are uncomfortable because of his appearance. They forget that, apart from his appearance, he is totally normal. In his case, his avatar helps to break down barriers.

4 Kim Nyvang from Denmark is medium-height, thin with short fair hair. He's happy the way he is, but he thinks it's funny to be a strong, well-built barbarian with long black hair in the online game he plays. He plays 27 hours a week. He's married in real life but has a different wife in his online game. He asked his real wife for permission before he got married in the virtual world!

5 Another player is Elizabeth Brown. Her avatar looks like her, but the way she wants to look when she's older. So, instead of having long brown hair, her avatar is grey-haired and her face is just a little fatter. Elizabeth likes older people who are nice and friendly and she wants to be like that in the future.

6 Then there is April Hatch, who says that she is a very shy person. At first, her avatar was very different from her real self, but she discovered that her avatar makes more friends when she is natural, more like the real April Hatch. Now April feels more confident and as a result she doesn't spend so many hours playing online.

7 It seems that avatars are becoming more and more popular. They're reading out the news, selling products and they're even teaching languages, for example at www.speak2me.cn where a beautiful avatar called Lucy helps Chinese-speaking people to practise their English. Avatars are everywhere. But don't forget the real people behind them.

EXAM SUCCESS

You are going to do a true/false reading exercise. What do you think is a good procedure for doing this type of exercise? EXAM SUCCESS ▶ page 150

3 Read the text again and decide if the statements are true (T) or false (F). Write the number(s) of the line(s) where you found the answer.

1 Robbie Cooper wrote his book because he is interested in online computer games. T/F ....
2 Not everybody creates avatars in the same way. T/F ....
3 Jason Rowe finds it difficult to make friends with his avatar. T/F ....
4 Kim Nyvang would like to have a different appearance. T/F ....
5 Kim's real wife knows that Kim has a virtual wife too. T/F ....
6 Elizabeth Brown wants to copy her avatar's appearance and personality one day. T/F ....
7 April Hatch's avatar now shows April as she would like to be, but isn't. T/F ....
8 April's avatar has made a positive change to her life. T/F ....

4 Correct the false sentences in 3.

5 Find words in the text with similar meanings to these words.

1 connected to the Internet *(paragraph 1)*
2 communicating with and reacting to somebody or something *(paragraph 1)*
3 from time to time *(paragraph 2)*
4 things that stop people from communicating or working with others *(paragraph 3)*
5 the right to be able to do something *(paragraph 4)*
6 has a similar appearance to *(paragraph 5)*
7 be similar to *(paragraph 5)*
8 believing in your abilities *(paragraph 6)*

6 SPEAKING What about *you*?

1 Do you like playing online games? Why/Why not?
2 If you have an avatar, is it similar to you or different?

GRAMMAR GUIDE

Present simple and present continuous

1a Look at sentences 1–7 and match them to rules a–g.

1 Avatars are becoming more and more popular.
2 Jason plays online 80 hours a week.
3 You're always playing on the computer. Stop it!
4 At this very moment, millions of people are using avatars.
5 People do things in different ways.
6 This journalist is studying the connection between avatars and their creators.
7 Computers use electricity.

We use the present simple for:

a routines and habits. ....
b things that are always or generally true. ....
c scientific facts. ....

We use the present continuous for:

d actions that are happening now or near the moment of speaking. ....
e actions that are temporary or not a normal routine. ....
f actions that happen very often and annoy the speaker. ....
g changing situations. ....

1b Rewrite sentences 1 and 2 in the negative and then in the question form.

GRAMMAR REFERENCE ▶ page 16

▶ STUDY SKILLS

What are the two main things we need to know about a grammatical structure to be able to use it correctly?

STUDY SKILLS ▶ page 146

2 Look at these sentences. The words in bold are all adverbs of frequency. Choose the correct alternative in the rules a–d.

1 I'm **never** late for school.
2 We don't **usually** eat much.
3 She **sometimes** comes at the weekend.
4 We **occasionally** go out during the week.
5 She's **always** the last person to arrive.
6 They're **always** telling me what to do.
7 I **rarely** travel by plane.
8 They **often** play this song in concert.

a Adverbs of frequency usually go *after/before* the verb *to be*.
b Adverbs of frequency usually go just *after/before* main verbs.
c Adverbs of frequency usually go with the *present continuous/present simple*.
d The adverb of frequency *always/sometimes* goes with the *present continuous/present simple* to talk about frequent actions that annoy the person who is speaking.

3 Complete the text with the present simple or present continuous form of the verbs and adverbs.

I **(a)** .... (be) really angry with my brother at the moment because he's **(b)** .... (always use) the computer when I want to use it. He **(c)** .... (not usually play) computer games but he **(d)** .... (become) more and more interested in online games at the moment. Right now he **(e)** .... (make) a new avatar for his favourite game. It's funny because my brother **(f)** .... (not usually wear) anything apart from jeans, T-shirts and trainers, but his avatar **(g)** .... (have got) really spectacular clothes. People **(h)** .... (usually say) that boys **(i)** .... (play) more computer games than girls but I think that **(j)** .... (change). The only reason that I **(k)** .... (not often play) is because when it's my turn to use the computer I **(l)** .... (always do) my homework on it first. Oh, good! My brother **(m)** .... (finish) now. It's 7pm and he **(n)** .... (usually go) to see his friend at 7pm. My turn to use the computer at last!

4 **Write two true sentences about you or other people with these words. Write one in the present simple and one in the present continuous. You can write negative sentences if necessary.**

do homework eat fast food go to school
play computer games read study English
watch TV wear jeans

My mum never wears jeans. I'm not wearing jeans at the moment because we can't wear them at our school.

5 **Read your sentences to your partner. How many of your sentences are the same?**

6 **SPEAKING Interview your partner using these questions.**

1 What are the first two things you do each morning?
2 What are the last two things you do each night?
3 What are people in your class doing right now?
4 In what ways are you, or people in your family, changing?
5 What do you usually do at the weekend?
6 What are members of your family doing now?
7 How do you usually spend your summer holidays?
8 Is anybody always doing things that annoy you? Who and what?

What are the first two things you do each morning?

I get out of bed and eat my breakfast.

7 **Write at least three more questions like the ones in 6. Use them to continue interviewing your partner.**

What subjects are you studying this year?

What is your favourite subject?

What sports are you doing this year?

Developing vocabulary

Synonyms and partial synonyms

1 **Look at these words. Do they have similar meanings? If there is a difference between the words, what is the difference?**

attractive beautiful good-looking
handsome pretty

2 **Match these words to their synonyms or partial synonyms. Each word can have more than one synonym or partial synonym.**

bright – intelligent – clever

bright cheerful clever difficult
elderly fat friendly glad
happy hard intelligent old
outgoing overweight skinny
slim sociable thin

3 **Choose the best alternative in each sentence. If there is no difference, choose both.**

1 Don't call your grandmother old/elderly! Call her old/elderly.
2 Why are you angry, Dad? I didn't say you're fat/overweight. I just said you're a little fat/overweight.
3 That actor is really attractive/good-looking.
4 My cousin is always smiling. She's a really glad/cheerful person.
5 You need to eat more. You don't look well. You look a bit skinny/slim.
6 This question is really hard/difficult. I'm not clever/bright enough to do it.

4 **Prepare a description of a famous person. Use words from 1 and 2 and from page 6.**

5 **Work with a partner. Describe the person you chose in 4. Can your partner guess who it is?**

She's a very beautiful actress. She's tall and slim. She's got long dark hair and big eyes. She isn't very old. I think she's probably quite bright. She makes a lot of action and adventure films.

Is it Angelina Jolie?

Yes it is!

He's a politician. He's got short dark hair. He's very intelligent. He isn't very old. He's quite slim.

Is it Barack Obama?

English national identity

International cultural knowledge
English icons

1 Look at the photos. They show some things that people often think of as 'typically English'. With your partner, can you think of any other things that are typically English?

2 Read the text. What other English 'icons' appear in the text? Did you predict any of them?

Icons: a Portrait of England

People usually have a clear idea of a Scottish, Welsh or Irish national identity. But when people think of England they often make the mistake of thinking that England is Britain. In fact, England has such a cultural mix that it can be difficult to decide on a national identity. The government decided to spend £1 million on an Internet project called *Icons: a Portrait of England*. The idea was to nominate English icons and then let the public vote to decide which they think are the best icons to show England's national identity. The project defined an icon as something of special importance in England's culture, history or way of life.

Not everybody in England agrees with the results, but they are often fascinating. Take food, for example. The whole world knows about English fish and chips or roast beef (whether they like them or not is another thing!). So it's not surprising that both dishes are in the final list of English icons. But some people might not expect chicken tikka masala to be in the list too. But of course this dish of Indian origin is a perfect example of how two cultures can come together to create something great. A famous politician recently named this curry the nation's favourite dish.

Three cars appear in the list of icons. First we have the ultimate status symbol, the Rolls Royce. More than 100 years ago, Charles Rolls and Henry Royce came together with one idea in mind – to make the best car in the world. The Rolls Royce is world-famous for its luxury and quality. The second iconic car became famous for its quality, not for luxury – the Land Rover. You can find Land Rovers in deserts, jungles, and other places where there aren't even any roads. They first appeared in 1948 and the quality is so good that people still drive 70% of all the original Land Rovers ever built. The third car is one of the world's smallest but most popular cars – the Mini. Winner of rallies, star of films like *The Italian Job* and TV series like *Mr Bean*, the Mini is as popular now as ever.

Two very different items of clothing appear as English icons. First, we have the bowler hat. This first appeared in 1850, made by the Bowler Brothers. Now we associate it (and a black umbrella, of course) with city businessmen and bankers. But originally this hard hat was for people working in the country, to protect their heads. And then we have the mini-skirt. The British fashion designer Mary Quant made the first mini-skirt in 1965. It quickly became a symbol of the 'swinging sixties', the decade when English music, films and fashion caught the attention of the world. Of course, one thing that could stop you wearing a mini-skirt is one of the most infamous English icons – the weather!

3 Read the text again and answer the questions.

1 Why did the government create the 'Icons' Internet project?
2 What exactly is an 'icon' in this project?
3 Why is chicken tikka masala such a good English icon?
4 Where does the Rolls Royce get its name from?
5 What is the secret of the Land Rover's popularity?
6 Which types of people wear bowler hats?
7 What was the origin of the bowler hat?
8 Why were the 1960s important for England?

P PROJECT

4a Work in groups. What icons are typical of your country? Make a list. They can be food, drink, sports or clothes.

4b Each person in the group should choose an icon, find out information about it, and look for photos or pictures.

4c In your group, decide how to present your information to the rest of the class.

Popular culture
She's Leaving Home by The Beatles

5 1.04 The album *Sgt. Pepper's Lonely Hearts Club Band* by The Beatles is the only album to appear in the Internet project *Icons: A Portrait of England*.

Listen to this song from the album and put the pictures in the correct order.

1 .... 2 .... 3 .... 4 .... 5 ....

6 Listen again and read the words. Who says the parts of the song in *italics*?

7 Before the daughter leaves home, she leaves a letter. Imagine you are the daughter. Write the letter.

8 Now you are the girl's parents. Write a reply to your daughter's letter.

9 What about *you*?

1 Do you know any Beatles songs? Do you like them? Why/Why not?
2 What type(s) of music do you like?

She's Leaving Home

Wednesday morning at five o'clock as the day begins
Silently closing her bedroom door
Leaving the note that she hoped would say more
She goes downstairs to the kitchen, clutching her handkerchief
Quietly turning the backdoor key
Stepping outside, she is free.

She (*We gave her most of our lives*)
is leaving (*Sacrificed most of our lives*)
home (*We gave her everything money could buy*)
She's leaving home after living alone (*Bye, bye*)
For so many years.

Father snores as his wife gets into her dressing gown
Picks up the letter that's lying there
Standing alone at the top of the stairs
She breaks down and cries to her husband
'Daddy, our baby's gone.
Why would she treat us so thoughtlessly?
How could she do this to me?'

She (*We never thought of ourselves*)
is leaving (*Never a thought for ourselves*)
home (*We struggled hard all our lives to get by*)
She's leaving home after living alone (*Bye, bye*)
For so many years.

Friday morning at nine o'clock she is far away
Waiting to keep the appointment she made
Meeting a man from the motor trade

She (*What did we do that was wrong?*)
is having (*We didn't know it was wrong.*)
fun (*Fun is the one thing that money can't buy*)
Something inside that was always denied (*Bye, bye*)
For so many years.
She's leaving home (*Bye, bye*)

INSIDE INFORMATION

- The Beatles are probably the most important group in the history of pop music.
- The four members of The Beatles were Paul McCartney, John Lennon, George Harrison and Ringo Starr. They were all born in Liverpool. Their first record appeared in 1962 and in 1970 they separated. John Lennon was murdered in New York in 1980. George Harrison died of cancer in 2001.
- *Sgt. Pepper's Lonely Hearts Club Band* appeared in 1967 and was an instant classic.

▸ WORD BOOSTER

Match the words and definitions.

1 clutching — a without thinking
2 snores — b makes sounds when sleeping
3 dressing gown — c not allowed
4 thoughtlessly — d something you wear at home e.g. over pyjamas
5 struggled — e tried hard to do something difficult
6 denied — f holding tight in your hand

Listening

1 Look at these people and pets. Work with a partner. Which pet do you think belongs to each person? Guess.

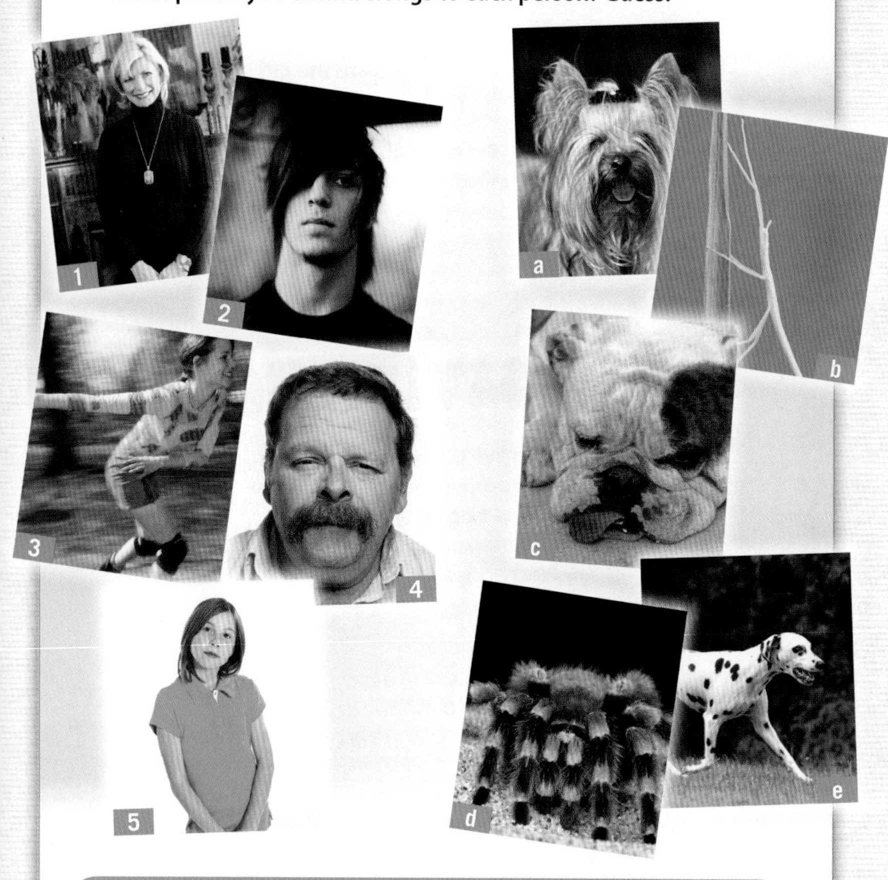

EXAM SUCCESS

In the next task you match the speakers with the correct information. What should you do before you listen? EXAM SUCCESS ▶ page 150

2 LISTENING 1.05 **Listen to the five people talking about their pets on a TV programme. Check your predictions in 1. How many did you get right?**

1 .... 4 ....
2 .... 5 ....
3 ....

3 Listen again. Which speaker …

		1	2	3	4	5
1	sounds like their pet?					
2	believes they understand what their pet is saying?					
3	doesn't own their ideal pet?					
4	isn't very active?					
5	owns a pet which tries to make them happy?					
6	enjoys physical activity?					
7	doesn't seem to enjoy doing housework?					
8	hasn't got a very healthy lifestyle?					

4 SPEAKING **What about *you*?**

1 Have you got a pet? If not, do you know anyone who has a pet?
2 Do you think you and your pet are similar in any way?
3 Do you know anyone who is similar to their pet?

Grammar in context

GRAMMAR GUIDE

State and action verbs

1a Look at these sentences. Do the verbs in bold describe states and situations or do they describe actions?

1 We**'ve** got a healthy lifestyle.
2 I **don't own** a pet at the moment.
3 We **love** animals.
4 Now she **likes** doing sport.
5 He **sounds** like his pet.
6 She **looks** like her pet.
7 Now I **know** that pets and their owners can be similar.
8 I **don't understand** why they're similar.

1b Look at the sentences again. Are they in the present simple or present continuous? Why?

1c Put the verbs in bold from 1a in the correct lists.

1 verbs of feeling:
.................., ...,
hate, want, prefer, need

2 verbs of thinking:
.................., ...,
believe, remember, mean

3 verbs of the senses:
.................., ...,
hear, see, taste, smell, feel, seem

4 verbs of possession:
.................., ...,
belong

GRAMMAR REFERENCE ▶ page 16

2 Decide if each verb describes a state or an action. Then choose the correct alternative.

1 I *look/am looking* for my pet snake. *Do you know/Are you knowing* where it is?
2 Isn't he attractive? He *looks/is looking* like a film star.
3 My sister *has got/is having* a new pet.
4 Jack can't speak to you at the moment. He *has/is having* a shower.
5 *Do you know/Are you knowing* the answer now?
6 I *don't understand/am not understanding* a word you're saying.
7 OK, OK, don't get angry. I *believe/am believing* you.
8 I *don't like/am not liking* this film. I *want/am wanting* to leave now.

3 Complete the sentences with the correct form of these verbs.

feel hear look seem smell sound taste

1. I love listening to that new Coldplay CD. It .... great.
2. Mmmm. What are you cooking? It .... delicious. I want to try it.
3. What's the matter? You don't .... very cheerful today.
4. Emma .... like her sister. Their personalities are very different but their appearance is almost identical.
5. There is too much sugar in this coffee. It .... too sweet.
6. Can you .... the sound that the bird is making?
7. Your hand is cold. It .... like ice!

4a Write sentences about the things in the pictures. For each sentence use one of the verbs and at least one of the adjectives.

Verbs

feel look smell sound taste

Adjectives

cold	delicious	frightening	great	hard
horrible	loud	soft	warm	wet

4b Read out your sentences to your partner, but do not give the name of the things you are describing. Can they identify which things you are describing?

I think it feels cold and wet, but I'm not sure. It looks frightening!

Is it a snake?

Yes, it is!

5 Complete the dialogue with the present simple or the present continuous form of the verbs given.

RYAN: Hi, Molly. How are you? You **(a)** .... (sound) really happy.
MOLLY: I am. I **(b)** .... (have) a great time.
RYAN: Where are you?
MOLLY: I **(c)** .... (stay) at my cousin Lily's house.
RYAN: Lily? Ah, yes. Now I **(d)** .... (remember). She's the one who **(e)** .... (have) a house near the coast.
MOLLY: That's right. Well, in fact, the house **(f)** .... (belong) to a good friend of my cousin. She always **(g)** .... (let) her stay when she **(h)** .... (want).
RYAN: And what **(i)** .... you .... (do) now?
MOLLY: I **(j)** .... (get) the table ready for dinner. Lily **(k)** .... (cook) really well. She **(l)** .... (make) something special for tonight. It **(m)** .... (smell) great.
RYAN: Stop! You **(n)** .... (make) me hungry. Anyway, I **(o)** .... (need) to go now. Somebody **(p)** .... (call) me. I'll phone again soon.
MOLLY: OK. Bye.

6 SPEAKING Now complete these sentences about yourself and then predict your partner's answers. Compare predictions.

YOU

1. You think .... sounds great.
2. You think .... looks really attractive.
3. You usually feel .... on Monday morning.
4. You always remember ....
5. You don't understand ....
6. You don't need .... to be happy.
7. You don't believe in ....
8. The most important thing you own is ....

YOUR PARTNER

1. Your partner thinks .... sounds great.
2. Your partner thinks .... looks really attractive.
3. Your partner usually feels .... on Monday morning.
4. Your partner always remembers ....
5. Your partner doesn't understand ....
6. Your partner doesn't need .... to be happy.
7. Your partner doesn't believe in ....
8. The most important thing your partner owns is ....

▶ STUDY SKILLS

How well did you do the last activity? Why is it important to reflect on activities when you finish them?

STUDY SKILLS ▶ page 146

1 LISTENING 1.06 **Listen to a conversation between two teenagers, Megan and Ellie, on their first day of school. What are each person's hobbies?**

Megan's hobbies: ...., ...

Ellie's hobbies: ...., ..., ...

2 Can you complete the dialogue? Listen again if necessary.

MEGAN: Hi. You're Lucy's cousin, aren't you?

ELLIE: Yes, that's right. My name's Ellie.

MEGAN: I'm Megan. This is your **(a)** .... year at this school, isn't it?

ELLIE: Yes, we moved house in the summer and this school is closer to where we live now.

MEGAN: Hey, Ellie, you don't play **(b)** ...., do you? We need new players for the team.

ELLIE: I play a little, but I'm not very good.

MEGAN: Do you play any other sports?

ELLIE: I really enjoy **(c)** ...., but I'm not in a club or team or anything.

MEGAN: So, what are your other hobbies then?

ELLIE: I'm mad about music.

MEGAN: Really? Me too. What kind of music do you like?

ELLIE: I like all sorts, but my favourite is **(d)** ....

MEGAN: Now I remember! You can play the **(e)** ...., can't you? Lucy told me once.

ELLIE: Yeah, I'm in a band. We aren't **(f)** .... but I need to practise more.

MEGAN: Do you know Josh, Josh Smith? He plays the guitar too. Come on. Let me introduce you to him …

3 SPEAKING **Practise the completed dialogue in 2 with your partner.**

4 Look at the question tags in the Speaking Bank. We use question tags when we want somebody to confirm something. Choose the correct alternative.

1 We use *nouns/subject pronouns* at the end of question tags.

2 We use *auxiliary verbs and 'to be'/main verbs* in question tags.

3 Usually the question tag in an affirmative sentence is *affirmative/negative* and the question tag in a negative sentence is *affirmative/negative*.

SPEAKING BANK

Question tags

- You're Lucy's cousin, **aren't you**?
- This is your first year at this school, **isn't it**?
- You like rock music, **don't you**?
- You don't play basketball, **do you**?
- You can play an instrument, **can't you**?

5 Complete the sentences with question tags.

1 You've got a sister, ...?

2 You can't play the piano, ...?

3 That girl sings really well, ...?

4 She's your best friend, ...?

5 Your brother would like to be at this school, ...?

6 That boy isn't very tall, ...?

7 Her dad doesn't like listening to that music, ...?

8 Jamie and Becky can swim really fast, ...?

6 SPEAKING **Test your partner. Tell your partner to close their book. Say the first part of the sentence and ask your partner to complete it with a question tag.**

You've got a sister, …

… haven't you?

Practice makes perfect

7a SPEAKING **Write down six things you think your partner likes or doesn't like doing in their free time.**

7b Ask your partner about their hobbies. Use question tags for confirmation and to keep the conversation going.

Tell me something about your hobbies. You like playing the guitar, don't you?

Yes, I do. I play in a band.

You play in a band with Jan, don't you?

7c When you finish, have a different conversation with a new partner.

1 Read Joe's email to his e-pal. Name the different people in the photo he attaches.

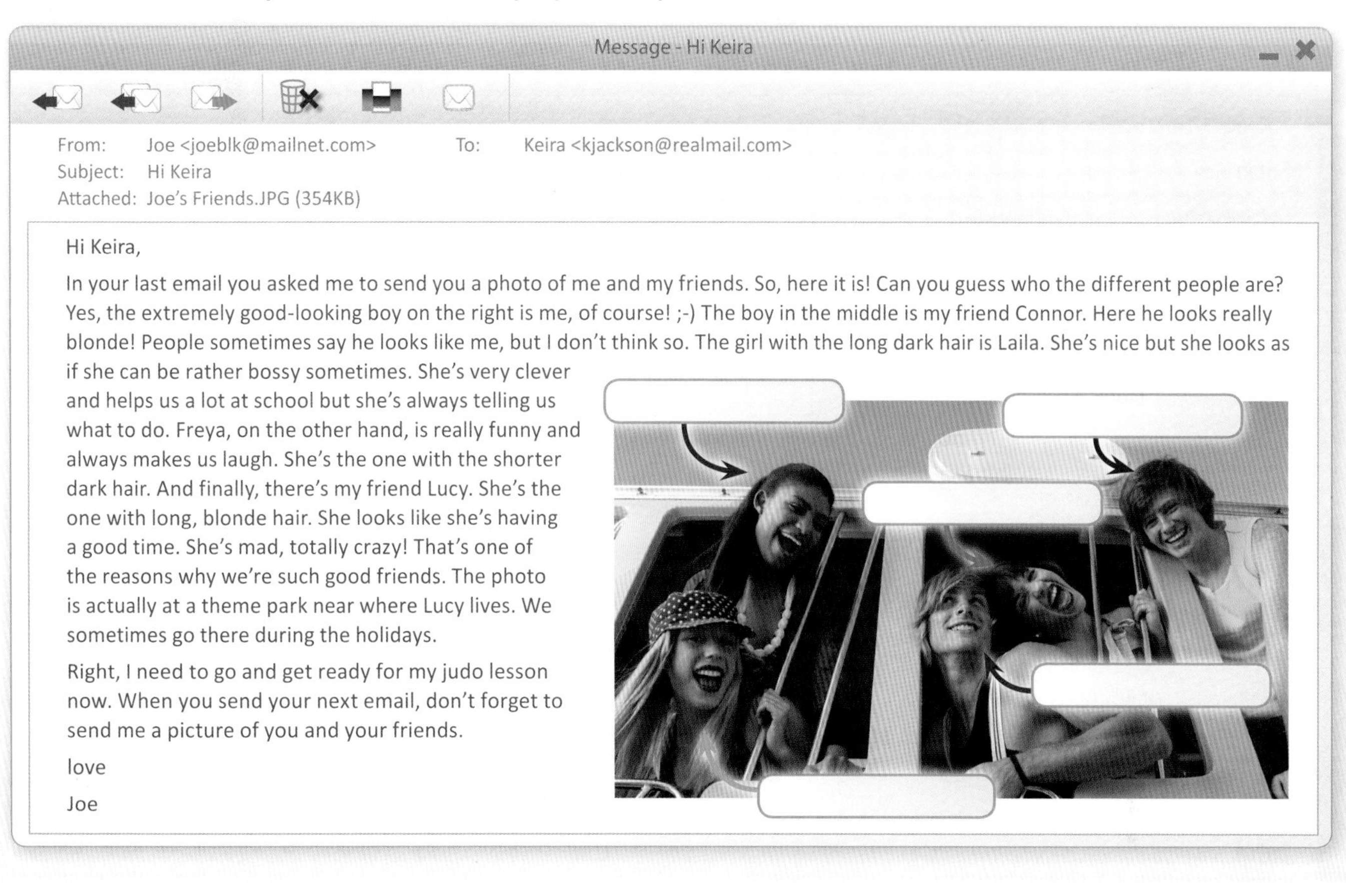

Message - Hi Keira

From: Joe <joeblk@mailnet.com> To: Keira <kjackson@realmail.com>
Subject: Hi Keira
Attached: Joe's Friends.JPG (354KB)

Hi Keira,

In your last email you asked me to send you a photo of me and my friends. So, here it is! Can you guess who the different people are? Yes, the extremely good-looking boy on the right is me, of course! ;-) The boy in the middle is my friend Connor. Here he looks really blonde! People sometimes say he looks like me, but I don't think so. The girl with the long dark hair is Laila. She's nice but she looks as if she can be rather bossy sometimes. She's very clever and helps us a lot at school but she's always telling us what to do. Freya, on the other hand, is really funny and always makes us laugh. She's the one with the shorter dark hair. And finally, there's my friend Lucy. She's the one with long, blonde hair. She looks like she's having a good time. She's mad, totally crazy! That's one of the reasons why we're such good friends. The photo is actually at a theme park near where Lucy lives. We sometimes go there during the holidays.

Right, I need to go and get ready for my judo lesson now. When you send your next email, don't forget to send me a picture of you and your friends.

love

Joe

2 Write notes about each person's personality.

Connor: ....

Lalia: ....

Freya: ....

Lucy: ....

Joe: ....

3 Look again at Joe's email and complete the examples in the Writing Bank.

Writing Bank

Descriptive language

To describe somebody's appearance we often use the verb 'look'. We can use:

1 *look + adjective* (*He looks* ....)

2 *look like + noun/pronoun* (*He looks like* ....)

3 *look like/as if + noun/pronoun + verb* (*She looks as if* ....)

We use modifying adverbs to make adjectives stronger or softer in order to give more accurate descriptions. For example, we use:

4 ...., *extremely* and *really* to make 'normal' adjectives (*good, bad*) stronger.

5 ...., *absolutely, really* and *completely* to make 'extreme' adjectives (*fantastic, awful*) stronger.

6 .... and *rather* to make 'normal' adjectives a little softer.

4 Complete these sentences to describe some of the people in the photo.

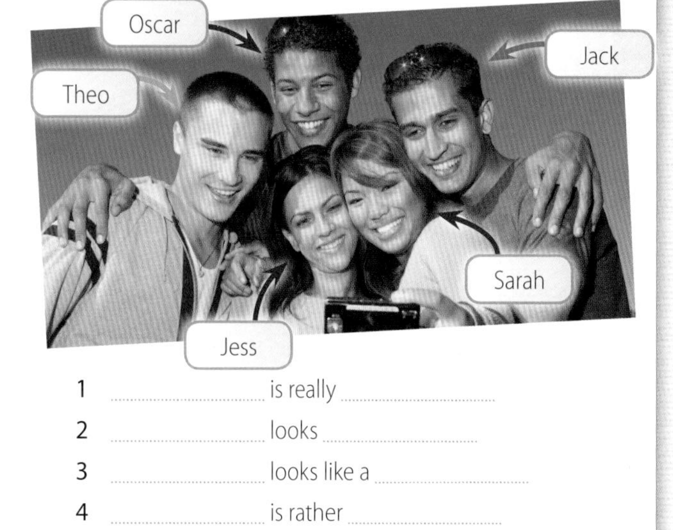

1 .... is really ....
2 .... looks ....
3 .... looks like a ....
4 .... is rather ....
5 .... is extremely ....
6 .... has got quite ....
7 .... looks as if ....

Practice makes perfect

5a Find a photo of you with friends or family. Write an email describing the people in the photo. Use the email in 1 as a model and include expressions from the Writing Bank.

5b Show your photo and description to a partner. Can they identify the people in your photo?

Language reference and revision

Grammar reference

Present simple

Form

Affirmative	I/You/We/They **start.** He/She/It **starts.**
Negative	I/You/We/They **don't (do not) start.** He/She/It **doesn't (does not) start.**
Question	**Do** I/you/we/they **start**? **Does** he/she/it **start?**
Short answers	Yes, I/you/we/they **do.** No, I/you/we/they **don't.** Yes, he/she/it **does.** No, he/she/it **doesn't.**

Use

We use the present simple to talk about:

1 regular habits and routines. *Our lessons start at 8 o'clock.*
2 permanent situations. *We live in this city.*
3 scientific facts. *The earth goes round the sun.*

Adverbs and expressions of frequency

Use

We often use **adverbs of frequency** with the present simple to talk about routines and habits. Adverbs of frequency usually go before the verb *to be* or just before main verbs.

He's always angry. She rarely goes out. We don't usually drive.

We also use other **expressions of frequency** with the present simple to talk about routines and habits. These usually go at the end of the clause/sentence.

I play tennis once/twice/three times a day/week/month/year.

Present continuous

Form

Affirmative	subject + **am/are/is** + verb+**ing** *We're working.*
Negative	subject + **am not/aren't/isn't** + verb+**ing** *She isn't watching.*
Question	**Am/Are/Is** + subject + verb+**ing?** *Are they talking?*
Short answers	Yes, subject + **am/are/is.** No, subject + **am not/ aren't/isn't**. *Yes, I am. No, they aren't.*

Use

We use the **present continuous** with time expressions such as *now, currently*, etc. to talk about:

1 actions that are happening now or near the moment of speaking. *I can't come out. I'm doing my homework now.*
2 temporary actions and situations. *I'm walking to school this week.*
  changing situations. *He's getting good at playing the guitar.*
3 actions that happen very often and annoy the speaker. *My sister is always taking my clothes.*

State and action verbs

Some verbs are not usually used in the present continuous because they describe states not actions. These are usually:

1 verbs of feeling: *like, love, hate, want, prefer, need*
2 verbs of thinking: *know, understand, believe, remember, mean, think (= have an opinion), see (= understand)*
3 verbs of the senses: *look, seem, sound, hear, see, smell, feel, appear*
4 verbs of possession: *have, own, belong*

Be careful because some verbs have different meanings. One can describe a state and the other an action.

I have two sisters. (state) *I'm having a great time.* (action)
You look angry. (state) *What are you looking at?* (action)

Vocabulary

1 Appearance

Build: overweight thin well-built
Height: medium-height short tall
Hair: bald blonde curly dark fair long short straight
General: good-looking handsome plain pretty ugly

2 Personality

arrogant bossy cheerful clever friendly funny hard-working impatient lazy nice patient quiet reliable selfish serious shy talkative tidy unfriendly untidy

3 Synonyms and partial synonyms

attractive beautiful bright cheerful clever difficult elderly fat friendly glad good-looking handsome happy hard intelligent old outgoing overweight pretty skinny slim sociable thin

4 Other words and phrases ▸ page 136

▶ Grammar revision

Present simple and present continuous

1 Are these sentences correct or not? If not, correct them.

1 I'm not usually going to school by bus.
2 You're always interrupting me. I don't like it.
3 My friends and I play sometimes football after school.
4 Adam is living in New York but he wants to come home soon.
5 Mia can't speak to you at the moment because she does her homework.
6 Where are penguins living, in the Arctic or the Antarctic?

WORKBOOK ▶ page 4 — */6 points*

2 Put the verbs given in the present simple or present continuous.

SARAH: Hey, Sam. Why **(a)** .... you .... (wear) a jacket and a tie? You **(b)** .... (not usually wear) such smart clothes.

SAM: I **(c)** .... (get ready) for a job interview. I **(d)** .... (start) to get bored this summer, sitting at home doing nothing.

SARAH: My sister and I are bored too, but that's because we **(e)** .... (work) every summer. We **(f)** .... (save) up money to buy a new computer.

WORKBOOK ▶ page 4 — */6 points*

State and action verbs

3 Choose the correct alternative.

1 Can we stop at the bank? I *need/am needing* some money.
2 Can you answer my question? *Do you know/Are you knowing* the answer?
3 How are you? *Do you have/Are you having* a good time?
4 He didn't have any money when he was small but now he *owns/is owning* three mansions!
5 What's the problem now? You *don't seem/aren't seeming* happy.
6 I loved drinking milk when I was a kid but now I *prefer/am preferring* juice or coke.
7 Why *do you look/are you looking* out of the window?
8 I don't know who this dog *belongs/is belonging* to.

WORKBOOK ▶ page 7 — */8 points*

▶ Vocabulary revision

Appearance

1 Look at the pictures and complete the sentences with these words.

bald curly overweight straight ugly well-built

1 Jane's hair is really ...., isn't it? It has no waves at all.

2 Suzanne ate a lot over Christmas and now looks a little bit ....

3 He's not very nice to look at, to be honest. He's a little bit ....

4 Steve goes to the gym three times a week so he's very strong and .... - ....

5 My dad went .... when he was in his twenties.

6 I've always wanted to have straight hair. My hair's too ....

WORKBOOK ▶ page 2 — */6 points*

Personality

2 What are the opposites of these words?

1 quiet ....
2 tidy ....
3 cheerful ....
4 stupid ....
5 friendly ....
6 hard-working ....
7 patient ....

WORKBOOK ▶ page 2 — */7 points*

Synonyms and partial synonyms

3 Write a synonym for each underlined word.

1 She's a very bright student.
2 Do you think he's attractive?
3 This question is really difficult.
4 She seems a very happy person.
5 Do you consider yourself to be an outgoing person?
6 Can you see that old lady over there?
7 Do you think that maths is hard?

WORKBOOK ▶ page 5 — */7 points*

Total */40 points*

2 Epic journeys

Grammar ‣ Past simple, past continuous and past perfect ‣ *Used to*
Vocabulary ‣ Transport and travel ‣ Accommodation
‣ Phrasal verbs connected with travel
Speaking ‣ At a train station
Writing ‣ A postcard

‣ Vocabulary

Transport and travel

1 Work with a partner. What types of transport can you see in the photos? Write them in the correct columns.

Land transport	Air transport	Water transport
motorbike		

2 With a partner, add these words to the columns. Can you think of any more words to add? Compare lists with another pair and add any new words.

ferry lorry rocket spaceship van

3 Complete the text with these words.

arrivals cancel catch delay departures fare
luggage miss platform return single ticket office

When you go to the station to **(a)** .... a train, if you don't already have a ticket you go and buy one at the **(b)** .... You can buy a **(c)** .... (if you're only going one way) or a **(d)** .... (if you're coming back). The **(e)** .... is more expensive when you travel first-class because it's more comfortable and you have more space. There isn't an extra cost for **(f)** .... – you can take at least two or three big bags.

When you have your ticket, you need to find the **(g)** .... where your train is leaving from. If you arrive late, you may **(h)** .... your train. But sometimes there can be a **(i)** .... and your train doesn't arrive on time. And sometimes, there's no train at all because they **(j)** .... it! It's important to keep looking at the information screens which show the **(k)** .... (the times that trains are coming into the station) and the **(l)** .... (the times that trains are leaving).

4 1.07 **Listen and check your answers.**

‣ STUDY SKILLS

What information do you need to write down and revise for new words which you add to your vocabulary list or notebook?
STUDY SKILLS ‣ page 146

Accommodation

5 Match the photos with these words.

bed and breakfast campsite caravan hotel
motel tent youth hostel

6 SPEAKING **Work with a partner. Explain the difference between these words.**

1 hotel/motel 2 hotel/youth hostel 3 hotel/bed and breakfast
4 tent/caravan 5 tent/campsite

A motel is a type of hotel. It's next to a big road. People usually stay there when they drive a long distance and want to rest and sleep.

7 LISTENING 1.08 **Listen to these conversations. Where are the people? Choose from these alternatives.**

bed and breakfast caravan hotel motel
platform tent ticket office youth hostel

1 ....
2 ....
3 ....
4 ....

1 **Look at the photo. It comes from a TV series called *By Any Means*. What do you think the idea of the programme is? Guess.**

2 **Read the text and check your prediction.**

BY ANY MEANS

1 The son of the well-known British film director John Boorman, Charley Boorman became famous by making two popular television series with the film star Ewan McGregor. In these series Boorman and McGregor rode huge distances on motorbikes.

2 Boorman was looking for a new challenge when his friend TV director Russ Malkin suggested going from Ireland to Australia using any means of transport. To be precise, the idea was to take any means of transport except planes, unless this was absolutely necessary. Boorman loved the idea and immediately began to plan the journey with Russ and a cameraman called Mungo. Together they made the trip into a TV series called *By Any Means*.

3 They began in Ireland because this was where Charley had grown up and started riding motorbikes at the age of just 15. The team began and ended the trip on motorbikes because these are Boorman's favourite type of transport. But they also went by express train, ferry, taxi, coach, bus, car, tractor, van, lorry, hot-air balloon, and helicopter. Sometimes there were delays and they missed a connection. On two occasions Boorman ended up catching a plane because there was no alternative. But he preferred more exotic types of transport like an elephant in India and a camel in Australia. It was good that they didn't have to carry much luggage!

4 At times Charley got very tired, especially on long-distance trains. He found it difficult to sleep on night trains, and sleep in general was a problem. The three travellers usually stayed in hotels and hostels, but sleeping in a different bed each night was exhausting. Once when they slept in a tent it was nearly a disaster. They'd spent the whole day on their bikes when it started raining. They were in the middle of the jungle in Cambodia during the monsoon. It rained all night and Charley slept with his camera in his hand. He was expecting something terrible to happen at any moment and wanted to make sure that he could at least film it.

5 Water gave Boorman one of his best moments on the trip, but also some of the worst. The best was when they were travelling on a 'rocket boat' in Cambodia. The boat really did go like a rocket and Charlie loved the thrill and excitement of the trip. But on other occasions when they were sailing, he thought he was going to die. On one trip from Bali to Borneo, the ship was very old and water started to pour in. Luckily another boat was going past and could rescue them. It was fortunate too that they were just beginning their trip and weren't in the middle of the ocean! And while they were sailing from Timor to Australia a storm hit them. The waves were over four metres high and they were only travelling in a very small boat. Again, luck was with them, and after 36 hours of sailing in terrible conditions they arrived safely. For Charley this was the hardest part of the trip.

6 By the time Boorman arrived in Sydney, Australia, he'd spent 102 days travelling, used 112 different types of transport, travelled across three continents and 25 countries, and had covered more than 32,000 kilometres!

3 **Read the text again and choose the best answers.**

1 Charley Boorman is
  a a film director.
  b a film star.
  c well-known on TV.

2 Charley, Russ and Mungo
  a didn't want to travel by plane.
  b didn't need to travel by plane.
  c couldn't travel by plane.

3 It was difficult to sleep because they
  a never stayed in the same place for long.
  b couldn't find places to sleep.
  c were usually travelling on trains at night.

4 Charley didn't sleep well in the tent in Cambodia because he
  a was filming a special event with his camera.
  b thought something bad was going to happen.
  c doesn't like rain.

5 Charley had some bad experiences at sea because
  a some of the boats they travelled in weren't ideal for the conditions.
  b he feels nervous and sick at sea.
  c the weather conditions were exceptionally bad.

4 **Find these words in the text. What do you think they mean? Use a dictionary to check your ideas.**

1 huge
2 means
3 grown up
4 no alternative
5 exhausting
6 monsoon
7 thrill
8 pour in
9 fortunate
10 waves

5 **SPEAKING What about *you*?**

1 Would you like to see the TV series *By Any Means*? Why/Why not?
2 Would you like to make a journey like the one in *By Any Means*? Why/Why not?

GRAMMAR GUIDE

Past simple, past continuous and past perfect

1a Look at these sentences. Which tenses are the verbs in?

a The team **began** and **ended** the trip on motorbikes.
b While they **were sailing** from Timor to Australia a storm **hit** them.
c They **had spent** the whole day on their bikes when it **started** raining.

1b Complete the rules with *past simple, past continuous* or *past perfect*. Then match sentences a–c with each rule.

1 We use the .... to talk about actions that happened before another action in the past. ....
2 We use the .... to describe finished actions or situations in the past, or to say that one thing happened after another. ....
3 We use the .... to talk about activities in progress at a moment in the past, to describe scenes in a story or description, or to talk about an activity in progress in the past that is interrupted by another action. ....

1c Rewrite these sentences, first in the negative form and then in the question form.

1 They began the trip on motorbikes.
2 They were sailing from Timor to Australia.
3 They had spent the day on their bikes.

GRAMMAR REFERENCE ▸ page 28

2a Put these verbs in the correct form of the past simple or past continuous.

buy catch hear look ride shine snow wait

1 When I left home this morning, the sun ....
2 I .... the bus at 8.45.
3 While I .... my bike to school this morning, I saw an accident.
4 When we arrived at the station, a lot of people .... to buy tickets.
5 She .... her ticket and got on the train.
6 Somebody stole his passport while he .... for something in his luggage.
7 There was a delay with the plane because it .... very hard.
8 As she was leaving the shop, she .... somebody call her name.

2b Look at the words *while* and *as* in sentences 3, 6 and 8. Do they usually go with the past simple or past continuous?

3 Choose the best alternative.

1 I fell asleep while I *watched/was watching* the film.
2 The teacher called me back as I *left/was leaving* the classroom.
3 The headmaster *came/was coming* in while we were doing the exam.
4 As we *drove/were driving* to the airport, I realised I didn't have my passport.
5 While you *shopped/were shopping*, three people called for you.
6 She *met/was meeting* one of her friends while she was taking the dog for a walk.
7 As we *talked/were talking*, I realised that I'd met her before.
8 They didn't speak while they *did/were doing* their homework.

4 Write sentences in the past perfect to explain the situations. Look at the example.

Why was she crying? **miss the plane**
Because she had missed the plane.

1 Why couldn't he find his bike? **somebody steal it**
....
2 Why did they buy a new car? **have the old one for 15 years**
....
3 Why were you scared of flying? **never fly before**
....
4 Why was everything white in the morning? **snow the night before**
....
5 Why didn't she pass her exam? **not study much**
....
6 Why didn't they let him board the plane? **lose his passport**
....
7 Why didn't Alex have any money? **spend it**
....
8 Why did she miss the bus? **not get to the bus stop on time**
....

5 Correct the mistakes in the sentences.

1 When everybody got on the train, it had left the station.
2 I was having lunch when my friend was calling me on my mobile.
3 She was running in the park while she saw her friend.
4 When I received her email I had read it.
5 When we were small we were going everywhere by bus.
6 When I was switching the light off I left the room.
7 I was making a sandwich when I was cutting my finger.
8 When I was putting my pyjamas on, I got into bed.

6 Complete the text with the past simple or past continuous form of the verbs.

My friends and I **(a)** .... (wait) to catch our plane at JFK airport when something very unusual **(b)** .... (happen). We **(c)** .... (see) a man who **(d)** .... (carry) a gun. He **(e)** .... (run) very fast. We thought that maybe he was a criminal. The next minute a police officer who **(f)** .... (look) like Brad Pitt suddenly **(g)** .... (appear). The criminal **(h)** .... (drop) a small packet on the floor. The police officer **(i)** .... (not see) it. Instead, the officer **(j)** .... (jump) quickly on top of the criminal and **(k)** .... (knock) him out. My friends and I quickly **(l)** .... (go) to pick up the packet. Suddenly somebody **(m)** .... (shout) 'Cut!' Then we **(n)** .... (realise) that there were cameras everywhere. They **(o)** .... (make) an adventure film in the airport. The film director was not happy!

7 Before you do exercise 8, do the Developing vocabulary section opposite.

8 Prepare notes about a journey that was special to you. Use some of these questions for ideas and phrasal verbs connected with travel.

1 Where was the journey to?
2 How did you travel?
3 When was it?
4 Who went?
5 Who had chosen the destination?
6 How had you prepared for the journey?
7 What special thing(s) happened on the journey?
8 What were you doing when these things happened?
9 What was the weather like?
10 How did the journey end?
11 How did you feel about what had happened?

9 Work in small groups. Tell your partners about your journey.

Developing vocabulary

Phrasal verbs connected with travel

1 Look at these sentences. Match the phrasal verbs in bold with the definitions below.

1 We **got on** the first train that came but we **got off** when we realised it was the wrong one.
2 When all passengers are in their seats, the plane can **take off**.
3 She **got into** the car and drove to the station. When she arrived she **got out of** the car and locked it.
4 This bus is really old. I think it's going to **break down** any minute.
5 Excuse me. Can you tell me what time the London train **gets in**? I'm meeting somebody on it.
6 They **checked in** their bags and went through passport control.
7 That was a long journey. We **set off** at 7 o'clock this morning and only arrived at 10pm.
8 I'm tired of working. I want to **get away** for a few weeks, maybe go to the beach.

a start a journey
b enter/leave (a train, bus, boat, plane)
c go somewhere different to have a rest or holiday
d arrive
e show your ticket/give your bags to an official at an airport
f stop working (for an engine or a type of transport)
g enter/leave (a car)
h start flying

2a PRONUNCIATION **Look at these sentences. Which of the words in bold are verbs and which are nouns?**

1 We need to **check in** at 7 o'clock.
2 Here's the **check-in** desk.
3 What time does the plane **take off?**
4 What time is **take-off?**
5 The car didn't **break down**.
6 There is a car **breakdown service**.

2b 1.09 **Listen to the sentences. Which part of the phrasal verb do we usually stress? Which part of the noun do we stress?**

Click onto... Life at sea

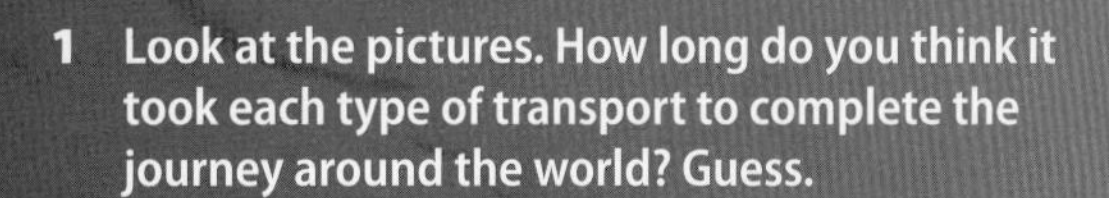

Cross-curricular – History
Sailing round the world

1 Look at the pictures. How long do you think it took each type of transport to complete the journey around the world? Guess.

1 .... 2 .... 3 .... 4 ....

2 Read the text and find the correct answers.

▸ WORD BOOSTER

Match the words and definitions.

1 expedition	a ways or roads that you use to go from one place to another
2 survived	b alone, with nobody helping
3 routes	c something you push with your foot
4 pedal	d make something start burning
5 Rollerblades™	e a long journey to a distant or dangerous place
6 set fire to	f continued to live after a difficult situation
7 solo/single-handed	g strong movements of water in one direction
8 currents	h boots with small wheels on the bottom in a line

3 Read the text again. Who ...

1 didn't use any type of transport with a motor on their journey? ....
2 died before finishing his journey round the world? ....
3 was the leader of a journey round the world from start to finish? ....
4 wanted food when he/she came back? ....
5 took a difficult route around the world? ....
6 stole things during the journey? ....
7 escaped a very dangerous incident? ....
8 didn't get much rest? ....

4 Work in groups. You are going to make a film about one of these journeys. Decide which one, choose actors, and make a list of reasons for your decisions. Then present your ideas to the rest of the class.

1

Many people think that Ferdinand Magellan was the first person to travel around the world. His expedition was the first to do this but Magellan himself died on the trip when he found himself fighting a battle on an island in the Philippines. The Spanish captain Juan Sebastian Elcano became the new leader of the expedition. He arrived back in Spain in 1522 after a journey of just over three years. Seventeen other members of the original expedition had survived with him.

The British sailor Sir Francis Drake became the first person to lead a complete expedition around the world. His three-year journey began in 1577. On the journey, Drake attacked many Spanish ships carrying gold from the New World. He also took their maps, which were better than his own. These maps helped him to find the best routes to complete his journey.

3

One of the strangest round the world journeys was by Jason Lewis. Lewis took 13 years to complete his journey. His method of transport? An eight-metre 'pedalo' – a pedal-powered boat. Lewis was the first person to go round the world by human power alone. On land, he travelled by bike and on Rollerblades™! The most terrifying incident during the whole trip was when a salt-water crocodile attacked him while he was in the water in a kayak. He reached a deserted beach and got out of the kayak but the crocodile started to eat the boat. In the end the crocodile left. Jason set fire to the rest of his kayak. A pilot in a small plane saw the smoke and rescued him.

Dee Caffari was born in Britain in 1973. In 2006 she became the first woman to sail solo non-stop around the world the 'wrong way'. The wrong way means going west, against the winds and sea currents. It took her 178 days. In 2008–9 it took her just 99 days to sail alone around the world in the usual direction. And so she became the first woman in history to sail around the world single-handed in both directions. On the voyage, she sailed through icebergs and could only sleep for periods of twenty minutes. When she got back, what she wanted most was a pizza, a diet cola and a bath!

4

5 What about *you*?

1 Would you like to travel around the world one day? Why/Why not?
2 Which type(s) of transport would you prefer to use on a trip around the world? Why?

I'd like to travel around the world, maybe after I finish university.

I'd like to go to Australia or New Zealand, but I don't want to sail there!

Cross-curricular – Geography
Hurricanes

6 How much do you know about hurricanes? Work with a partner and guess whether these sentences are true (T) or false (F).

Hurricane Quiz

		T	F
1	Hurricanes and typhoons are basically the same thing.		
2	Hurricanes usually have more power than typhoons.		
3	Hurricanes are really bad when the water is cold.		
4	Typhoons kill more people than hurricanes.		
5	Hurricanes lose their strength when they leave the sea and go inland.		
6	In the past they only used men's names for hurricanes.		
7	When a hurricane is really bad, they never use the name of the hurricane again.		
8	You can fly right through a hurricane.		

7 1.10 Listen to a radio programme about hurricanes. How many answers did you get right? Correct the false sentences.

8 Work with a partner. Choose the correct alternative.

1 Warm air *rises/falls*.
2 Evaporation is when *gas changes into liquid/liquid changes into gas*.
3 Humid air is *more/less* dense than dry air.

9 Look at this diagram and put the three pieces of information in the correct places.

a Winds come together and push the air up.
b Light winds outside the hurricane push it and help it to get bigger.
c Warm water (27°C or higher) from the ocean gives the hurricane energy. It causes more evaporation and makes humid air and clouds.

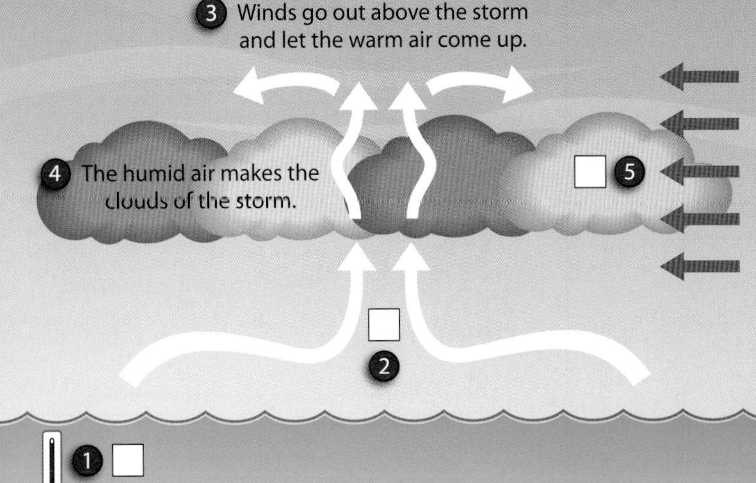

10 Answer the questions with a partner.

1 Most hurricanes happen just after the summer. Why do you think this is?
2 When hurricanes hit the land, they can be very dangerous. Do you think they are more dangerous in situation A or in situation B? Why?

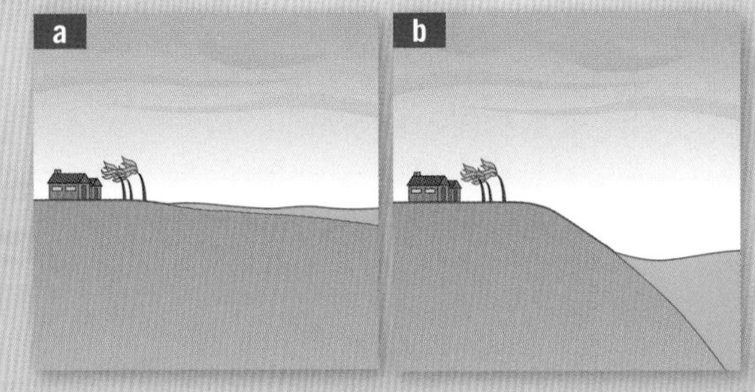

3 Hurricanes start near the equator. They go across the warm oceans of the world and then go north, to colder lands. Can you think of any positive effects that this has on global weather conditions?

11 What about *you?*

1 Do you know any books or films about hurricanes, storms or extreme weather? What happens in the story or film?
2 What types of extreme weather do you have where you live?

Do you remember that hurricane in the USA a few years ago?

Yes, it was awful. It was worse than anyone expected and thousands of people lost their homes.

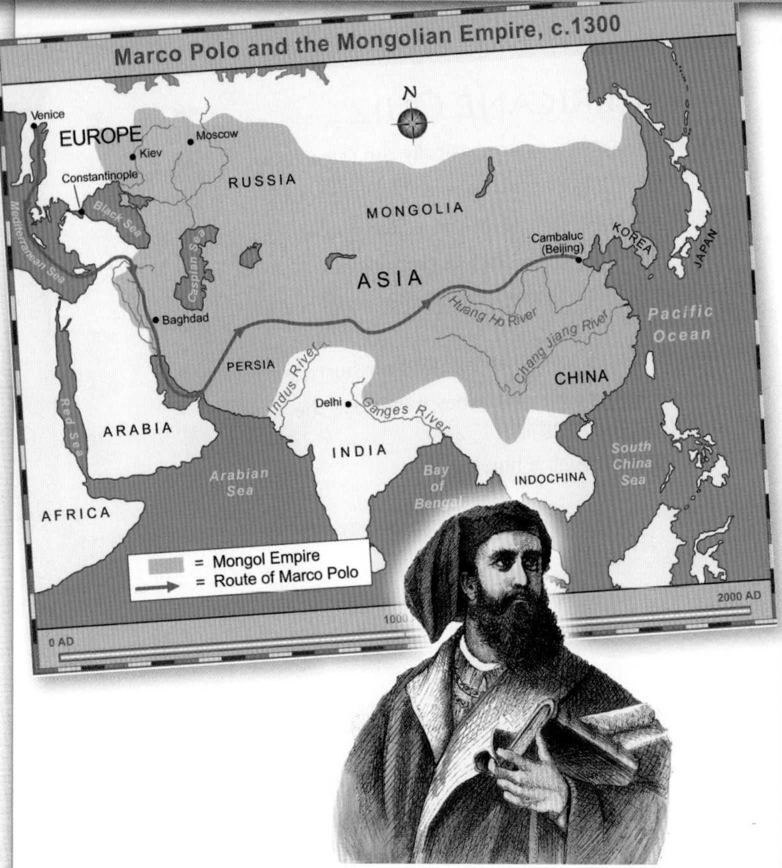

1 **Work with a partner and guess the answers to these questions.**

1 What year was Marco Polo born?
 a 1254
 b 1496
 c 563

2 What was the title of the book he wrote?
 a *Epic journeys*
 b *The description of the world*
 c *Around the world in 80 days*

3 Why was he famous?
 a He was the first European to travel to China.
 b He became an emperor.
 c He created famous Chinese and Italian recipes.

4 Was his book fact or fiction?
 a Fact
 b Fiction
 c Fact with some fiction

2 LISTENING 1.11 **Listen to an expert talking about Marco Polo. What answers does she give for the questions in 1?**

3 **There are six mistakes in this text about Marco Polo. Listen again and correct the mistakes.**

Marco Polo used to exaggerate and invent details. For example, he said that a big city in China had 500 bridges, but it only had thirty. That's why some people call him the 'man of a thousand lies'. For example, he talked about an island with big elephants and men with the heads of dogs. He was in hospital in Italy when he wrote his book. He gave interesting details of life in China and Europe in it. For example, we can read that in Europe people used to have paper money but they didn't in China. Also many Europeans didn't use to have baths at that time. And in the 13th century the Chinese already had a postal service and could send letters, but they couldn't do this in Europe.

GRAMMAR GUIDE

Used to

1a Look at the sentences then match the correct halves of the rules.

Sentences

1 Marco Polo **used to** invent pieces of information.
2 They **didn't use** to have baths.
3 **Did** they **use to** believe that unicorns existed?
4 They **usually** mention this story.
5 Marco Polo **died** on this day.

Rules

1 We use *used to* to talk about ....
2 We use the past simple to talk about ....
3 We use the present simple and *usually* to talk about ....

a present habits.
b past habits that do not happen now.
c single actions in the past.

1b Write the negative and question forms of this sentence.

They used to travel by horse in 1254.

GRAMMAR REFERENCE ▶ page 29

2 **Complete the sentences with the correct form of *used to*.**

1 Some people .... think unicorns existed.
2 They .... wear jeans in the thirteenth century.
3 Transport .... be much slower three hundred years ago.
4 A long time ago people .... believe that the sun went around the earth.
5 In Britain in 1600 most children from poor families .... go to school.
6 People .... drive cars in 1750.
7 Before DVDs, people .... watch VHS videos.
8 People .... travel by train and ship before the invention of the aeroplane.
9 People .... have mobile phones.
10 Many people .... believe Marco Polo's book was fact, not fiction.

3 Decide if the sentences describe a past habit, a single action in the past or a present habit. Then complete the sentences with the correct form of *used to*, the past simple or the present simple.

1 My friend .... (go) to China to see the Olympic Games in 2008.
2 We .... (walk) to school, but now we go by car.
3 She .... (cycle) to school usually but yesterday she caught the bus.
4 I .... (not/like) pepper when I was small but now I love it.
5 She .... (be) born in 1999.
6 They .... (play) football on Wednesdays but now they play basketball.
7 I .... (not/go) to the cinema at the weekend because it was too expensive, but now I go every Saturday.
8 Oliver usually .... (come) to my house at the weekend because we're really good friends.

4 Look at this picture of a scene from the life of Marco Polo. Find eight historical mistakes in the picture and write as many sentences as possible, affirmative and/or negative.

They used to drink tea. They didn't use to drink cola.

5 Write eight questions to ask your partner about what they used to do when they were five years old.

Did you use to like football when you were five years old?

6 SPEAKING Use your questions from 5 to interview your partner.

7a SPEAKING Work with a partner. Make notes about how life was different in your country fifty years ago. Use these topics:

1 Transport
2 Food and drink
3 Entertainment
4 Work
5 Health
6 Education

7b Report back to the class with your ideas.

Fifty years ago people didn't use to fly much here. Journeys used to be much longer than now.

1 Look at this British train ticket and complete the information below.

1 Place of departure ....
2 Destination ....
3 When travelling ....
4 Number of people travelling ....
5 Single/Return? ....
6 First class/Standard? ....
7 Price ....

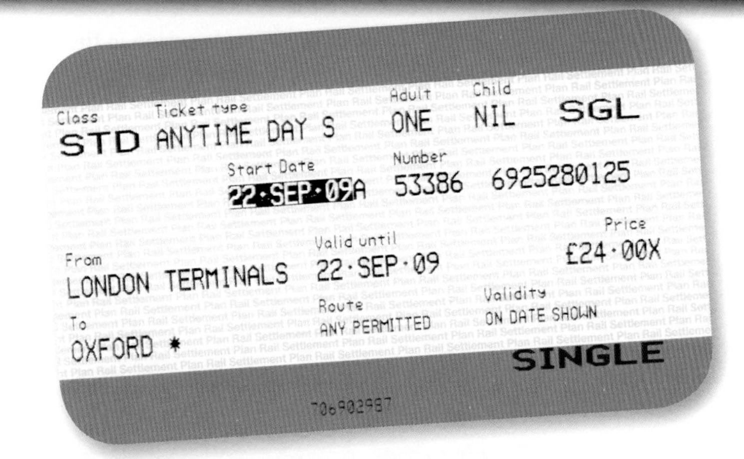

2 LISTENING 1.12 Listen to a conversation between a girl and a ticket agent. Choose the correct alternative and complete the missing details.

1 Destination: *Cambridge/Canterbury*
2 When travelling: *Today/Tomorrow*
3 Time of departure: *3.55pm/6.05pm*
4 *Direct train/Change trains?*
Details: ....
5 *Single/Return?*
Details: ....
6 Price: *£27.60/£36.70*
7 *Cash/Credit card*
8 Platform: *8/9*

3 Listen again. Circle the expressions in the Speaking Bank which you hear.

Speaking Bank

When you understand:

- I see.
- OK.
- That's great.
- Right.
- Really?

When you don't understand:

- Pardon?
- Could you repeat that, please?
- Sorry, I didn't catch that.
- Sorry, I missed that.

STUDY SKILLS

What is the best way to learn useful everyday expressions in English?

STUDY SKILLS ▶ page 146

4 Work with a partner. Make a list of useful questions to ask when you want to buy a train ticket. Listen again to the conversation in 2 if necessary.

5 Work with a partner. Prepare a dialogue using the Guide below.

Conversation Guide

TICKET OFFICER:	Offer to help the customer.
CUSTOMER:	Ask for the times of trains to Newcastle.
TICKET OFFICER:	Give the time of the next train.
CUSTOMER:	Ask if the train is direct.
TICKET OFFICER:	Say yes.
CUSTOMER:	Ask for a ticket.
TICKET OFFICER:	Ask if the customer wants a single or return.
CUSTOMER:	Say you want a return and say when you want to come back.
TICKET OFFICER:	Give the price.
CUSTOMER:	Ask how to pay.
TICKET OFFICER:	Reply.
CUSTOMER:	Find out the platform number.
TICKET OFFICER:	Reply and say goodbye.

Practice makes perfect

6a SPEAKING Look at the task.

You are in Britain and you want to buy a train ticket. Find out:

- the departure and arrival times of trains to your destination
- if the train is direct or not
- the price
- if you can pay by credit card
- which platform the train leaves from.

6b Work with a partner.

Student A: Look at page 146 for information about the ticket you want to buy.

Student B: You work in the ticket office. Look at page 149 for information about different trains. Begin the conversation: *Good morning. Can I help you?*

Remember to show that you understand or don't understand by using expressions from the Speaking Bank.

EXAM SUCCESS

In this type of exam activity, how important is it to know what specific information you need to ask for and give?

EXAM SUCCESS ▶ page 150

Developing writing *Giving emphasis*

1 Read this postcard from Lily. Which picture shows where Lily is now? Put the other two pictures in the order that Lily is going to visit them.

Hi Max!

I can't believe it! Here we are in L.A.... at last! What a journey! It was so long! We had a big delay at the airport and then, when we'd arrived, it took ages to collect our bags. Anyway, they did appear in the end, so that's OK. L.A. is such an amazing place and the weather is brilliant. Our hotel is close to an enormous shopping mall. We didn't have time to go shopping yesterday but we do have time today – yippee! Tomorrow we're going to Hollywood. Ben and I want to see Universal Studios. And later this week we're going to the beach at Santa Monica.
Now it's time for our shopping expedition!
Missing you lots – hope you are well.
See you soon,
Lily xxx ☺

Max Johnson
6 Hobson Road
Wytham
Oxfordshire
OX2 8WA
UNITED KINGDOM

2 Read the postcard again. What does Lily say about ...

1 the journey to Los Angeles?
2 Los Angeles?
3 shopping?
4 Universal Studios?

3 Look at Lily's postcard and complete the examples in the Writing Bank.

> **Writing Bank**
>
> **Useful words and expressions to give emphasis**
>
> **Here are some ways of giving emphasis to what we write, to make our writing more interesting.**
>
> - We can use *What + (adjective) + noun!*,
>   e.g. *What a* .... *! What a beautiful day!*
> - We can use *so + adjective* or *such + (adjective) + noun*,
>   e.g. *It was so* .... *. L.A. is such* ....
> - We can use *do* and *did* in affirmative sentences,
>   e.g. *We do* .... *to go shopping today. They did* .... *in the end.*

4 Make these sentences more emphatic by using the word given.

1 It's a busy city. (what)
2 The flight was awful. (such)
3 We were tired when we arrived. (so)
4 I love Paris. (do)
5 We had a good time. (did)
6 We were happy to get back. (so)
7 It's a great holiday. (what)
8 It's a fantastic place for shopping. (such)
9 We wish you were here. (do)
10 It rained a lot yesterday. (did)

5 Think of an amazing holiday destination and make notes for a postcard. Use these questions to give you ideas.

1 Where are you?
2 Where are you staying?
3 When did you get there?
4 Did anything good or bad happen during your journey?
5 How did you get there?
6 What is the place like? Are you very happy there? Why/Why not?
7 What did you do yesterday?
8 What are your plans for the next few days?

Practice makes perfect

6a Look at the task.

> You are on holiday. Write a postcard to an English-speaking friend. Tell your friend:
>
> - where you are and where you're staying
> - what happened on the journey
> - what the place is like
> - what you did yesterday and what your plans are for the next few days.

6b Use your notes from 5 to write your postcard. Use the expressions in the Writing Bank to add emphasis and interest.

> **EXAM SUCCESS**
>
> When you finish a piece of writing in an exam, what different things do you need to check before you hand it in?
>
> EXAM SUCCESS ▸ page 150

Language reference and revision

Grammar reference

Past simple

Form

Affirmative	I/You/He/She/It/We/They **worked** yesterday. I/You/He/She/It/We/They **began** yesterday.
Negative	I/You/He/She/It/We/They **didn't (did not) work** yesterday. I/You/He/She/It/We/They **didn't (did not) begin** yesterday.
Question	**Did** I/you/he/she/it/we/they **work** yesterday? **Did** I/you/he/she/it/we/they **begin** yesterday?
Short answers	Yes, I/you/he/she/it/we/they **did**. No, I/you/he/she/it/we/they **didn't**.

Spelling

Many common verbs are irregular.
See the list of irregular verbs on page 159.

Use

We use the **past simple** to:

1 describe finished actions or situations in the past.
I flew to London last year.

2 say that one thing happened after another.
When the train arrived, we got on it and sat down.

Past continuous

Form

Affirmative	I/He/She/It **was** go**ing**. You/We/They **were** go**ing**.
Negative	I/He/She/It **wasn't (was not)** go**ing**. You/We/They **weren't (were not)** go**ing**.
Question	**Was** I/he/she/it go**ing**? **Were** you/we/they go**ing**?
Short answers	Yes, I/he/she/it **was**. No, I/he/she/it **wasn't**. Yes, you/we/they **were**. No, you/we/they **weren't**.

Use

We use the **past continuous** to:

1 talk about activities in progress at a moment in the past.
At four o'clock this morning we were sleeping.

2 describe scenes in a story or description.
The old woman was wearing a long coat and she was carrying a big, heavy bag.

3 talk about an activity in progress when another, shorter activity happened or interrupted it. It tells us that an action was in progress, but not that the activity was finished.
I was talking to Cathy when suddenly I heard a loud noise.

4 We often use *while* and *as* with the past continuous.
While/As I was walking to school, I heard somebody call my name.

5 Remember that some verbs are not usually used in the continuous (see page 16).
I had a green bike. not *I was having a green bike.*

Past perfect

Form

Affirmative	subject + **had ('d)** + **past participle** *She had seen the film before.*
Negative	subject + **had not (hadn't)** + **past participle** *They hadn't seen the film before.*
Question	**had** + subject + **past participle** *Had you seen the film before?*
Short answers	Yes, subject + **had**. No, subject + **hadn't**. *Yes, I had. No, they hadn't.*

Use

1 We use the **past perfect** to talk about actions that happened before another action or actions in the past.
When I had brushed my teeth I got into bed.
(= First I brushed my teeth and then I got into bed.)

2 We often use time expressions such as **when, after, by the time as, as soon as …** with the past perfect.
I had finished my lunch by the time he arrived.

Vocabulary

1 Travel and transport

arrivals cancel catch coach delay departures fare ferry hot-air balloon lorry luggage miss motorbike office platform return rocket single ticket van yacht

2 Accommodation

bed and breakfast campsite caravan hotel motel tent youth hostel

3 Phrasal verbs connected with travel

break down check in get away get in get into/out of get on/off set off take off

4 Other words and phrases ▸ page 137

Grammar revision

Past simple and past continuous

1 Choose the correct alternative.

1 We were travelling fast when the train suddenly *stopped/was stopping*.
2 I saw an old friend of mine when I *waited/was waiting* to buy my ticket.
3 My friends and I *put/were putting* our coats on and left the house.
4 When the train stopped we *got/were getting* off.
5 You looked sad yesterday because you *cried/were crying*.
6 Nobody paid attention to me when I arrived because they *watched/were watching* something on TV.
7 He *dropped/was dropping* the plate and it broke.

WORKBOOK ▸ page 12 / 7 points

Past simple and past perfect

2 Decide which action happened first and then join the two sentences with a time expression. Put one of the verbs in the past perfect.

1 She started driving. She got into the car.
She ....
2 He finished using the computer. He switched it off.
When ....
3 They went into the cinema. They bought their tickets.
They ....
4 She did her homework. She went to bed immediately after.
As soon as ....
5 The police identified the criminal. They arrested him.
After ....
6 We ate our meal. We paid the bill.
When ....
7 They went into the house. They unlocked the door.
They ....

WORKBOOK ▸ page 12 / 7 points

Used to

3a Match the correct halves of the sentences.

1 He didn't use to wear jeans ....
2 He wore jeans ....
3 He used to wear jeans ....
4 He usually wears jeans ....

a last Wednesday.
b because he likes wearing them.
c but now he wears them all the time.
d but he never wears them now.

3b Write the question with the correct form of used to **and then answer the question.**

you/wear jeans when you were 5?

Question: ....
..........?
Answer: ....
....

WORKBOOK ▸ page 15 / 6 points

Vocabulary revision

Transport and travel

1 What are the words?

1 A type of transport that goes on the road and takes a lot of people from one city to another: ....
2 The place where you stand to catch a train: ....
3 The situation when something happens later than planned: ....
4 The money that you pay for a journey: ....
5 A type of sea transport that takes people and cars on journeys that are not very long: ....
6 A ticket for a journey where you go and come back to the same place where you started: ....
7 When you arrive too late for a bus, train or other type of transport: ....
8 When you stop something that was going to happen: ....

WORKBOOK ▸ page 10 / 8 points

Accommodation

2 What are these types of accommodation?

1 A place near a big road where travellers stop to sleep: ....
2 A small hotel that gives you a room and a meal: ....
3 A place where lots of people camp: ....
4 Something you need to sleep outside: ....
5 A vehicle that people can live and travel in on holiday: ....
6 A place where young people can stay without spending much money: ....

WORKBOOK ▸ page 10 / 6 points

Phrasal verbs connected with travel

3 Choose the correct alternative.

1 We arrived at the airport and checked *in/off* our bags.
2 It was going to be a very long journey so he set *on/off* early.
3 What time does your brother's train get *in/off* at the station?
4 She got *into/on* the car and started driving.
5 The bus broke *up/down* so he had to walk.
6 A lot of people get *away/around* from the city at the weekend.

WORKBOOK ▸ page 13 / 6 points

Total / 40 points

▸ Reading

▸ Tip for Reading Exams

In true/false activities, remember …

First read the text quickly to get a general understanding. Then read the sentences that you need to prove true or false. Find the parts of the text where you think the information comes and read them again in more detail. **EXAM SUCCESS ▸ page 150**

1 Work with a partner. Imagine that you are in the UK and you want to go to Switzerland. Decide how to travel – by plane, train or car – and give reasons.

2 Read the text from a guidebook. How long does it take to get to Switzerland from the UK by plane, train and car?

Switzerland

Getting there from the UK

1 The easiest way to get to Switzerland is, of course, to catch a plane. Zurich and Geneva have major international airports and many European flights arrive 5 at Basel every day. Other smaller airports in the south of the country and in the Alps are useful entry points for specific regions.

Flying from the UK

From the UK, there are over fifty flights a day to 10 Switzerland, from 12 or more UK airports. British Airways and Swiss have many flights, and the fares are similar to cheap airlines. When you fly with Swiss, they offer everyone unlimited free chocolate!

Because routes and airlines can change quickly, the best 15 thing to do is to check the website of your home airport and/or your destination airport.

Flight time from London is around an hour and a half. From the north of England or Scotland it is two to three hours.

20 Fares

For the cheapest fares, always book online. With cheap airlines, book early (at least two or three weeks in advance). You can sometimes find tickets for £50–£70 return. But remember that these flights are usually only 25 in the middle of the week, early morning or late evening. And if you cancel your flight, you lose your money.

'Fly rail luggage'

The Swiss have a great way of taking away some of the stress of 30 travelling by air. For a small cost you can send your luggage direct from the check-in desk at your home airport through to one of seventy or more train stations in Switzerland. That means when you arrive at your destination airport, you don't need to think about your bags. All you need to do is complete a special green form and 35 attach it to your luggage. Each green label costs about £10. You can usually collect your bag eight hours after your plane lands, depending on the distance of the train station from the airport.

By train from the UK

Travelling to Switzerland by train still has lots of romance – 40 it can be both relaxing and very scenic. But it's usually more expensive than flying. Time is also a factor – the fastest route from London to Geneva (which still involves changing trains in Paris) takes about 7 hours 30 minutes.

From Paris, many trains go to Switzerland but not from the Gare 45 du Nord. This is the station that you arrive at when you catch the Eurostar train from London. That means you need to plan your route in advance and be prepared to carry your luggage through the Paris underground.

Driving from the UK

50 You can also get to Switzerland by car. It takes about one day. The Swiss border is approximately 850km from the channel coast. You could start early and be in Basel for dinner. You can drive onto a train which then passes through the Eurotunnel. These trains are frequent, they operate 24 hours a day, and the journey 55 takes 35–45 minutes. The alternative is driving onto a ferry. Fares depend on what time you travel, the time of the year, and how far in advance you book.

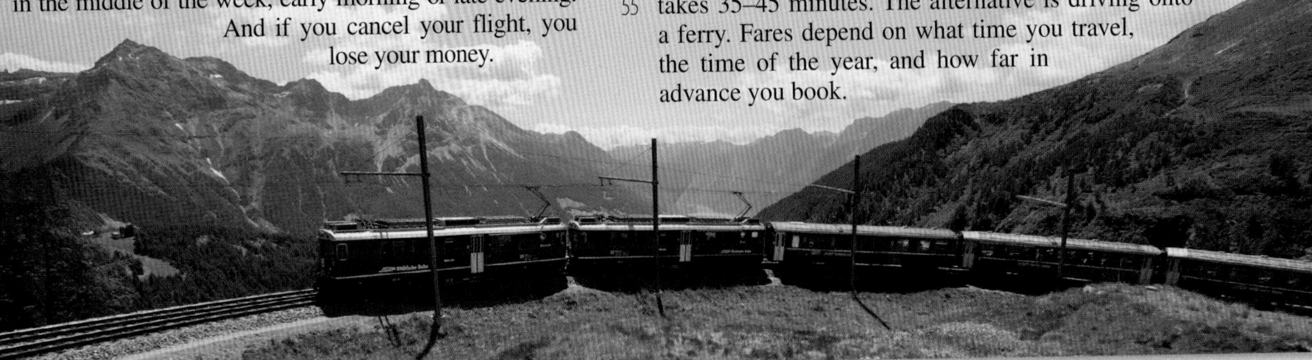

3 Read the text again and decide if the statements are true (T) or false (F). Write down the number(s) of the line(s) where you found the answer.

1 There are only three airports in Switzerland that you can fly to from the UK. T/F ....

2 British Airways and Swiss flights are not more expensive than other companies. T/F ....

3 You can't get very cheap flights at the weekend. T/F ....

4 You can send your bags from a UK airport to a Swiss train station so that you don't need to carry them. T/F ....

5 You can't go direct by train from the UK. T/F ....

6 If you drive from the UK to Switzerland, you must always travel by sea at some point. T/F ....

7 The text mentions six types of transport in total. T/F ....

Listening

Tip for Listening Exams

In matching activities, remember ...

Before you listen, read the statements. But remember that you may hear the same ideas expressed in different words.

EXAM SUCCESS ▸ page 150

4 Work with a partner. Discuss the problems people sometimes have with travel or accommodation when they go on holiday.

5 1.13 You are going to hear four people talking about problems they had the last time they travelled. Match the statements with the speakers. There is one extra statement which you do not need.

A I didn't make any plans.
B Bad weather ruined my holidays.
C I couldn't get home on the right day.
D I took the wrong train.
E I had a problem with my luggage.

Speaker 1 ☐
Speaker 2 ☐
Speaker 3 ☐
Speaker 4 ☐

Writing

Tip for Writing Exams

In writing exams, remember ...

When you finish, check carefully for mistakes with punctuation and capital letters, word order, spelling, tenses, vocabulary, missing words and agreement between the subject and verb. Check also the style and content.

EXAM SUCCESS ▸ page 150

6 Work with a partner. Look at the photo and describe the people. Use these words and expressions.

look + adjective
look like + noun/pronoun
look like/as if + noun/pronoun + verb
extremely/really/quite

7 The people in the photo are some new friends that you made on holiday. Write an email to your family about your new friends. Describe their appearance and personality.

Speaking

8 Look at these questions about a holiday you went on. Make notes for your answers, but do not write full sentences.

- Who did you go with?
- Where and how did you go?
- Where did you stay and what did you do?
- What were the best and worst things about the trip?

9 Work with a partner. Look at this exam task and take it in turns to ask and answer. You can use your notes but don't just read them out.

An English-speaking friend is asking you about your last holiday. Tell him/her:
- where and how you went
- who you went with
- where you stayed and what you did
- the best and worst things about the trip.

Tip for Speaking Exams

In speaking exams, remember ...

Make sure that, before you begin, you understand the situation and the specific information that you need to ask for or give.

EXAM SUCCESS ▸ page 150

'Can Do' Progress Check

CEF

1 **How well can you do these things in English now? Give yourself a mark from 1 to 4.**

1 = I can do it very well.
2 = I can do it quite well.
3 = I have some problems.
4 = I can't do it.

a I can talk about routines and what's happening now using the present simple and present continuous. ☐
b I can ask for and give personal information. ☐
c I can use synonyms. ☐
d I can understand written and spoken texts about people's identity. ☐
e I can describe people's appearance and personality. ☐
f I can talk about past events, situations and habits using the past simple, past continuous, past perfect and *used to*. ☐
g I can talk about trips and travel. ☐
h I can understand written and spoken texts about journeys. ☐
i I can ask to buy a train ticket at a station. ☐
j I can write a basic postcard on holiday. ☐

2 **Now decide what you need to do to improve.**

1 Look again at my book/notes.
2 Do more practice exercises. → WORKBOOK pages 2–19
3 Other: ____________________

3 City life

Grammar ‣ Present perfect simple and past simple ‣ *ever, never, for, since, yet, already, just* ‣ Present perfect continuous
Vocabulary ‣ Cities and houses ‣ Adjectives describing a city ‣ Extreme adjectives
Speaking ‣ Giving personal opinions
Writing ‣ An informal letter describing a place

‣ Vocabulary

Cities and houses

1 Work with a partner and match the photos with these words.

bungalow cottage detached house flat/block of flats semi-detached house terraced house

2 1.14 Listen, check and repeat.

3 Work with a partner. Make a list of typical rooms in a flat or house.
kitchen, bedroom ...

4 SPEAKING Tell your partner what type of house or flat you live in and describe it.

I live in a terraced house. It's got three bedrooms …

5 Match the photos below with these words. There are more words than photos.

city centre factory inner city port skyscraper square suburbs town hall

6 1.15 Listen, check and repeat.

7 Which word in 5 describes …

1 a very tall building with offices or flats?
2 a poor area near the centre of a big city?
3 the part of a city where there are many shops, banks or restaurants?
4 an open area in a city or town with buildings around it?
5 a richer area near a city but away from its centre where there are a lot of houses and trees?

Adjectives describing a city

8 Match these words with their definitions.

busy crowded dirty historic lively noisy quiet

1 important because it is old and interesting
2 not very busy, or without much noise
3 not clean
4 with lots of noise
5 full of people who are very active and/or having a good time
6 with lots of people doing things
7 with a lot of people

9 Look at the photo of the square in 5 (photo b). Can you use any of the adjectives in 8 to describe it?

10 LISTENING 1.16 Listen to four people talking about houses or places in a city. Which place from 1 or 5 does each person talk about?

1 .... 3 ....
2 .... 4 ....

11 SPEAKING Work with a partner. Prepare a description of the area where your school is and then practise describing it.

Our school isn't in the city centre but it's quite near the centre. It isn't very noisy. There are a lot of blocks of flats here …

1 **Work with a partner. Look at the photo and take it in turns to describe it. Look at the title of the text. What do you think the text is about? Guess.**

2 **Read the text and check your predictions. Ignore the gaps in the text.**

STUDY SKILLS

Why is it useful to look at pictures and the title of a text before you read it? STUDY SKILLS ▶ page 147

An Old English town … in China

a ....

Enjoy the green grass in front of the old castle. But when you look past the red telephone boxes you can see that this is not England at all. This is Thames Town, just 20 miles from the busy centre of China's biggest port, Shanghai.

b ....

The idea of Songjiang City is to offer houses to millions of people from the suburbs of Shanghai, making it into one of the biggest cities in the world. It has seven universities (one of the main aims is to attract University students and their families to live there), the biggest shopping centre in the world, and some of the most important high-tech companies too. And they've already built a new train line to cut the journey from Shanghai city centre to just 15 minutes.

c ....

Experts have calculated that approximately 400 million people are going to move into cities in the next few years. That means that China needs 3,000 new towns or cities by 2020. But Thames Town is not a crowded inner city project. It is a suburban paradise where rich residents can relax, watch English football and shop at Next and other UK shops. Just like in historic towns in Britain, they've built the town around a market square, with medieval buildings around it. Architect Paul Rice has worked on Thames Town for over three years. Some people have described Thames Town as a theme park, but Rice says that this is not Disneyland. 'We've built this as a real town. Thames Town is unique.'

d ....

There is a German New Town which is perfect for people who love cars. It has a Formula 1 race track and a giant Volkswagen factory. In Barcelona Town you can walk along a Chinese Las Ramblas. Italian Town, in the suburbs of Pujiang, has 100,000 people living next to canals just like in Venice.

e ....

She moved in 2005 when the first houses appeared. 'I like the town because of its beautiful British buildings,' she says. 'I've never known a town like this in China. It's the first. More and more people here have started to live in satellite towns and work in the city.' So for Chinese people who prefer quiet English cottages to the usual enormous skyscrapers, Thames Town could be the perfect place for them.

EXAM SUCCESS

You are going to do a missing sentences reading activity. In this type of activity you have to find the best place to put different sentences taken from a text. What do you think should be the first thing you do in this type of activity?

EXAM SUCCESS ▶ page 151

3 **Put sentences 1–5 into gaps a–e in the text.**

1 But Songjiang City does not just have an English town.
2 Take a walk along the quiet roads with their terraced houses.
3 Wang Haijun is one pioneer who has already moved from Shanghai to Thames Town.
4 In China in recent times more and more people have moved from the country to urban areas.
5 Thames Town is a 200 million-pound project which has just opened as part of Songjiang City.

4 **Read the text again and answer the questions.**

1 Where exactly is Thames Town?
2 Why does China need more cities?
3 How can you spend your time in Thames Town?
4 What different nationality towns does the text mention?
5 Who is Thames Town good for?

5 **Find words in the text which mean:**

1 a common green plant that covers the ground *(paragraph a)*
2 objectives *(paragraph b)*
3 reduce/make shorter *(paragraph b)*
4 people who live in a particular place *(paragraph c)*
5 special/different from everything else *(paragraph c)*
6 a town that is next to a big city and depends on the city *(paragraph e)*

6 **SPEAKING** **What about *you?***

1 Would you like to live or study in Thames Town? Why/Why not?
2 Which type of town would you like to live in – British, German, Spanish, Italian or another nationality? Why?

I think Thames Town seems a good place to live. It's quiet and clean.

I think it's strange. The town doesn't seem real at all!

GRAMMAR GUIDE

Present perfect simple and past simple

1a Look at these sentences and choose the correct alternative.

1 She **moved** to Thames Town in 2005.
2 He **has worked** on the project for over three years.
3 They**'ve built** the town around a market square.
4 They **lived** in Shanghai for four years but then they moved to Thames Town.

a We use the *present perfect/past simple* for actions or experiences which happened at a specific moment in the past, or actions which started and finished in the past.
Examples: sentences *1, 2, 3, 4.*

b We use the *present perfect/past simple* for actions or experiences which happened at an unspecified moment in the past, actions which started in the past and continue to the present, or past actions which have a result in the present.
Examples: sentences *1, 2, 3, 4.*

1b Complete this rule for the formation of the present perfect.

has/have + ...

GRAMMAR REFERENCE ▸ page 42

2 Complete each sentence with the correct form of the verb in the present perfect or past simple.

1 Ian .... (be) in New York since last Friday. He's leaving on Sunday.
2 Kate ....(live) in this city all her life. She loves living here.
3 In 2002 my cousin .... (go) to live in Milan.
4 Matt and Jo love travelling. They .... (visit) lots of different countries.
5 My great grandfather died last year. He .... (spend) his whole life living in the country.
6 Two years ago Sophie .... (move) to a bigger flat.
7 When you look around you can see that this city .... (change) a lot.
8 Charlie .... (be) a builder for ten years and then he changed jobs.

GRAMMAR GUIDE

ever, never, for, since, yet, already, just

3a These words are frequently used with the present perfect. Complete each explanation with the correct word.

already ever for just never since yet

1 We can use .... in questions with the present perfect. It means 'at any time in your life'.
2 We use .... with the present perfect to talk about very recent activities.
3 We use .... with the present perfect to say that something has happened, possibly earlier than we thought.
4 We can use .... to make negative sentences in the present perfect. It means 'at no time in your life'.
5 We use .... and .... with the present perfect to talk about things that started in the past and continue in the present. We use .... with periods of time, and .... with specific moments in time.
6 We use .... with the present perfect to say that something has not happened but we think it is going to happen soon. We use it in negative sentences and questions.

3b What is the usual position of the words in 3a in a sentence? Complete the table with the words in 3a.

1 Words that go just before the past participle: ....
2 Words that go just before a time expression: ....
3 A word that usually goes at the end of the sentence: ....

GRAMMAR REFERENCE ▸ page 42

4 Complete the sentences with the present perfect form of these verbs. Put the other word in the correct place in the sentence.

already/visit ever/live have/for just/rain love/since never/live not finish/yet ~~not sell/yet~~

1 They *haven't sold* their flat *yet*.
2 I .... in a big city but one day I'd like to.
3 We .... this exercise ....
4 My brother .... New York. He went there for a holiday five years ago.
5 We .... this car .... ten years.
6 Why is it wet here? .... it ....
7 I .... this city .... the day I arrived here.
8 .... you .... in a cottage?

EXAM SUCCESS

You are going to do a multiple-choice cloze activity. In this type of activity you have to choose which answer best fits a space in a sentence or text. What do you think is a good procedure for this type of activity? EXAM SUCCESS ▸ page 151

5 Read the text below and decide which answer (A, B, C or D) best fits each gap.

The new commuter

Have you **(1)** .... seen people travelling to work in the morning and felt sorry for them? These people are called 'commuters'. Of course, commuting has existed **(2)** .... many years. A commuter **(3)** .... to be somebody who travelled to work each day, either from a suburb or maybe from a nearby town or city where it was cheaper to buy or rent property. They caught a bus or train or the underground or drove into work. But recently a new type of commuter has **(4)** .... come into existence. These commuters work in one country but live in another. High house prices, cheap flights, flexible working hours, email and the Internet have **(5)** .... it easier to work from home. And they have also contributed to create this new type of long-distance commuter. Take Carrie Frais, for example. She has **(6)** .... become a pioneer of long-distance commuting. She works as a TV news presenter in London but finds it cheaper to live in Barcelona. She **(7)** .... there a year ago. With a minimum of a four-hour journey, this trip to work hasn't become a daily habit for her **(8)** .... She usually works in London for a few days, staying with friends and family, and then she **(9)** .... back to Barcelona. It can be difficult but Carrie has found a much higher quality of life **(10)** .... she moved to Barcelona. Experts have predicted a list of cities where London commuters could live in the future. The list includes Palma, Dubrovnik, Faro, Marrakech, Tallinn and Valencia!

	A	B	C	D
1	A not	B ever	C just	D always
2	A for	B since	C during	D through
3	A usually	B used	C is	D was
4	A been	B yet	C only	D just
5	A make	B did	C made	D done
6	A already	B yet	C never	D decided
7	A has moved	B have moved	C moves	D moved
8	A life	B always	C yet	D sometimes
9	A go	B goes	C has gone	D went
10	A for	B since	C while	D due to

Extreme adjectives

1 Match the extreme adjectives (1–10) with the normal adjectives (a–j).

1 ancient	a bad
2 boiling	b beautiful
3 dreadful	c big
4 enormous	d cold
5 filthy	e crowded
6 freezing	f dirty
7 packed	g hot
8 silent	h old
9 stunning	i quiet
10 tiny	j small

2 Look at the example sentences. Then match the correct halves of the rules.

The film was really bad.
The film was really awful.
The film was absolutely awful.
The film was quite bad.
The film was very bad.

1 We use *totally*, *completely* and *absolutely*
2 We use *very* and *extremely*
3 We use *really*
4 We use *quite* and *rather*

a with normal adjectives.
b with normal adjectives.
c with extreme adjectives.
d with both normal and extreme adjectives.

3 Complete the sentences with the correct adjectives.

1 The view from our window wasn't just beautiful. It was absolutely ....
2 The city of Athens isn't just old. It's .... It's existed for over 3,000 years!
3 It was very .... in the city yesterday – over 35°C.
4 It's .... here in the winter.
5 At Christmas the shops in the city centre are totally .... with people.
6 The streets are usually quite .... because nobody cleans them.

4a PRONUNCIATION **1.17 Listen and check your answers. Which words do we stress more – normal adjectives or extreme adjectives?**

4b Practise saying the sentences in 3 with the correct stress.

5a SPEAKING **Write down the names of places in your city or country which are: ancient, usually packed, boiling, freezing, stunning, filthy and enormous.**

5b Tell your partner, in a different order, the places you have written. Can they guess the extreme adjective for each place?

Did you write Moscow because it's freezing there in the winter?

Good idea, but no, I didn't.

London

International cultural knowledge
Sightseeing in London

1 Work with a partner. Ask and answer the questions.

1 Have you ever been to London? If so, what do you remember about it?
2 Would you like to go to London one day? Why/Why not?

2 You are in London and you see this leaflet for the London Pass. What is the main advantage of a London Pass?

3 Read the leaflet and find out the information.

1 You have a French friend with you who doesn't speak any English. Do you think they will be able to understand the free guidebook? Why/Why not?
2 How does the London Pass save you time?
3 You want to see a play when you are in London. How does the London Pass help you?
4 Do you lose all your money if you buy a pass and don't use it?
5 The leaflet says the London Pass is a type of 'smart card'. What does this mean?

▸ WORD BOOSTER

Match the words and definitions.

1 sightseeing	a special places or things to visit
2 attractions	b money you pay, e.g. to visit something
3 benefit from	c money in notes and coins
4 fee	d an agreement that something will happen in a particular situation
5 guarantee	e activity of travelling and seeing interesting things
6 insurance	f get good things from
7 cash	g service where you pay and if something goes wrong they fix the situation for you

4 Work with a partner. Each piece of information (1–7) has a connection with the London Eye. What do you think the connection is?

1 3.5 million people
2 Harry Potter
3 seven years
4 40 kilometres
5 30 minutes
6 getting married
7 Christmas Day

5 1.18 Listen and check your ideas. Were you right?

Get a
London Pass
for all your sightseeing needs!

Visit over 55 attractions for just one price!

With its history, culture and exciting attractions, London always has lots to offer the visitor. However, sometimes sightseeing in London isn't the easiest or cheapest experience! We at London Pass have spent years understanding the needs of our customers and have made sure that the Pass gives the value and convenience that visitors to our great city need!
The London Pass has been making customers happy for over 10 years. It's simply the best way to see all that London has to offer while saving both money and time!

How does the London Pass work?

The London Pass is a 'smart card' – like a credit card with a computer chip inside – which allows you to go to 56 London tourist attractions without paying cash. Simply show your card at the entrance of the attraction, they will put it through a special machine, and that's it, you can go in!

Activating the London Pass

The smart card remembers when and where you first use your London Pass. Your London Pass is then valid for the number of days that you purchased – 1, 2, 3 or 6 days. It is important to note that a 'day' is based on a calendar day, so if you first use your pass at 4pm on Monday, Monday counts as Day One of your pass usage.

How you benefit from the London Pass

* Free entry to over 55 attractions – including the Tower of London, St. Paul's Cathedral, Windsor Castle, HMS Belfast and many more.
* A free 128-page guidebook – available in 7 different languages, containing lots of detailed information including maps and directions as well as great suggestions about how to get the most from London.
* Saving time at attraction entrances – use your London Pass to get inside attractions faster.
* Save money on entrance fees.
* Added travel option – add a London Travelcard to your Pass. This means you can use all public transport in London.
* Other special offers – with the guidebook, we will also give you access to other great offers for visitors to London, including special prices on West End theatre tickets and at restaurants, plus much more!
* Guarantee – an optional insurance extra offers comfort and the peace of mind knowing you will get your money back for any non-used passes if you change your travel plans.

Literature
The London Eye Mystery by Siobhan Dowd

6 These are paragraphs from the start of a novel called *The London Eye Mystery*. Read them and put them in the correct order.

1 .... 2 .... 3 .... 4 ....

a

We waited for the next capsule and the next and the one after that. He still didn't appear. Somewhere, somehow, during the thirty minutes of riding the Eye, in his sealed capsule, he had vanished off the face of the earth. This is the story of how I discovered how he had disappeared …

b

We took Salim to the Eye because he'd never been up before. A stranger came up to us in the queue, offering us a free ticket. We took it and gave it to Salim. We shouldn't have done this, but we did. He went up on his own at 11.32, 24 May, and was due to come down at 12.02 the same day. He turned to wave at Kat and me as he boarded, but you couldn't see his face, just his shadow. They sealed him in with twenty other people he didn't know.

c

Kat and I tracked Salim's capsule as it made its orbit. When it reached its highest point, we both said 'NOW!' at the same time and Kat laughed and I joined in. That's how we knew we'd both been tracking the right one. We saw the people bunch up as the capsule came back down, facing north-east towards the automatic camera for the souvenir photograph. They were just dark bits of jackets, legs, dresses and sleeves.

d

Then the capsule landed. The doors opened and the passengers came out in twos and threes. They walked off in different directions. Their faces were smiling. Their paths probably never crossed again. But Salim wasn't among them.

WORD BOOSTER

Match the words and definitions.

1 track (v.)
2 bunch up
3 sleeves
4 seal (v.)
5 queue
6 wave

a get very close to other people
b follow
c a line of people waiting for something
d the parts of a shirt, coat, or jacket which cover your arms
e move your hand to say hello or goodbye
f close something so that nothing or nobody can get in or out

7 Are the sentences true (T) or false (F)?

1 Salim bought a ticket to the London Eye. T/F
2 The writer saw Salim clearly when he went into the capsule. T/F
3 Salim went into the capsule with another friend. T/F
4 Kat and the writer laughed because they said the same word at the same time. T/F
5 Nobody finds out where Salim went. T/F

8 What about *you*?

1 Would you like to read the rest of the story? Why/Why not?
2 What do you think happened to Salim?

I'd like to read the rest of the story because I want to know how Salim disappeared.

Me too. I love mystery stories.

INSIDE INFORMATION

- This book was written in 2007 and has won several awards.
- The narrator of the story is an autistic child.
- The book is for children but, as one reviewer said, it's perfect for readers from 8 to 88.

1a SPEAKING **Work with a partner. Look at the photos and take turns describing them. Do you think the people are having a good time? Why?**

1b LISTENING **1.19 Listen to a radio programme about the Erasmus project – a programme where European students can go and study in a different country for up to a year. A student called Eda describes her experiences of living in a new city. Complete this information.**

1 Eda is originally from ....
2 On the project, she's been living in ....
3 She's been speaking a lot of .... and ....

2 **Listen again and complete the notes.**

Eda has been living in this new city since **(a)** .... and she is leaving in **(b)** .... She likes the city because there are **(c)** ...., exhibitions and **(d)** .... She also loves the countryside and **(e)** .... She thinks the best part of her stay has been the **(f)** .... This is when people come together and make **(g)** .... The worst part of her stay has been **(h)** ....

3 **What about *you*?**

1 Would you like to live in another country for a year? Why/Why not?
2 Where would you most like to live in the world?

I don't know if I'd like to live abroad. And you?

I'd like to go to a country where they speak English. I want to practise my English.

GRAMMAR GUIDE

Present perfect continuous

1a Look at these sentences from the dialogue in 1. Which sentences are in the present perfect continuous and which are in the present perfect simple?

1 I**'ve been living** here for four months.
2 I**'ve seen** two or three brilliant concerts.
3 I**'ve made** friends with people from all over Europe.
4 Recently we**'ve been doing** lots of exams.

1b Which of these two tenses gives more importance to ...

a the completion and result of an action?
b the process and duration of an action?
c how many times an action happens?
d the fact that an action is temporary, incomplete or has finished very recently?

1c Complete this rule for the formation of the present perfect continuous.

has/have + ... + ...

GRAMMAR REFERENCE ▶ page 42

2 **Write about what these people have been doing.**

1

....

....

2

....

....

3 Are these sentences correct? Why/Why not? If they aren't correct, change them.

1 Ouch! I've been cutting my finger.
2 We've been studying English for eight years.
3 Have you been crying?
4 She's been reading this book three times.
5 My brother has painted his bedroom but he hasn't finished.
6 We've been waiting for the bus for half an hour and it still hasn't come.
7 Oh no! I've been breaking the window.
8 This week I've been staying with my grandparents but I'm going home tomorrow.

4 Choose the best alternative.

1 Stop singing that song! You've *sung/been singing* it all afternoon!
2 That's it! I've *done/been doing* all my homework!
3 It's terrible! Max has *had/been having* an accident!
4 She's *looked/been looking* for her keys all day but she still hasn't found them.
5 Why are you dirty? What have you *done/been doing*?
6 That actor has *made/been making* twenty films.
7 My eyes hurt. I've *worked/been working* on the computer all day.
8 You've *played/been playing* computer games since ten o'clock this morning. It's time to switch it off!

5 Complete the dialogue with the present perfect simple or present perfect continuous form of the verb.

INTERVIEWER: Assen, you're Bulgarian but at the moment you're living here in Edinburgh. How long **(a)** .... you .... (live) here?

ASSEN: For six months. I **(b)** .... (study) at the university but I **(c)** .... (not finish) my course yet.

INTERVIEWER: What **(d)** .... you .... (study)?

ASSEN: Business Studies. I **(e)** .... (complete) three written projects already and for the last two weeks we **(f)** .... (work) in a company in the city centre. That finishes next month.

INTERVIEWER: Where exactly **(g)** .... you .... (live)?

ASSEN: Well, I **(h)** .... (make) two really good friends on the course. We **(i)** .... (live) in a flat in the old town. Edinburgh is an amazing place!

6 SPEAKING Work with a partner. Take it in turns to ask and answer the questions. Use the present perfect continuous or present perfect simple in your answers. Which answers are the most imaginative?

1 Why are you hiding behind the sofa?
2 Why are your shoes so dirty?
3 Why are you crying?
4 Why are you so happy?
5 Why are you bored?
6 Why are you so tired?
7 Why aren't you watching your favourite TV programme?

Why are you hiding behind the sofa?

I've been watching a really frightening horror film.

1 **SPEAKING** Work with a partner. Make a list of words that describe each photo.

2 **SPEAKING** Take it in turns to describe one of the photos to your partner.

3 **LISTENING** 1.20 Listen to a student talking about the photos. Where would the student prefer to live? Why?

4 Listen again. Which of the words or expressions in the Speaking Bank does the speaker use?

Speaking Bank

Expressions of opinion

- Personally,
- I think (that) …
- I don't think (that) …
- I'm convinced that …
- I don't really know if …
- In my view …
- In my opinion …
- As I see it …

5 **SPEAKING** Tell your partner which place you prefer. Give reasons for your opinion.

Personally, I'd prefer to live in the village in photo a. It looks so peaceful and beautiful!

I don't really know if I'd like it. Living there would be really boring. I think that I'd prefer to live in the city. In my view city life is much more exciting.

Practice makes perfect

6 **SPEAKING** Work wth a partner. Take it in turns to do the task. Use some of the expressions in the Speaking Bank, and give reasons for your opinions.

Describe the two photos. Then:

- say which home you would prefer to live in
- give reasons for your opinion.

1 **SPEAKING** **Look at this photo of the city of Liverpool. Work with a partner. What do you know about Liverpool?**

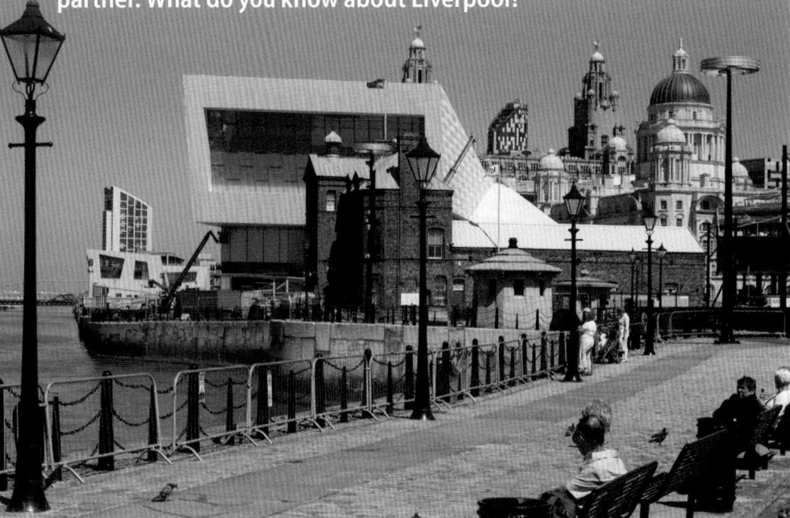

2 **Read this letter written by somebody from Liverpool and answer the questions.**

1. How have the docks in Liverpool changed in the last twenty years?
2. What is the Liverpool Arena?
3. What has been happening to Liverpool city centre?
4. What doesn't the writer like so much about the new city centre?

Dear Oana,

Thanks for your last letter. It was great to hear from you! It was really interesting learning all about your family. I'm looking forward to meeting them one day.

Well, in your last letter you asked me to tell you something about my hometown. Most people think of The Beatles and football when they think of Liverpool, but there's a lot more than just that. Actually, Liverpool has changed quite a lot in the last twenty years. It's always been an important port but the old docks used to be very depressing and dirty. They've changed a lot. Now in the Albert Dock area there are lots of cool shops, bars and restaurants. The nightlife is great. They've built a big stadium for concerts too. It's called the Liverpool Arena and a lot of big groups have already played there.

As for the city centre, they've been building an enormous new shopping centre there, called Liverpool One. They've just finished it and it's really cool! It has all the usual shops. That's the only problem with it, in my opinion. All city centres in England have started to look the same!

Anyway, write back soon and tell me about your hometown. Has it changed much in the last few years?

Love

Holly xxx

3 **The letter in 2 is informal. Which one of these things is *not* typical in informal letters?**

1. Beginning *Dear* or *Hi*
2. Calling the person by their surname
3. Using short forms of words (e.g. *Thanks* instead of *Thank you*)
4. Using contractions
5. Using interjections like 'Oh' and 'Well'
6. Using informal expressions
7. Using exclamation marks

4 **Look again at the letter in 2. Complete the expressions in the Writing Bank.**

Writing Bank

Useful words and expressions in informal letters

- To begin: *Thanks* ....
  It was .... *from you.*
- To change the subject: ....
- To end: *Write* ....
  ....

5 **Work with a partner. Make notes about your hometown. What type of place is it? What is special about it? Has it changed in the last few years? How?**

STUDY SKILLS

The first thing to do before you write a text is to read the questions carefully, and then brainstorm ideas, to decide what you are going to write about. What should you do next?

STUDY SKILLS ▶ page 147

Practice makes perfect

6 **Do the task. Include all the information and organise your notes from 5 into paragraphs. Use the information in 3 and words and expressions from the Writing Bank.**

An English-speaking friend has asked you to write them a letter about your hometown. Write the letter. Include this information.

- Say what type of place your hometown is and what is special about it.
- Describe any recent changes there.

Language reference and revision

Grammar reference

Present perfect simple

Form

Affirmative	subject + **have/has** + **past participle** *She has bought a flat.*
Negative	subject + **haven't/hasn't** + **past participle** *We haven't painted the house.*
Question	**have/has** + subject + **past participle** *Have you been to the city centre?*
Short answers	Yes, subject + **has/have.** No, subject + **hasn't/haven't** *Yes, I have. No, they haven't.*

Use

We use the present perfect simple to talk about:

1. an experience in someone's lifetime, without saying the exact time when the event occurred.
   I've travelled around Europe.
2. recent events which have a result in the present.
   She's bought a new house. (= She has a new house now.)
3. actions or situations that began in the past but continue in the present.
   Mark's lived here for ten years. (= Mark still lives here now.)

Present perfect simple and past simple

We use the present perfect to describe actions in the past, without saying when they happened. *I've been to Paris.*

If we say the exact time something happened, we must use the past simple. *I went to Paris last year.*

The present perfect can describe an action which started in the past but continues in the present. *I've lived in Paris since 2006.*

The past simple describes completed actions in the past.
I lived in Paris for five years. I arrived in 2001 and left in 2006.

ever, never, for, since, just, already, yet

We can use **ever** in questions with the present perfect. It means 'at any time in your life'. **Ever** comes just before the past participle.
Have you ever been to London?

We can use **never** (at no time in your life) in negative sentences.
I've never lived in a big city.

We use **for** and **since** when the present perfect is describing past actions or situations which continue in the present. We use **for** with periods of time and **since** with moments in time. We also use the question 'How long ...?' *How long have you lived here?*
I've lived here for three months/since May.

We use **just** to emphasise what happened very recently.
I have just seen Liz. (= I saw Liz a minute ago).

Just goes immediately before the past participle.

We use **already** to talk about something that has happened earlier than we expected. *I 'm not going. I've already been there.*

Already usually goes before the main verb, or at the end of the sentence for emphasis.

We use **yet** at the end of questions or negative sentences to ask if something we expect has happened, or to say that it hasn't.
Have you bought a flat yet? I haven't bought a flat yet.

Present perfect continuous

Form

Affirmative	subject + **have/has** + **been** + **-ing** *I've been living with my cousin.*
Negative	subject + **haven't/hasn't** + **been** + **-ing** *He hasn't been studying enough.*
Question	**have/has** + subject + **been** + **-ing** *Have you been staying here long?*

Use

We use the present perfect continuous when we want to emphasise the process and duration of an action.
I've been living here for more than five months.

If an action is very short, we cannot use the continuous form.
~~*I've been breaking my leg.*~~

We also use the continuous to emphasise that an action finished very recently or is incomplete.

I've been painting my room (=I'm dirty because I only finished a second ago or I still haven't finished.)

If we want to emphasise the completion and result of an action, or how many times an action happens, we must use the present perfect simple. *I've washed the dishes.* (=They are all finished.)

I've written seven books. not ~~*I've been writing seven books.*~~

Remember that some verbs do not usually go in the continuous form. (See page 16). ~~*I've been knowing you for three years.*~~

Vocabulary

1 Cities and houses
block of flats bungalow city centre cottage detached house factory flat inner city port semi-detached house skyscraper square suburbs terraced house town hall

2 Adjectives describing cities
busy crowded dirty historic lively noisy quiet

3 Extreme adjectives
ancient boiling dreadful enormous filthy freezing packed silent stunning tiny

4 Other words and phrases ▸ page 138

Grammar revision

Present perfect simple and past simple

1 Complete the text with the present perfect simple or past simple form of the verbs and choose the correct alternative.

I **(a)** .... (live) in this city **(b)** *for/since* many years and I love it here. The city **(c)** .... (change) a lot in the last five years. The biggest change is that the city **(d)** .... (get) a lot bigger recently. They **(e)** .... (build) a lot of offices and shops in the city centre, and there are more planned. In 2005 they **(f)** .... (start) to build an enormous new sports stadium near the port but they **(g)** .... (not finish) building it **(h)** *already/yet*. They have **(i)** *ever/just* pulled down a lot of buildings in the area. In the past, everybody **(j)** .... (want) an office there, but not now.

WORKBOOK ▸ page 22 **/ 10 points**

Present perfect continuous

2 Complete the sentences with the present perfect simple or present perfect continuous form of the verbs.

1 .... you .... (switch) the light off?
2 Come on, you need a rest. You .... (study) for five hours non-stop.
3 My hands are dirty because I .... (fix) the car.
4 Did you hear about Jacob? He .... (break) his leg.
5 My friend Charlie .... (study) in Cambridge all summer, but next week he's coming home.
6 They .... (build) more and more shopping centres in the city for a while now and I don't think they're going to stop.
7 That group .... (make) more than ten CDs.
8 I'm very sorry. .... you .... (wait) for long?
9 My legs are tired because I .... (walk) all day.
10 That's it! We .... (finish) this exercise.

WORKBOOK ▸ page 25 **/ 10 points**

Vocabulary revision

Cities and houses

1 Write the words.

1 A house which is separate, not touching other houses:
....
2 A small house, usually in a village or in the country:
....
3 A building for the offices of the local government:
....
4 The area where ships stop, where there are usually buildings:
....
5 An area where many people live, and there are often social problems there: ....
6 An area away from the centre of the city where richer people live: ....
7 A house which is attached to houses on both sides:
....
8 A tall building where there are many homes:
....

WORKBOOK ▸ page 20 **/ 8 points**

Adjectives describing cities

2 What adjectives describe these situations?

1 A concert in a small room with hundreds of people: c....................
2 A place which nobody ever cleans: d....................
3 A place which is old and interesting: h....................
4 A place where there is no noise: q....................
5 A place where there are a lot of exciting things happening: l....................
6 A place with lots of people, movement and activity: b....................

WORKBOOK ▸ page 20 **/ 6 points**

Extreme adjectives

3 Write the normal equivalent of these extreme adjectives .

1 stunning ....
2 boiling ....
3 filthy ....
4 dreadful ....
5 enormous ....
6 packed ....

WORKBOOK ▸ page 23 **/ 6 points**

Total / 40 points

4 Food for thought

Grammar ‣ *Will, be going to,* present simple and present continuous for future ‣ Future continuous and future perfect
Vocabulary ‣ Food ‣ Describing food ‣ Prefixes
Speaking ‣ Making plans
Writing ‣ Invitations and replies

‣ Vocabulary

Food

1 Look at these photos. What food and drink can you see?

a

b

c

d

2 Work with a partner. Put these words in the correct column.

bread chewing gum chicken chips corn doughnut oil pea pie plum semi-skimmed milk strawberry tuna turkey

Fruit	Vegetables	Meat/ Fish/ Seafood	Dairy products	Sweets/ Bakery products	Other

3 With your partner, you have five minutes to add as many words as possible to the different columns. When you finish, compare words with another pair of students and add any new words.

4a Look at these two lists. Which word is the 'odd one out' in each list? Why?

1 milk, butter, bread, yoghurt

2 lemon, strawberry, banana, corn

4b Work with a partner and prepare your own 'odd one out' exercise with food and drink.

4c See if other students can do your exercise.

5a SPEAKING Look at the questions and check that you understand the words in *italics*.

1 What do you usually have for *breakfast*?
2 Which is usually bigger for you, *lunch* or *dinner*?
3 What is a typical *starter* in a restaurant in your country?
4 What is a popular *main course*?
5 What is your favourite national *dish*?
6 What is your favourite *dessert*?
7 Do you usually have a *snack* in the morning or afternoon? What do you have?

5b Use the questions to interview your partner.

Describing food

6 Match these words with the definitions.

fresh fried frozen healthy junk raw spicy stale sweet tasty vegetarian

1 with a hot, strong flavour ....
2 good, with lots of flavour ....
3 not cooked ....
4 for people who don't eat meat or fish ....
5 good for your body ....
6 preserved by becoming very cold ....
7 cooked in hot oil ....
8 recently picked, caught or prepared ....
9 not good for you because it has a lot of salt, sugar or fat ....
10 with a lot of sugar ....
11 old and bad, not fresh ....

7 Choose two types of food that go with each of the words in 6. Does your partner agree with you?

fresh – fresh fish, fresh strawberries

8 LISTENING 1.21 Listen. For each dialogue, choose a word from 6 to describe the food.

1 .... 3 ....
2 .... 4 ....

9 SPEAKING Work with a partner. Describe a type of food or drink and see if your partner can identify it.

It's a type of meat. It's quite healthy. It comes from a bird. The bird's bigger than a chicken.

Turkey!

The future of food

1 When you eat your dinner tonight, will you really know what you're eating? Yes, it certainly looks like fried chicken, chips and peas, but do you know what's hiding
5 inside? Be careful, because soon not everything is going to be what it seems, thanks to nanotechnology.
The word 'nano' simply means 'small'. Nanotechnology is the name we give to
10 an area of science which studies how to control matter on a tiny, molecular scale.
So, how is nanotechnology going to affect the food of the future? One example is a new product that the big multinational
15 company Kraft are working on. It's a transparent drink with no taste. It doesn't sound very exciting, does it? But the idea is that you, the consumer, will decide what colour and flavour you want when you get
20 home. You can even decide what nutrients it will have in it. When you arrive at your house, you'll put your drink in a special microwave transmitter. This will activate nanocapsules. Each nanocapsule is about
25 2,000 times smaller than the width of a hair. These nanocapsules will contain the necessary chemicals for the drink which you choose. So you can make a blue drink, tasting of strawberry, with some omega-3
30 oil in it. The other nanocapsules will stay in the drink but will pass through your body, unused.
Does this sound like science fiction? Well, already in Australia one of the
35 most popular types of bread, Tip-Top, contains nanocapsules of tuna oil. The nanocapsules contain the oil but they keep the taste inside so that the bread doesn't taste of fish. Kids who hate fish
40 get the health benefits of omega-3 but without suffering! And the good news for older eaters is that it will be possible to use nanocapsules to take away the cholesterol from meat. Nanofilm will
45 be able to cover food so that it will take longer before it goes stale. And soon a new type of chewing gum is coming. It will contain chemicals that will actively clean your teeth.
50 Not everybody is happy, though. One of the main problems is precisely that we won't know what our food, or even an innocent bottle of water, actually contains. And, anyway, if humans have
55 managed to live so long eating natural, fresh food, do we really need to turn everything, from an apple to a glass of milk, into some complicated, scientific experiment?
60 Some scientists say that nanotechnology is completely safe and natural. It only uses the same old natural substances, but it makes them smaller. But others disagree. They say that matter doesn't
65 act in the same way when it gets much bigger or much smaller. There are different risks associated with nanotechnology and nobody knows what the risks are yet. As one top scientist
70 says: 'We are giving very toxic chemicals the ability to go where they've never gone before. Where will they end up? We have to ask ourselves if it's a good idea.'
Tomorrow I'm having lunch at my
75 favourite restaurant. I just hope the 'chicken surprise' doesn't contain too many surprises!

1 You have three minutes to read this text about nanotechnology and food. Answer these two questions.

1 What is nanotechnology?
2 Is the text in favour of nanotechnology in the world of food, is it against it, or is it a mixture?

2 Read the text again and decide if the statements are true (T) or false (F). Write the number of the line(s) where you found the answer.

1 Nanotechnology has already made a big change to the food we eat. T/F .....
2 Kraft's new drink can taste of different things, depending on what you want. T/F .....
3 You will need a special gadget to create your Kraft drink. T/F .....
4 Tip-Top bread is good for people who don't like the taste of fish. T/F .....
5 All the benefits of nanotechnology in food are for children. T/F .....
6 Nanotechnology can help food to stay fresh for longer. T/F .....
7 There are scientists who are in favour of nanotechnology and scientists who are against it. T/F .....
8 One problem with nanotechnology is that, because it is new, it is difficult to know exactly what effects it will bring. T/F .....

3 What is the meaning of these words in the text? Look at the words in context and then use a dictionary to check your ideas.

1 hiding ....
2 matter ....
3 scale ....
4 nutrients ....
5 width ....
6 managed ....
7 risks ....

4 SPEAKING What about *you*?

1 What do you think about nanotechnology in food?
2 Which of the products in the text do you think is the most interesting? Why?

I think nanotechnology will be a good thing.

Maybe, but I prefer natural food.

GRAMMAR GUIDE

Will, be going to, present simple and present continuous for future

1a Match the sentences 1–4 with the explanations (a–d).

1 Tomorrow I'**m having** lunch at my favourite restaurant. ....
2 When you **eat** your dinner tonight, will you really know what you're eating? ....
3 It **will** contain chemicals to clean your teeth. ....
4 From what we can see, nanotechnology **is going to** affect the food of the future. ....

a We use the present simple with time expressions like *when, after, before, as soon as* to talk about the future.
b We use the present continuous to talk about fixed, confirmed future arrangements.
c We use *will* to make general predictions.
d We use *be going* to to make predictions based on some sort of evidence.

1b Read the sentences and complete rules a–d with *will, be going to* or the present simple.

1 The conference **begins** at ten o'clock tomorrow.
2 I'**m going** to attend the conference.
3 It **will** be the second annual conference.
4 Hey! I know. I'**ll** invite Scott.

a We use .... for decisions that we make at the moment of speaking.
b We use .... to talk about an objective truth, a 'fact'.
c We use .... to talk about a future event that is part of a timetable or routine.
d We use .... to talk about plans or intentions.

GRAMMAR REFERENCE ▸ page 54

2 Complete the sentences with the correct form of the present simple or *will*.

1 When the waiter .... (come), we .... (order) our food.
2 My dad .... (call) you as soon as he .... (finish) his dinner.
3 I .... (do) my homework before the lesson .... (start).
4 When you .... (go) to the shops tomorrow, ... you .... (buy) some bread?
5 Before my mum .... (get) home tonight, I .... (clean) the kitchen.
6 When Christmas .... (come), she .... (have) enough money to buy a present.
7 I .... (not take) the pie out of the oven until it .... (be) ready.
8 As soon as the adverts .... (come) on, we .... (make) the coffee.

3 What do you think is going to happen in each situation? Write predictions with these words.

burn cut drop fall

1

....
....

2

....
....

3

....
....

4

....
....

4 **Look at this poster for an event. How many sentences in the present continuous can you make?**

The future of food

Next Monday! A talk by two experts!

Where? Town Hall

Start: 6pm

First speaker: Film director Stephanie Brand talks about her new film *What is in our food?*

7pm Watch a preview of the film

8pm Second speaker: Scientist Oliver Reeves explains the dangers of nanotechnology

8.30pm Drinks

9pm Prize-giving ceremony for school projects

TV cameras will be there to make a programme about the talk.

Two experts are talking next Monday. They're having the event at the town hall.

5 **Look at these pairs of sentences. Choose the correct alternative. If you think both are correct, mark them both, but be ready to explain any difference in meaning.**

1a What do you do this weekend?
1b What are you doing this weekend?

2a I think it'll rain tomorrow.
2b I think it's raining tomorrow.

3a Someone's calling. I'll see who it is.
3b Someone's calling. I'm seeing who it is.

4a She's going to win the election.
4b She'll win the election.

5a When mum comes home, she'll make the dinner.
5b When mum will come home, she'll make the dinner.

6a What time does your plane leave?
6b What time is your plane leaving?

STUDY SKILLS

When you choose between two different grammatical structures, is it always a question of one is right and the other is wrong?
STUDY SKILLS page 147

6a SPEAKING **Make notes on these topics with predictions for this year.**

clothes entertainment music sport technology your city your country

6b **Compare your predictions with your partner. Are they similar or different?**

Who do you think will win the Champions' League this year?

I don't know, but I think it'll be an English team.

Prefixes

1a **Match these words with the explanations.**

overcooked **pre**cooked **re**cooked **under**cooked

1 not cooked enough ....
2 cooked again ....
3 cooked before ....
4 cooked too much ....

1b **The parts of the word in bold are prefixes. What do prefixes do? Do they change the meaning of the word or do they change the type of word (noun, verb, adjective, verb, etc)?**

STUDY SKILLS

How can prefixes and suffixes help us when we are reading? STUDY SKILLS page 147

2 **Match these prefixes and their meaning.**

1 pre	a again
2 over	b not enough
3 mis	c the opposite
4 inter	d wrong, incorrect
5 dis	e before
6 co	f too much
7 re	g with, together
8 under	h between

3 **Complete the sentences by adding the correct prefix to the word in bold.**

1 You have to ....***do*** the exercise because the first time you did it you made a lot of mistakes.
2 Sorry, I ....***understood*** what you said. I thought you said 30, not 13.
3 There are lots of advantages and .... ***advantages*** with nanotechnology in food.
4 They've ....***booked*** the flight – there aren't enough seats for everyone.
5 Food is still a terrible problem in many countries. Some people ....***estimate*** the problem and don't think it's so important.
6 The governments of the world need to ....***operate*** and work together.

4a **Complete these questions with words from 1 and 3.**

1 Have you ever .... something that somebody said to you in English? When?
2 Forget the good things. What do you think are the .... of new technology?
3 Do you ever eat .... meals or do you always eat freshly prepared meals?
4 Have you ever had to .... an exam? Why?
5 What do you think is the biggest .... problem at the moment? Which countries does it affect?
6 When you work in a team, do you think that you .... well?

4b SPEAKING **Now interview your partner using the questions.**

Food, American-style

Literature
A poem about food

1 Look at this famous poem written by an American poet called William Carlos Williams. What is the poet doing in this poem?

1 Asking somebody to do something
2 Saying he is sorry for something
3 Explaining how to do something

2 Work with a partner. Do you like this poem? Why/Why not?

3 Work with a partner. Try to write a simple poem apologising to somebody for doing something wrong. Use the poem here as a model. Begin:

This is just to say
I have ...

This is just to say
I have eaten
the plums
that were in the icebox

and which
you were probably
saving
for breakfast

forgive me
they were delicious
so sweet
and so cold

INSIDE INFORMATION

- William Carlos Williams lived from 1883 to 1963.
- In theory, this poem was a note to his wife.
- He inspired some of the famous Beat Generation poets, like Allen Ginsberg.

Cross-curricular – Economics
The US Fast Food Industry

4 Work with a partner. Ask and answer the questions.

1 Do you like fast food? What is your favourite type?
2 How often do you eat fast food?
3 How popular is fast food in your country?
4 Which section of the population eats the most fast food in your country?
5 Are there many adverts for fast food in your country? Where?
6 Why do you think fast food is so popular generally?
7 What are the disadvantages of fast food?

5 You are going to listen to a radio programme about the fast food industry in the USA. Before you listen, look at the Word Booster.

6 1.22 Listen. Are these sentences true (T) or false (F)?

1 The fast food industry grew quickly because of the changing role of women in society. T/F
2 One in eight Americans works or has worked in a McDonald's restaurant. T/F
3 The fast food industry has always made adverts for children. T/F
4 Fast food is not permitted in US school canteens. T/F
5 Some fast food companies use text books and TV programmes in school classrooms. T/F
6 Half of American children are obese at the moment. T/F
7 In *Super Size Me*, a man had to eat one meal every day in a fast food restaurant. T/F
8 Generally, fast food companies don't care about bad publicity. T/F

7 Can you explain why the false statements in 6 are false? Listen again if necessary.

8 What about *you*?
Do you think young people are becoming more unhealthy in your country? If so, why?

WORD BOOSTER

Match the words and definitions.

1 economic growth
2 global economy
3 expand
4 canteen
5 TV channel
6 obese
7 improve

a a TV station and the programmes it makes
b get bigger
c get better
d a room at school, work or in a hospital where people eat
e overweight, in a way that is dangerous for your health
f the economies of the world considered as one economic system
g bigger production of goods and services

International cultural knowledge
Thanksgiving Day

9 Work with a partner. How much do you know about Thanksgiving Day in the USA? Answer the questions. If you don't know the answers, guess.

1 When is Thanksgiving Day?
2 What is the origin of Thanksgiving Day?
3 When was the first Thanksgiving Day?
4 What food do people eat?
5 Are there any other popular customs in American cities on Thanksgiving Day?
6 Are there any unusual customs?

10 Read the answers to the questions in the text. Match each question in 9 with the answer.

11 Why do these people, places or things appear in the text? Write one or two sentences to explain each one.

1 sharing food
2 Stars and Stripes
3 Florida
4 George Washington
5 Macy's

PROJECT

12a Work in groups. What food is traditional at festivals in your country? Make a list of special dishes, sweets or cakes and write down when you eat them. Then choose one.

12b Each person in the group should find out information about the dish you have chosen. For example, how, why and when did it start to become popular? How exactly do you make it? Look for photos or pictures.

12c In your group, decide how to present your information to the rest of the class. Prepare it and present it.

Question ....

The traditional meal on Thanksgiving Day is based around turkey. In fact, people sometimes call Thanksgiving Day 'Turkey Day'. With their roast turkey, people usually eat boiled potatoes and corn. Freshly baked pumpkin pie is another common element of Thanksgiving Day meals. These ingredients were all common types of food that were natural to North America.

Question ....

It has similarities with ancient festivals which were to celebrate the fruits of the harvest, to give thanks for all the food that they had collected. Traditionally, harvest festivals have also been about sharing this food, offering food to people who are in need of it.

Question ....

The National Turkey Federation gives three turkeys as a present to the US president. Nowadays, one of the turkeys becomes part of the president's Thanksgiving meal, but the other two are allowed to go free in a special ceremony in front of the White House. Recently, the American public has been able to vote for the names of these turkeys (one recent pair of turkeys was called Stars and Stripes – the name of the US flag). The two turkeys then fly first-class from Washington to Los Angeles, where they appear in a parade organised by Disneyland!

Question ....

There is a record from 1565 of a Thanksgiving celebration by Spanish people living in Florida. The first English people who came to North America in the 17th century also started to have Thanksgiving celebrations. George Washington, the first president of the United States of America, created the first official Thanksgiving Day on October 3, 1789.

Question ....

Thanksgiving Day is always on the fourth Thursday of November. The end of November is also the end of the harvest season, the time when farmers have finished collecting all their crops.

Question ....

On Thanksgiving Day, there are often parades in the streets. The famous New York department store, Macy's, organises a big parade where famous people often appear. American football matches are also very popular on Thanksgiving Day.

WORD BOOSTER

Match the words and definitions.

1 roast
2 boiled
3 baked
4 pumpkin
5 harvest
6 share
7 crops
8 parade
9 department store

a cooked in an oven with oil
b a big round vegetable with a thick orange skin
c plants grown for food
d a big shop where you can buy lots of very different things
e give a part of something to another person
f cooked in very hot water
g an organised walk in the streets to celebrate something
h the activity of collecting plants grown for food
i the way bread, cakes and pies are prepared in an oven

1 SPEAKING **Work with a partner. Look at the imaginary scene of life in the future. Take it in turns to describe what you can see.**

2 LISTENING 1.23 **Listen to four people talking about their predictions for life in the year 2050. Is each speaker generally optimistic or pessimistic about the future?**

Speaker 1: Speaker 3:
Speaker 2: Speaker 4:

3 **Listen again. Match the speakers and their opinions.**

		1	*2*	*3*	*4*
a	We won't be destroying the atmosphere when we use transport.				
b	Some serious health problems will have stopped existing.				
c	The planet will have become too dry.				
d	It won't be easy for everybody to get medical treatment.				
e	People in poorer countries will be eating more.				
f	Everybody will be able to send emails and communicate all over the world.				
g	Our food will come from laboratories.				
h	Life won't be very different.				
i	Doctors won't be able to save everyone.				

4 SPEAKING **What about *you*?**

Which of the opinions about the future do you agree with? Share your ideas with the rest of the class.

I think it'll be hotter and drier in the future.

GRAMMAR GUIDE

Future continuous and future perfect

1a Look at the sentences. Which sentences are in the future continuous and which are in the future perfect?

1. They **will have found** a cure for cancer by the year 2050.
2. In the year 2050 **we will be using** new types of transport.
3. We**'ll be living** in more comfortable homes in 2050.
4. Most of the planet **will have turned** into desert by the year 2050.

1b Choose the correct alternative.

1. We use the *future continuous/future perfect* to talk about activities in progress at a particular time in the future.
2. We use the *future continuous/future perfect* to talk about activities that will be finished before a particular time in the future.
3. We often use the preposition *by/in* with the future perfect. It means 'some time before'.

1c Complete the rules.

1. To make the future .... we use ***will/won't*** + **be** + ...
2. To make the future .... we use ***will/won't*** + **have** + ...

GRAMMAR REFERENCE ▶ page 54

2a Complete the predictions with these verbs in the future continuous.

do eat have live not drive not grow speak work

1. We .... our holidays on the moon in 2050.
2. I think people .... in high-technology homes.
3. We .... cars that use petrol in 2050.
4. Perhaps we .... genetically-modified food in the future.
5. Most people .... at home via the Internet, not in an office.
6. Everybody in the world .... English in the year 2050.
7. Robots .... jobs like cleaning or building.
8. Farmers .... any fresh fruit or vegetables because there won't be enough water.

2b Which predictions do you agree with?

3 Complete these predictions about the year 2050 with the future perfect form of the verbs. Make the sentences affirmative or negative depending on your own opinion.

1 By 2050 we .... (find) a cure for all illnesses.
2 We .... (use) all the world's petrol.
3 Polar bears .... (become) extinct.
4 The North Pole .... (disappear).
5 Astronauts .... (land) on Mars.
6 They .... (invent) clothes that can make you invisible.
7 Temperatures .... (get) much higher.
8 Coasts .... (change) because of the rising water level.

4 Look at the schedule of the US President for next Monday.

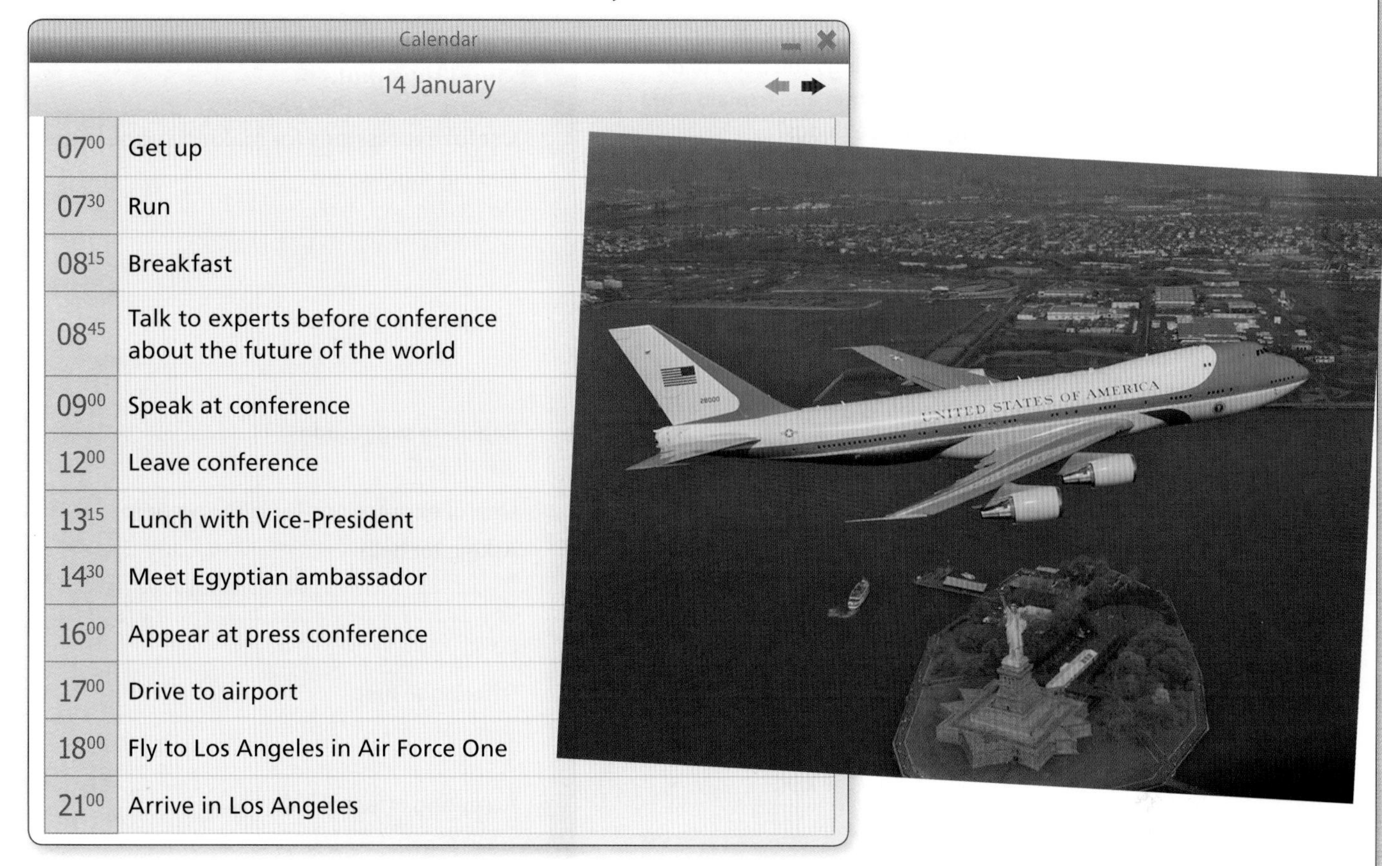

Calendar

14 January

Time	Activity
07^{00}	Get up
07^{30}	Run
08^{15}	Breakfast
08^{45}	Talk to experts before conference about the future of the world
09^{00}	Speak at conference
12^{00}	Leave conference
13^{15}	Lunch with Vice-President
14^{30}	Meet Egyptian ambassador
16^{00}	Appear at press conference
17^{00}	Drive to airport
18^{00}	Fly to Los Angeles in Air Force One
21^{00}	Arrive in Los Angeles

5 Complete the sentences with either the future continuous or future perfect form of the verb.

1 At half past seven next Monday the President .... (get up).
2 At quarter to eight he .... (run).
3 At twenty past eight he .... (have) breakfast.
4 At quarter to nine he .... (have) breakfast.
5 At ten to nine he .... (talk) to experts.
6 By twelve o'clock he .... (speak) at a conference.
7 By half past two he .... (eat) with the Vice-President.
8 At half past two he .... (meet) the Egyptian ambassador.

6 SPEAKING Compare your answers in 5 with a partner. How many answers are similar?

7 SPEAKING In pairs, ask and answer questions about what you will be doing or will have done at different times.

What will you be doing at seven o'clock this evening?

I think I'll be watching TV. And you?

8a SPEAKING Think about your life when you're thirty years old. What will you be doing? What will you have done? Think about these ideas and events.

become famous buy a house get married
live at home live in a different country
make a lot of money study work

8b Ask your partner questions about how they imagine their life when they are thirty.

Do you think you'll be studying when you're thirty?

No, I think I'll have finished.

1 SPEAKING **Look at the pictures of different things you need to do when you organise a party. Work with a partner and explain what each one is. Have you ever done any of these things?**

2 LISTENING 1.24 **Listen to a conversation between Toby and Amy. Toby is having a party on Saturday. What jobs in 1 does Amy offer to help Toby with?**

3 **Now read and listen to the conversation. Which two jobs isn't Amy going to help with? Why not?**

TOBY: Hi Amy. Listen. What are you doing on Saturday?
AMY: Nothing much.
TOBY: I'm having a party at my place in the evening. Do you fancy coming?
AMY: Yes, I'd love to. Would you like any help getting things ready for the party?
TOBY: That would be great.
AMY: How can I help?
TOBY: Would you mind helping to prepare some food?
AMY: Hmm. I'm sorry but I'm not a very good cook.
TOBY: Well, could you give me a hand buying some food and drink?
AMY: OK. When are you going shopping?
TOBY: How about tomorrow afternoon?
AMY: OK, why not?
TOBY: Thanks! And would you mind helping me to get the room ready on Saturday?
AMY: OK. Why don't we have lunch together on Saturday and then get the room ready in the afternoon?
TOBY: Great! Could you help me to tidy up on Sunday too?
AMY: Sorry, I can't. I'm going out for the day with my parents.
TOBY: That's OK. I'll ask Dylan to help me.

4 **Complete the Speaking Bank with the expressions from the dialogue.**

a That would be great!
b Yes, I'd love to
c How can I help?
d How about (going tomorrow afternoon)?
e Would you mind (helping to prepare some food)?

5a PRONUNCIATION 1.25 **Listen and check your answers to 4. What do you notice about the intonation in each sentence?**

5b **Listen and repeat the sentences with the correct intonation.**

Speaking Bank

Useful expressions for making suggestions

Making suggestions
Do you fancy (coming)?
Why don't we (have lunch together)?
1 ....

Accepting suggestions
2 ....
Great! OK. Why not?

Rejecting suggestions
Sorry, I can't.

Useful expressions for offering help

Asking for help
3 ....
Could you give me a hand (buying some food)?
Could you help me to (tidy up)?

Offering to help
Would you like any help?
4 ....

Accepting offers of help
Thanks!
5 ....

EXAM SUCCESS

You are going to do an oral activity that is sometimes called 'negotiating'. You usually work with another person (a student or the examiner). The examiner explains a situation where you and the other speaker need to make a decision. Who should speak more in this type of exercise – you or your partner?

EXAM SUCCESS ▸ page 151

Practice makes perfect

6a SPEAKING **Work with a partner. One of you is going to invite a group of friends for a meal. The other person offers to help with some (but not all) of the preparations. Prepare the dialogue. Use the dialogue in 3 and the expressions in the Speaking Bank to help you.**

6b **Practise the dialogue and then act it out for other students.**

1 **Read these two invitations (1 & 2). What is the special occasion in each invitation?**

1

Dear Mr and Mrs Pearson

Mr and Mrs George Smith request the pleasure of your company at the wedding of their daughter Lily to Mr Thomas Derby on Saturday 27th August.

The ceremony will be held at seven o'clock at Mount Olive Church, Chester.

There will be a dinner reception at Chester Golf Club immediately following the ceremony.

RSVP

2

Dear Luke,

I'm having a BBQ in my garden next Sunday. There'll be lots of food (for vegetarians too!) so you only need to bring your own drinks. I'll be serving the first sausages at 12.30. So don't be late!

If it rains, we'll have the BBQ the following Sunday.

Hope you can make it! Matt x

2 **Read these replies (a and b). Which invitations are they responding to? Complete the spaces with the correct information.**

a

Dear ....,

Thanks for the invitation. I'm really sorry but I won't be able to come. On .... it's my parents' wedding anniversary and they're taking us out for the day. I hope you have a great time and that the weather's fine. Don't eat too many burgers!

from

....

b

Dear ....,

Thank you very much for your kind invitation. We regret to say that we will be unable to attend the .... since we will be out of the country at that time. We wish the happy couple all the best and will be thinking of you all.

Best wishes,

....

3 **Look again at the invitations and replies and complete the examples in the Writing Bank.**

Writing Bank

Useful expressions in invitations and replies

In **informal** invitations we:

- use contractions like ....
- use *Please* .... or *I'd love to see you there* to invite people.
- finish the invitation with *Hope to see you there* or ....

In **formal** invitations we:

- do not use contractions.
- use *We* .... *of your company* to invite people.
- often finish the invitation with the letters .... (French: *Répondez S'il Vous Plaît*), which means that we want people to confirm if they are accepting the invitation or not.

In **informal** replies we:

- use contractions.
- thank the person who has invited us with .... *for the invitation.*
- use *I'm really* .... *but I/we won't be able to come* if we cannot accept the invitation.
- explain why we can't accept the invitation if this is the case.

In **formal** replies we:

- do not use contractions.
- thank the person who has invited us with .... *you very much for your* .... *invitation.*
- use *We* .... *to say that we will be unable to attend* if we cannot accept the invitation.
- explain why we can't accept the invitation if this is the case.

EXAM SUCCESS

You are going to do a piece of writing where the instructions tell you who you are writing to and what information you need to include in the letter. This is sometimes called a 'transactional' piece of writing. Do you think the style is important in this type of task?

EXAM SUCCESS ▶ page 151

Practice makes perfect

4a **Look at the task and write the invitation.**

You are having a party next Saturday. Write an invitation to an English friend. Include this information:

- why you are having the party
- what day, date and time the party is
- where the party is, and why you decided that place
- how to get to the place
- which other people are coming
- what food, drink, music or other entertainment there will be
- what time the party will end.

4b **Swap invitations with another student. Write replies to each other's invitations explaining why you cannot go.**

Language reference and revision

Grammar reference

Be going to and will

We use **be going to** to talk about plans and intentions which we have already decided to do in the future.

We've decided that we're going to order a pizza.

We can also use **be going to** to make predictions about the future, particularly when we have evidence for the prediction.

The waiter isn't very strong. I think he's going to drop all those plates.

We use **will** and **won't** to make general predictions about the future. We often use **think**, **hope**, **expect**, etc with **will** and **won't** to express our opinion.

I think the future will be amazing.

We also use **will** and **won't** when we decide to do something at the moment of speaking.

A: I can't do this exercise. B: I'll help you.

We use **will** and **won't** to talk about the future when it is an objective truth.

It's her birthday next month. She'll be sixteen.

We use **definitely**, **probably**, **perhaps** and **it's possible that** with **will** to say how certain we think something is.

Definitely and **probably** come just after **will** but just before **won't**.

We'll definitely like the food. The food definitely won't be bad.

Present continuous and present simple for future

We use the present continuous to talk about future arrangements or plans that have been confirmed.

Tomorrow I'm flying to London. I bought the tickets last month.

We use the present simple with time expressions like **when**, **as soon as**, **until**, **after** and **before**. We cannot use **will** with these time expressions. *When I see him, I'll give him the note.*

We can also use the present simple to talk about the future when the action is part of a timetable or routine.

My plane leaves at 8am tomorrow.

Tomorrow I have my English class at two o'clock.

Future continuous

Form

Affirmative	subject + **will** + **be** + **-ing** *She will be having lunch at one o'clock tomorrow.*
Negative	subject + **will not/won't** + **be** + **-ing** *We won't be having dinner at 6pm tomorrow.*
Question	**will** + subject + **be** + **-ing** *Will you be having breakfast at 9 o'clock tomorrow?*
Short answers	Yes, subject + **will**. No, subject + **won't**. *Yes, I will. No, they won't.*

Use

We use the future continuous to talk about activities in progress at a particular time in the future. The activities are in progress and so they are unfinished.

At this time tomorrow, I'll be watching a film at the cinema.

Future perfect

Form

Affirmative	subject + **will** + **have** + **past participle** *She will have had lunch by 3pm.*
Negative	subject + **will not/won't** + **have** + **past participle** *We won't have finished the exam by half past nine.*
Question	**will** + subject + **have** + **past participle** *Will you have done your homework by 9pm tonight?*
Short answers	Yes, subject + **will**. No, subject + **won't**. *Yes, I will. No, they won't.*

Use

We use the future perfect to talk about activities that will be finished before a certain time in the future.

I will have read this book by Saturday.

We often use the preposition *by* with the future perfect. It means 'some time before'.

Vocabulary

1 Food

Dairy products: semi-skimmed milk
Fruit: plum strawberry
Meat/fish/seafood: chicken tuna turkey
Sweets/bakery products: bread doughnut pie
Vegetables: chips corn pea
Others: chewing gum dessert dish main course oil snack starter

2 Describing food

fresh fried frozen healthy junk raw spicy stale sweet tasty vegetarian

3 Prefixes

co-operate **dis**advantage **inter**national **mis**understand **over**book **over**cooked **pre**-cooked **re**-cooked **re**-do **under**cooked **under**estimate

4 Other words and phrases ▶ page 139

Grammar revision

Present simple for future

1 Complete the dialogue with *will* or the present simple form of the verb.

Alex: What time **(a)** .... your train .... (leave) tomorrow?
Liam: I don't know. When I **(b)** .... (arrive) at the station tomorrow, I **(c)** .... (look) at the information board.
Alex: **(d)** .... you .... (remember) to call me as soon as you **(e)** .... (get) to the conference?
Liam: Don't worry. I **(f)** .... (call) you.

WORKBOOK ▶ page 30

/ 6 points

Will, be going to, present continuous for future

2 Choose the best alternative.

1 A: What are you going to do this weekend?
B: *I'll have/'m having* a party at my house. I've invited fifty people!
2 A: What are you going to do this weekend?
B: I haven't made any plans. I know! *I'll call/'m calling* my friends. We can go out together.
3 A: Look at those black clouds.
B: Yes. It's *raining/going to rain* this afternoon.
4 In my opinion, temperatures *will get/are getting* higher in the next twenty years.
5 Tomorrow my sister *will be/is being* twenty-one.
6 I'm sure that Johnson *will win/is winning* the elections next year.
7 I can't go out with you on Saturday. *I'll go/'m going* to my grandmother's house.

WORKBOOK ▶ page 30

/ 7 points

Future continuous and future perfect

3 Look at the situations and complete the sentences with the future continuous or future perfect form of the verb.

1 I'll do my homework between 6pm and 8pm.
By 9pm ....
(do my homework)
2 She's going to study English for one month next August.
On 15th August ....
(study English)
3 Tomorrow I'll get up at 11am.
At 10am .... (sleep)
4 Tomorrow I have an appointment at the dentist from 4 o'clock to 4.30.
By 5pm ....
(leave the dentist)
5 We have to give our teacher the project before Thursday.
By Friday ....
(give our teacher the project)
6 I'm going for a run tomorrow between 5 and 6pm.
Tomorrow at 5.15pm ....
(run)
7 He's reading the last chapter of the book right now.
By tomorrow ....
(read the book)

WORKBOOK ▶ page 33

/ 7 points

Vocabulary revision

Food

1 Write the names of the food.

1 .... 2 .... 3 ....
4 .... 5 .... 6 .... 7 ....

WORKBOOK ▶ page 28

/ 7 points

Describing food

2 Complete the sentences with these words. There are two words you don't need.

fresh fried frozen junk raw spicy stale sweet tasty

1 Waiter! This fish isn't .... It smells terrible.
2 This bread is .... It's at least a week old!
3 I don't like eating too much .... food because a lot of oil can be bad for you.
4 .... food is really convenient. We buy lots, keep it all in the freezer and then get it out when we need it.
5 This coffee is too .... How much sugar did you put in it?
6 I don't think it's fair to call all hamburgers .... food because in some restaurants they make them with top quality ingredients.
7 Sashimi is a Japanese dish with .... fish. They don't cook it.

WORKBOOK ▶ page 28

/ 7 points

Prefixes

3 Underline the prefix and write its meaning.

1 disadvantage ....
2 re-cook ....
3 co-operate ....
4 underestimate ....
5 international ....
6 misunderstand ....

WORKBOOK ▶ page 31

/ 6 points

Total */ 40 points*

Gateway to exams *Units 3–4*

Reading

Tip for Reading Exams

In reading activities where you complete a text with missing sentences, remember …

First read the text quickly to get a general idea. Then read the missing sentences and find the sections of the text where you think the sentences go. Read those sections again slowly and carefully.

EXAM SUCCESS ▸ page 151

1 Work with a partner. You are going to read about the coldest city on earth. Make predictions about life there.

2 Read the text and check your predictions. Ignore the gaps.

Yakutsk: life in the coldest city on earth

1 ____. The metal sticks to your face and it's extremely painful when you try to take your glasses off. I know this because I've just arrived in Yakutsk, a place where friendly local people suggest not wearing glasses when you go outside.

2 ____. It's famous because it is probably the coldest city on earth. In January, the coldest month, the *highest* temperature is -40ºC. Today it is -43ºC and the city is covered in freezing fog which only allows you to see ten metres in front of you. I decided to come to Yakutsk myself to find out how people can survive in the coldest city on earth.

3 ____. In fact one person told me that last November was exceptionally warm – -25ºC! Before I go outdoors in Yakutsk for the first time I put on two pairs of socks, long underwear, two big jumpers, a heavy winter coat with hood, two pairs of gloves, and a hat. And when I walk out, I feel … fine. In fact, I feel good.

4 ____. Then I just can't feel it, and that is dangerous. Then the cold penetrates my two pairs of gloves and starts to attack my fingers. Next it's my ears. And then my legs. Finally my whole body hurts and I decide to go back indoors. I look at my watch. I've been outside for just 13 minutes.

5 ____. Now it takes six hours by plane. There are no trains to Yakutsk. The other alternatives are a 1,000 mile boat ride up the Lena River (only during summer, when the river isn't frozen) or a 1,200 mile drive on the 'road of bones' (only during winter), which runs over the frozen rivers.

6 ____. Workers continue working on building sites up to -50ºC. When it gets colder than this the metal becomes too fragile to work with. Children go to school unless it's below -55ºC. 'Of course it's difficult to live here' says Vladimir Fyodorov, editor of the regional newspaper. 'But the people here were born here. It's our home. What can you do about it?'

3 Read the text again and put sentences a–f in gaps 1–6.

- **a** The inhuman temperatures are just part of daily life for the residents of the city.
- **b** In the past it took more than three months to get to Yakutsk from Moscow.
- **c** I soon discover that local people describe -40ºC as 'cold, but not very cold'.
- **d** Yakutsk is a remote city in eastern Siberia with a population of 200,000.
- **e** But after a few minutes, the cold weather starts to make my face feel uncomfortable.
- **f** At -45ºC wearing glasses is not a good idea.

Writing

4 Read this invitation and answer the questions.

1 What is the invitation for?
2 What does Matt want?
3 Is the invitation formal or informal? How do you know?

Dear ___________

I'm having a party at 8pm on Saturday 18th April to celebrate the end of term and I'd love you to come. You don't need to bring any drinks but I'm asking everyone to bring something to eat. And it would be great if some of you could come early to help me get everything ready! I really hope you can make it!

Matt

Tip for Writing Exams

In transactional activities, remember …

It is essential to write in the correct style – informal, semi-formal or formal. Use contractions and informal expressions in informal texts but not in formal or semi-formal ones.

EXAM SUCCESS ▸ page 151

5 Write a reply to Matt's invitation.

- Tell Matt what food you are going to bring.
- Explain why you can't come early to help.
- Ask if you can bring a friend to the party.
- Offer to help tidy up after the party.

▶ Use of English

▶ Tip for Use of English Exams

In multiple-choice cloze activities, remember …

Read the complete text first without thinking about the gaps. Then read again and think of words that could go in each gap. Look at the alternatives. Are any words the same as yours?

EXAM SUCCESS ▶ page 151

6 Read this text about genetically-modified foods. What are they and what good and bad aspects of these foods appear in the text? Ignore the gaps.

Genetically-modified foods

Genetically-modified (GM) foods are foods which come from plants and animals that scientists **(1)** .... changed through genetic engineering. For example, you can make a strawberry plant more resistant to the cold by adding a gene from an alpine plant that is able to live even when the weather is **(2)** .... freezing. These organisms are stronger than natural organisms and so they can grow **(3)** .... difficult conditions. The biotech companies that make GM organisms say that they will help to end world hunger. But organisations like Greenpeace are **(4)** .... that the real reason for their development is not to help poor countries that need food, but to control food production and make lots of money.

The truth is that nobody knows what the effects of GM foods may be. Scientists have **(5)** .... investigating the possible consequences **(6)** .... more than ten years but they still can't predict all the possible impacts on plants, animals and human health. By the time we understand the effects, it could be too late and the biotech companies may **(7)** .... contaminated the environment so badly that it is impossible to fix the problem. Because GM organisms grow faster and stronger **(8)** .... natural organisms, once they mix with natural varieties they could change the natural species forever.

But some scientists have already predicted that we **(9)** .... all be eating GM foods in the future because they will be so good for our health. They give the example of a new genetically-modified purple tomato which scientists have **(10)** .... created. This tomato will help to fight some types of cancer. However, other experts say that this is absurd and that it is better for people to eat just normal, healthy, organic food.

7 Read the text again and decide which answer (A, B, C or D) best fits each gap.

	A	B	C	D
1	**A** are	**B** has	**C** have	**D** will
2	**A** really	**B** very	**C** quite	**D** extremely
3	**A** by	**B** on	**C** for	**D** in
4	**A** true	**B** convinced	**C** thinking	**D** considering
5	**A** wanted	**B** had	**C** been	**D** already
6	**A** for	**B** since	**C** already	**D** yet
7	**A** finish	**B** have	**C** be	**D** already
8	**A** that	**B** then	**C** than	**D** with
9	**A** will	**B** are	**C** have	**D** can
10	**A** yet	**B** since	**C** just	**D** been

▶ Speaking

▶ Tip for Speaking Exams

In negotiating activities, remember …

Work with your partner and take turns to speak. Help your partner to speak if you think you are speaking too much or if your partner is not speaking enough.

EXAM SUCCESS ▶ page 151

8 Decide if the sentences are making suggestions (MS), asking for help (AH) or offering help (OH). Then write down words or expressions we can use to accept suggestions or offers of help.

1 Could you give me a hand organising a trip? *AH*
2 How about drawing a poster?
3 How can I help?
4 Why don't we plan the trip together?
5 Do you fancy coming?
6 Would you mind helping me?

9 Work with a partner. Prepare a dialogue for this task. When you finish, change roles.

You are organising a school trip to London. You need to do things like:

- Plan a list of places to see and things to do on the trip
- Make posters to advertise the trip
- Collect the money

Ask a friend to help you to do these things.

▶ 'Can Do' Progress Check

CEF

1 How well can you do these things in English now? Give yourself a mark from 1 to 4.

1 = I can do it very well.
2 = I can do it quite well.
3 = I have some problems.
4 = I can't do it.

a I can talk about past activities which are relevant in the present using the present perfect simple and present perfect continuous ☐
b I can describe cities and use extreme adjectives. ☐
c I can express personal opinions. ☐
d I can write informal letters describing places. ☐
e I can understand written and spoken texts about city life. ☐
f I can talk about the future using different verbs and tenses including the future perfect and future continuous. ☐
g I can talk about food and describe it. ☐
h I can form new words by adding prefixes. ☐
i I can make plans and suggestions, and offer help. ☐
j I can write simple invitations and plans. ☐

2 Now decide what you need to do to improve.

1 Look again at my book/notes.
2 Do more practice exercises. → WORKBOOK pages 20–37
3 Other: ....

5 Learning for life

Grammar ‣ Modal verbs of obligation, prohibition, advice and permission ‣ First and second conditional
Vocabulary ‣ School and university subjects ‣ Words connected with school and university ‣ Noun suffixes *-ist, -er, -or, -ian, -ee*
Speaking ‣ Describing photos 1
Writing ‣ A formal letter applying for a scholarship

Vocabulary

School and university subjects

1 Work with a partner. How many of these subjects do you know? Match the subjects with the book covers.

art biology business studies chemistry drama engineering English geography history information and communication technology (ICT) law literature maths media studies medicine music physical education (PE) physics psychology

2 When do you usually study these subjects for the first time – at nursery school (3–4 years old), primary school (5–10), secondary school (11–18) or at university (18+)? Complete the table.

Nursery	Primary	Secondary	University
art	*English*	*biology*	*business studies*

3 LISTENING 1.26 **Listen to four teachers giving instructions and asking questions. What subject is each one teaching?**

1 ....
2 ....
3 ....
4 ....

4 SPEAKING **Find out your partner's opinion of the different subjects. Do they like studying the subjects? Would they like to study them one day?**

Do you like studying physics?

No, I don't like physics much. I prefer biology.

Words connected with school and university

mark/grade essay about the Roman Empire fail pass certificate coursework cheat terms timetable resit it

5 Complete the sentences with these words.

1 Last week in history I wrote an ....
2 9 out of 10 is a really good ....
3 I didn't do the exam very well so next week I'm going to ....
4 I don't know what lesson we have now because I didn't bring my ....
5 Usually you need to get more than 50% in an exam to ....
6 When you don't get more than 50% in an exam you usually ....
7 Usually the school year is divided into three ....
8 When I finished my karate course, they gave me a ....
9 The teachers watch us during our exams so that we can't ....
10 The teachers evaluate us by looking at our exams and the work we do all year, our ....

6a SPEAKING **Work with a partner. Ask and answer the questions. Make a note of your partner's answers.**

1 What is your school timetable for Friday? Do you like it?
2 Which is your favourite term and why?
3 What's your best mark in an exam this year?
4 Did you have to resit any exams last year? Which one(s)?
5 Have you got any certificates? What are they for?
6 What was the last essay that you wrote?

6b Report back to the class with information about your partner.

What is your school timetable for Friday?

My first lesson is maths, then I have ...

1 You have two minutes to write down any words you associate with university. Compare your words with the rest of the class. Explain your choices if necessary.

2 Work with a partner. Discuss these questions.

1. Do you want to go to university when you finish school? Why/Why not?
2. What do you think are the biggest differences between studying at school and university?

3 You have three minutes to read the text and answer these questions.

1. Who do you think the text is for?
2. Who do you think the text is by?
3. What do you think is the purpose of the text?

University: the basics

A different way of learning and teaching

At university, you ought to have sufficient maturity to work on your own for longer periods, without somebody in the room to guide you. You have more responsibility for your own success than at school. This can be frightening, but it can also make you feel free. You don't always have to do things in the way that people tell you. You have more freedom to study in the ways that are best for you.

Making choices

It is your responsibility to make sensible choices of options within your programme, as well as to plan extra-curricular activities. Your choices will affect your studies and your future career. It's a big responsibility but it's exciting to be more in control of your own life.

Assessment

Different courses have different ways of assessing your work. Exams are usually at the end of each term, but some courses leave exams until the end of the year. If the course assesses your coursework, you usually have to hand in essays, reports, project work, or you have to make an oral presentation. You mustn't hand in your work late because university regulations do not usually permit it.

Essential characteristics for success at university

Whether you are a mathematician, a historian or a physicist, here are some qualities that all your professors, tutors and lecturers will want to see:

- Independence: You must be able to stand on your own two feet.
- Self-motivation: You have to be able to work alone a lot.

- Ability to work with others: You must be ready to organise study sessions with friends.
- Ability to set objectives to improve your work.
- Ability to organise your time: You need to manage your time well. You must know when and where you should be for classes, events and exams and you must know when you have to hand in your work.
- Ability to decide when, how, and where you learn best.

On second thoughts maybe I do work better indoors, in the daytime.

Typical worries when you start university

Worries about studying and learning

It is important to give yourself time to feel comfortable. You should plan your own life instead of worrying about how well other students are doing. Some people play psychological games by saying that they do no work and can write essays the night before handing them in. Very few people can actually do this and you shouldn't really try.

Meanwhile, many other students will be worrying about some aspect of their study and it helps to be able to talk about your worries and problems. So you should find time to meet other students in your classes. All students and trainees make mistakes at times but think of the course as an adventure.

Other worries

University students often have to combine their studies with work and family obligations. Students have to be very organised and creative to solve some of these problems. Student Services normally offer advice on finding work, on grants, childcare, health care, disability, discrimination and many other problems that come up.

Adapted from *The Study Skills Handbook* by Stella Cottrell, (Palgrave Macmillan; Third Edition) 2008

STUDY SKILLS

Read the next task. What is the biggest difference between this task and the one before? STUDY SKILLS ▸ page 147

4 Read the text again and answer the questions.

1. What is the biggest difference between studying at school and at university, according to the writer?
2. What are the positive and negative sides to making your own choices at university?
3. What examples of coursework does the text describe?
4. Why is time management important at university?
5. What does the writer think about students who say they can write essays quickly, at the last minute?
6. Why is it important to get to know other students, in the writer's opinion?
7. Apart from academic work, what other difficulties do students find at university?

5 Match the underlined words in the text with the explanations.

1. job, or a part of your life that you spend in a job
2. intelligent, reasonable, practical
3. something that you do at school or university that is not part of your course
4. looking after children when their parents are working or studying
5. unfair treatment of somebody because of their race, sex, religion or appearance
6. the services that look after people's health
7. teaching staff at a university
8. people who are training for a job

6 SPEAKING What about *you*?

1. Do you think the information in the text is useful? Why/Why not?
2. What do you imagine are the best and worst things about studying at university?

GRAMMAR GUIDE

Modal verbs of obligation, prohibition, advice and permission

1a Read the sentences and complete the rules with the words in bold.

1 You **should** find time to meet other students in your classes.
2 You **must** be able to stand on your own two feet.
3 You **have to** hand in essays on time.
4 You **mustn't** hand in your work late.
5 You **can't** copy other people's work.
6 You **ought to** think of university as an adventure.
7 You **had better** plan your own life, not worry about others.
8 You **can** decide how you want to study.
9 You **don't have to** do what other people tell you.

a We use .... and .... for obligation.
b We use .... when there is no obligation.
c We use .... and .... for prohibitions or when there is no permission to do something.
d We use ...., ... and .... for advice and recommendations.
e We use .... to give permission.

1b Are these sentences true (T) or false (F)?

1 The contraction for *had better* is *'d better*. T/F
2 We use *to* with *ought*, but not with *should* or *'d better*. T/F
3 We usually use *must* in questions. T/F
4 The correct question is *Do you have to (go)?*, not *Have you to go?* T/F

GRAMMAR REFERENCE ▸ page 68

2 Look at these school rules and choose the correct alternative.

1 You must/mustn't/don't have to smoke.

2 You have to/don't have to/mustn't wear a school uniform if you're 15.

3 You have to/don't have to/mustn't wear a school uniform if you're 17.

4 You can/can't/don't have to wear make-up.

5 You must/mustn't/can't arrive on time.

6 Students must/mustn't/don't have to use mobile phones in class.

3 Write rules for your school using *must, mustn't, can, can't, have to, don't have to* and these verbs.

arrive early | carry ID | cheat in tests | eat or drink in class | participate in class | wear special shoes and clothes for PE

4a Look at the information about legal ages in Britain. Complete the second sentence using the correct form of the modal verbs and any other words.

1 It is obligatory to go to school until you are at least 16.
You .... to school until you are at least 16. (have to)

2 You have permission to go into a pub when you're 14 but you don't have permission to drink or buy alcohol.
You .... into a pub when you're 14 but you .... alcohol. (can)

3 Voting in a general election is prohibited until the age of 18.
You .... in a general election until you are 18. (can)

4 It is obligatory to be at least 17 to drive a car.
You .... at least 17 to drive a car. (have to)

5 It is possible to ride a moped when you're 16.
You .... 18 to ride a moped. (have to)

6 It is obligatory to be 18 before you can get married without your parents' permission.
You .... 18 before you can get married without your parents' permission. (must)

7 It is impossible to change your name until you are 16.
You .... your name until you're 16. (can)

8 It is possible to buy a ticket for the National Lottery when you are 16.
You .... 16 to buy a ticket for the National Lottery. (have to)

4b What are the legal ages for these things in your country? Do you know?

EXAM SUCCESS

The next activity is a cloze activity. You have a text with gaps, but you do not have the words to fill the gaps. What type of words do you think you will have to put in?

EXAM SUCCESS ▸ page 151

5 Complete the text by filling in each gap with one word.

You **(a)** .... better be careful if you drive **(b)** .... fast near a school in Lancashire in England. Everybody knows you **(c)** .... pay attention to speed limits (in the UK the legal speed limit in cities is 50 km/h). But it's even more important to respect speed limits where **(d)** .... are many children crossing the road. So, the police have decided to punish drivers **(e)** .... a very original way. The police think that drivers ought **(f)** .... realise what they are doing when they are driving fast in areas near schools. They have decided that the best punishment is to make the bad drivers sit at school and answer **(g)** .... from school children. The students ask **(h)** .... drivers to think about what they **(i)** .... done. The result is that the drivers quickly change the way they think about driving. **(j)** .... it isn't only the drivers who think about the consequences of dangerous driving. One of the 15-year-old students at the school said that it would help her to be a good driver when she was **(k)** .... enough to drive. So you **(l)** .... have to be a driver already to learn about the rules of the road!

6a SPEAKING Work with a partner. You have a friend who wants to become a maths teacher one day. Think of advice to give them. Use *must, mustn't, have to, should, shouldn't, had better, ought to*. Make a list of your ideas.

6b Compare your list with another pair. Are your ideas similar?

You have to get very good marks in maths. You should be patient with people when they don't understand.

Noun suffixes *-er, -or, -ist, -ian, -ee*

1 Look at these words. They all have suffixes which make nouns. Are they nouns for people or things?

histor**ian**	lectur**er**	physic**ist**
profess**or**	train**ee**	

2 Match these words and the words from 1 with the definitions. One of the definitions goes with two words.

direct**or**	electric**ian**	employ**ee**
employ**er**	instruct**or**	journal**ist**
photograph**er**	scient**ist**	technic**ian**

1 somebody who teaches at a university
2 somebody who teaches you to do a particular skill, e.g. ski or play a sport
3 somebody who is paid to work for another person or company
4 somebody who pays someone to work for them
5 somebody with technical training who works with special equipment or machines
6 somebody whose job is to report the news
7 somebody who is training for a job
8 somebody whose job is to repair electrical systems or equipment

3a PRONUNCIATION 1.27 Listen to the words in 1. Which is the only noun suffix which we stress?

3b 1.28 Listen to the words in 2. Underline the stress. *journalist*

3c Practise saying the words with the correct stress.

4 Complete the sentences with words from 1 and 2.

1 I don't want to be a professional .... but I enjoy taking pictures.
2 I'd like to be a swimming .... because I love swimming and I'd like to teach other people how to do it.
3 I'd like to be a .... or a .... because I'm good at science, especially physics.
4 I'd prefer to have my own company and be an ...., not an .... working for somebody else.
5 I wouldn't like to be the .... of a company because you're responsible for everything.

5 SPEAKING Work with a partner. Ask and answer questions about the sentences in 4. You can ask other questions to find out more details.

Do you want to be a professional . . . ?

Click onto...

University life in the UK

International cultural knowledge
Finding out about a British university

1 **Work with a partner. Make a list of information you would like to know about a British university before you go to study there.**

2 **Look at this leaflet for an open day at Lancaster University. Can you find all the information on your list?**

3 **Read the *Annual Open Days* section again. When you visit the university, can you:**
1. talk to tutors or professors?
2. see the places where students work or do sport?
3. go to the places where the students live?
4. take books from the library?
5. go by bus to the university at 5 o'clock without paying?
6. find out about studying in other countries, not just Britain?

4 **In the section *Why Lancaster?*, they describe it as the 'ideal university city'. Why?**

You can get to the city easily.

5 **Read the *Campus Tours* section again and answer the questions.**
1. How long is the campus tour in total?
2. Which part is longer – the talk or the tour?
3. Where does the tour begin and end?
4. Who takes you on the tour?
5. Is it possible to talk to professors?
6. What do you have to do if you want to go on the campus tour?

6 **What about *you*?**
Do you think open days and campus tours are a good idea? Why/Why not?

WORD BOOSTER

Match the words and definitions.

1 staff
2 labs
3 lecture theatres
4 facilities
5 accommodation
6 finances
7 campus
8 book (v.)

a place for someone to live
b large rooms for lessons at university
c buildings or rooms where people do scientific experiments
d money and decisions about how to spend or save it
e area of land with all the important buildings of a university
f reserve (e.g. a table at a restaurant, or a place on a trip)
g group of people who work for an organisation
h places and things that somebody lets you use to do an activity

LANCASTER UNIVERSITY

Annual Open Days

Thinking of going to university?

Come and visit Lancaster and see what we have to offer!

During your visit you will be able to:
- talk to departmental staff in the subjects you are interested in
- find out about courses and subjects
- visit labs and lecture theatres
- see academic facilities
- visit student accommodation
- tour the library
- see our sports facilities
- discover what Lancaster has to offer you!

Between 9.00am and 4.00pm, free buses will run from Lancaster train station to Lancaster University. Food will be available.

We will give information about:
- getting a place at Lancaster
- studying in Europe
- studying in USA/Canada

There will also be general information on:
- questions of interest to parents
- the city: questions of interest to students
- clubs, sports and societies
- student finances
- accommodation

Why Lancaster?
- excellent teaching
- flexible degree structure
- a friendly, safe campus
- easy access by road or rail
- low cost of living
- first class facilities
- good employment prospects
- a multi-cultural experience
- the ideal university city

Campus Tours
Regular organised campus tours take place twice a month from February to December.

Campus Tour Programme:

1.00pm: Meet outside the main library in Alexandra Square.
1.05pm: The Lancaster Experience: a guide to student life at Lancaster (talk).
1.50pm: Guided tour with current students, including accommodation, library, sports centre and much more!
3.00pm: Tour finishes back in Alexandra Square or, on special dates only, tour guides will take you to the department of your choice to meet academic staff and look around the department.

If you would like to join a tour it is essential to book your place (http://domino.lancs.ac.uk) in advance.

Travel information (http://www.lancs.ac.uk/travel/travel.htm), including downloadable campus maps.

For further information, contact the open day team on:
Email: **visitus@lancaster.ac.uk**
Tel: **01524 593724**

INSIDE INFORMATION
- Most universities in Britain organise visit days or open days for school students.
- On open days, school students interested in going to a university can visit it to find out more information and to see if they like it.

International cultural knowledge
Student life in Britain

7 A university student called Francesca is answering questions about life at university. Work with a partner. Guess her answers to these questions.

1 Apart from studying, what is student life like?
2 Why did you decide to study chemistry?
3 Do you prefer exams or continuous assessment? Why?
4 Do you like your teachers? Why/Why not?
5 What is your course like?
6 Why did you decide to come to this university?

8 1.29 Listen. Which three questions does Francesca answer?

1 .... 2 .... 3 ....

9 Listen again and answer the questions.

1 What is special about Francesca's university?
2 Do British students study in their hometown or city?
3 What is the big difference between studying at school and at university in Francesca's opinion?
4 Why does Francesca think clubs and societies are a good thing?
5 What does Francesca think about part-time jobs?

10 What about *you*?

Do you think university life in your country is similar to university life in the UK? Why/Why not?

International cultural knowledge
The biggest university in Britain

11 Work with a partner. You are going to read about a British university called the Open University. Why do you think it has this name? Guess.

12 Read the text. Did you guess correctly?

13 Read the text again and decide if the sentences are true (T) or false (F). Write the number of the line(s) where you found the answer.

1 The Open University is the biggest university building in Britain. T/F
2 Distance learning is when you can learn with different materials in your home. T/F
3 TV was the starting point of the Open University. T/F
4 It is essential to have a school certificate to study at the Open University. T/F
5 It is possible to be seventy and study at the Open University. T/F
6 The university pays special attention to people with disabilities. T/F

14 Make a list of different groups of people that the Open University is open to.

disabled people

15 What about *you*?

1 What do you think are the good and bad things about distance learning?
2 Would you prefer to do a distance learning course at home or attend a university? Why?

I think one good thing is that you can stop and start when you like.

Yes, and you are more comfortable at home.

The Open University

The biggest British university, in terms of student numbers, is the Open University, with around 180,000 students in 2009. The Open University began in the 1960s and was the first university in the world dedicated to distance learning. Students don't have to go to classes, they study at (5) home with books, videos, CDs, DVDs and the Internet. In fact, the idea for the Open University came from the increasing popularity of television in the sixties and seventies. Instead of going to class, people could learn by watching special academic programmes on TV and then following this up with independent study and coursework. Nowadays, students can (10) usually communicate with their lecturers by phone or the Internet, or occasionally meet them face to face.

You don't have to have any previous qualifications to study at the Open University, you just have to be over 16. But, importantly, there is no maximum age limit. 10,000 disabled people study at the Open (15) University, where there is special material for different disabilities, for example special computer software for visually impaired students. Disabled people are officially a priority group in the university. The Open University is also ideal for people who are working. Approximately 70% of students work full-time. Distance learning gives these students (20) flexibility to study where and when they like, at their own speed. Most Open University courses are available throughout Europe. Some of them are available in many other parts of the world. More than 25,000 Open University students live outside the UK.

▸ WORD BOOSTER

Match the words and definitions.

1 increasing	a of most importance
2 previous	b from before
3 visually impaired	c having difficulty seeing
4 priority	d ability to make changes and adapt
5 flexibility	e getting bigger and bigger

▶ Listening

1a Work with a partner. Look at these photos. They show different extra-curricular activities that you can do at school or university. Name the activities.

a

b

c

d

1b Make a list of any other extra-curricular activities that are typical in schools or universities in your country.

2 LISTENING **1.30 Listen to four people talking about extra-curricular activities. What clubs or societies do you think they are talking about?**

1 ....
2 Octo..............................
3 .... and ....
4 ....

3 Listen again and complete the sentences.

1 This society is organising a .... at Christmas. They need people who can ....
2 The boy doesn't want to join this club because .... and ....
3 The girl's mother likes the first club because ....
The girl's mother thinks the second club isn't a good idea because ....
4 The boy doesn't have time to join this club because he .... The girl thinks that the boy should ....

4 What about *you*?

1 What extra-curricular activities do you do, or would you like to do?
2 Do you think extra-curricular activities are good or bad for your studies?

▶ Grammar in context

GRAMMAR GUIDE

First and second conditionals

1a Look at the sentences. Which are first conditionals and which are second conditionals?

1 If I had time, I'd join the team, but I just don't have the time.
2 If you join now, you'll be able to take part in our Christmas show.
3 If I were you, I'd do one course and play tennis.
4 You won't have time to study if you go climbing every weekend.
5 If I could swim, maybe I would join.

1b After each rule, write: first conditional, second conditional or both.

1 It describes an improbable or imaginary situation in the present or future, and its consequence. ....
2 It describes a possible situation in the present or future and its consequence. ....
3 We use the present simple in the half of the sentence with *if*, and *will/won't* + infinitive in the other half. ....
4 We use the past simple in the half of the sentence with *if*, and *would/wouldn't* + infinitive in the other half. ....
5 The half of the sentence with *if* can come after the other half, but we don't use a comma. ....
6 We can use it to give advice when we have *If I were/was you* in one half of the sentence. ....

GRAMMAR REFERENCE ▶ page 68

2 Put the verbs in the correct form to make first conditional sentences.

1 My friend Omar wasn't at school yesterday. If he .... (not come) today, I .... (ring) him to find out how he is.
2 Don't worry. If the exam .... (be) tomorrow, I .... (lend) you my notes.
3 If they .... (have) a party for new students tonight, I .... (go).
4 You .... (not like) the Drama Club if you .... (not enjoy) acting.
5 She .... (learn) Italian if there .... (be) free Italian classes.
6 If you .... (not know) some of the answers, the teacher .... (help) you.
7 If we .... (arrive) late today, the teacher .... (get) angry.

3 Complete the dialogues with these verbs in the second conditional.

be do get have not work spend study

1 BEN: What **(a)** .... you .... to improve the world if you **(b)** .... a world leader?
BETHANY: I **(c)** .... more money on schools and universities.

2 EMMA: You never do any schoolwork at the weekend. If you **(d)** .... more, you **(e)** .... higher marks in your exams.
MEGAN: I know, but I have to work at my dad's shop. If I **(f)** .... there, I **(g)** .... time to study.

4 Complete the text with the verbs in the correct form of the first or second conditional.

My name's Lizzy. I'm 18 and I've just started university. There are hundreds of extra-curricular activities at my university but right now I can't decide which ones I want to do. The problem is that I'm not very good at sport. If I **(a)** .... (be) good at sport, I **(b)** .... (play) tennis or basketball or something like that. I love singing but I haven't found a choir yet. It can't be difficult to find one. If I **(c)** .... (find) a choir, I **(d)** .... (join). I imagine it's free. I haven't got much money. If I **(e)** .... (have) more money, I **(f)** .... (think) about joining the Snow Club. They organise lots of trips to the mountains. The thing is, if we **(g)** .... (be) closer to the mountains, it **(h)** .... (not be) so expensive but we're about 200 kilometres away! Anyway, I'm going to make my final decisions in the next three or four days. If I **(i)** .... (have) problems deciding, I **(j)** .... (talk) to my older sister, but I don't think that'll be necessary in the end.

5 Complete the sentences with true information about you.

1 If a Martian stole my homework on the way to school …
2 If I pass all my exams …
3 If I haven't got any homework this weekend …
4 If I have time this weekend …
5 If I had enough money …
6 If I met my favourite film star …
7 If I was a superhero …
8 If I go out with my friends this weekend …

6 Work with a partner. Compare your sentences from 5 and choose the three best ones.

7a SPEAKING Write six questions. You must have three questions beginning 'What *will* you do if …?' and three beginning with 'What *would* you do if … ?' Look at these photos for ideas.

What will you do if you don't have any homework this weekend?
What would you do if you met Kate Moss at a party?

7b Interview different people with your questions. Choose the best answers and report them to the class.

1 SPEAKING **Look at this photo. Work with a partner and write six words which you could use to describe it.**

2 LISTENING 1.31 **Listen to somebody talking about the photo in 1. Tick any of the words in your list that you hear.**

3 Are the statements true (T) or false (F)?

1 The speaker thinks the man is the director of the university. T/F
2 He thinks the photo shows the students' final graduation. T/F
3 He thinks the students have just received books. T/F
4 He has been in a similar situation in his life T/F
5 He thinks it's strange that all the people look serious. T/F

4 Listen to the speaker again. Tick the expressions he uses in the Speaking Bank.

Speaking Bank

- In the photo I can see …
- The photo shows …
- In the foreground …
- In the background …
- At the top of the photo …
- At the bottom of the photo …
- In the middle of the photo …
- On the right …
- On the left …
- In the top/bottom right/left corner …
- It looks/doesn't look like …

5 Look at this photo and complete the sentences with words from the Speaking Bank.

1 ………………………… three students in a classroom.
2 ………………………… a science lesson.
3 In the ………………………… there's a student wearing a white coat.
4 On the ………………… there's a boy with short brown hair.
5 On the ………………… there's a girl wearing a blue shirt.
6 ………………………… there's a large window.
7 It ………………………… they are doing an experiment.

Practice makes perfect

6a Look at the photo and prepare the task.

Describe the photo. Then talk about:
- what it makes you think of
- if you have had a personal experience of something similar.

6b Work with a partner. Each person should choose one of the photos of the photos on this page. Take it in turns to describe your photo. Remember to use expressions from the Speaking Bank.

STUDY SKILLS

Spoken language is not exactly the same as written language. In what ways is it different? Do we generally have more time to think when we write or when we speak? **STUDY SKILLS ▸ page 147**

1 Read this information about a scholarship at a university. Underline the qualities that an ideal candidate should have. Do you think *you* would be a good candidate for the scholarship? Why/Why not?

St. George's College

STUDENTS & APPLICANTS

Society Scholarship

A number of annual scholarships are given to students of English who have a special interest in British history and/or who would like to study in Britain in the future. Applicants must have good grades and should be active in extra-curricular activities such as sports (emphasis on swimming, tennis, football and hockey) and social activities. Please send a letter of application to this address.

2 Read the letter of application for this scholarship. Do you think this person is a good candidate or not? Why? Make a list of reasons for your answer.

Dear Sir or Madam,

I am writing to apply for the St. George's Society Scholarship which I saw advertised on the university website.

I believe I would be perfect for this scholarship for the following reasons. Firstly, my best subjects at school are English and History and my ambition is to study one day in the United Kingdom, to discover more about the people, places and traditions. My grades this year have been very good, with an average mark of 80% in my exams.

I also love sports, particularly football. I am the captain of my school football team. As captain of the team, I am responsible for organising social activities such as parties and events to raise money for the team.

I would be very grateful to receive the chance to study at your university with a St. George's Scholarship and I am sure that I could make a valuable contribution to the English department.

I look forward to receiving your reply.

Yours faithfully

Marcus Reeves

Marcus Reeves

3 Look again at the letter in 2 and complete the information in the Writing Bank.

Writing Bank

Useful expressions and conventions in formal letters

- If we know the name of the person we are writing to, we begin *Dear Mr/Mrs/Ms* and their surname. We finish *Yours sincerely.*
- If we don't know the name of the person we are writing to, we begin *Dear* .... or .... We finish *Yours* ....
- In formal letters we do not use ...., e.g. we write *I would*, not *I'd*.
- We often use more formal words and expressions, e.g. .... instead of *I'd be really happy to get the chance.*
- We often start formal letters with *I am writing to ...* and then explain why we are writing.
- We often end formal letters with expressions like *I* .... to receiving your reply.

Practice makes perfect

4a Look at the task and write the letter. Use the expressions and conventions in the Writing Bank to help you.

Read the information below about a scholarship. Write a letter of application. Include information to make yourself the ideal candidate. Write between 150 and 200 words.

STUDENTS & APPLICANTS

Combined English Scholarship

We have two scholarships for students who are interested in combining their chosen subject (any subjects are possible) with an English Studies program. Applicants need to have good academic marks and should have an interest in extra-curricular activities such as music, theatre, literature, or debating, etc. Active participation in a sport is also an advantage. Send your letter of application to this address.

EXAM SUCCESS

How many words should you write in your text? Who are you writing to? Why is it important to know this in an exam?

EXAM SUCCESS ▶ page 151

4b When you finish your letter, exchange it with a partner. Prepare seven questions to ask them in an interview to get the scholarship.

In your letter you say that your marks are usually high. Which are your best and worst subjects?

4c Role-play your interviews. Would you give your partner the scholarship?

Language reference and revision

Grammar reference

Have to, don't have to

Form

Affirmative	*You have to go to school until you are 16.*
Negative	*You don't have to wait until you're 20 to vote.*
Question	*Do you have to be 18 to vote?*
Short answers	*Yes, you do./No, you don't.*

Use

We use **have to** to talk about things which are obligatory or necessary. It often describes obligations imposed on us by other people and authorities. *You have to have a passport to check in.*

We use **don't have to** to talk about things which are not obligatory or necessary. *Students don't have to pay tax.*

Must, mustn't

Affirmative	*You must listen to what the teacher says.*
Negative	*You mustn't copy in exams.*

Must is not very common in questions. We usually use **have to**.

We use **must** to talk about rules, regulations, and obligations. It often describes obligations that come internally, from ourselves. *I must remember to get my passport.*

We use **mustn't** to talk about prohibitions. *You mustn't smoke here.*

Can, can't

We use **can** to give permission and **can't** to refuse permission.

You can use the computers but you can't eat in the classroom.

Should, shouldn't, ought to, had ('d) better

Affirmative	*You should/ought to/had better respect others.*
Negative	*You shouldn't study too late at night.*
Question	*Should I stop now?*
Short answers	*Yes, you should./No, you shouldn't.*

We use **should, shouldn't, ought to, had ('d) better** to give and ask for advice and recommendations.

You should read this book.

Ought to and **had ('d) better** are slightly less common in the negative and question forms.

First conditional

If + present simple, ... **will/won't** + infinitive

If you study more, you will get better marks.
If we don't do the exam, we won't get a certificate.

The present simple comes in the part of the sentence with **if**.

We use the first conditional to talk about possible and probable situations in the future, and their consequences.

If you aren't careful (possible future situation), *you will have an accident* (the consequence of this situation).

Second conditional

If + past simple, ... **would/wouldn't** + infinitive

If I had a million pounds, I'd travel around the world.
If we didn't revise, we wouldn't remember much.

If can go at the start or the end of the sentence. If the part with **if** goes at the start of the sentence, we must use a comma before the second half of the sentence.

If we had more free time, we'd do more sport.

We can use **were** instead of **was** with **if**.

If I were/was a teacher, I would make my students work hard.

We use the second conditional to talk about imaginary or improbable situations and their consequences. The sentences are in the present or future, not in the past.

If I made films I would live in Hollywood.

We use **If I were you, I'd ...** to give advice.

Vocabulary

1 School and university subjects

art biology business studies chemistry drama engineering English geography history information and communication technology (ICT) law literature maths media studies medicine music physical education (PE) physics psychology

2 Words connected with school and university

certificate cheat coursework essay fail grade mark pass resit term timetable

3 Noun suffixes *-er, -or, -ist, -ian, -ee*

direct**or** electric**ian** employ**ee** employ**er** histor**ian** instruct**or** journal**ist** lectur**er** photograph**er** physic**ist** profess**or** scient**ist** technic**ian** train**ee**

4 Other words and phrases ▸ page 140

Grammar revision

Must, mustn't, have to, don't have to, can, can't

1 Rewrite the sentences with *must, mustn't, have to, don't have to, can* and *can't*.

1 I haven't got permission to go to the party.
I ....
2 It isn't necessary for students to wear a uniform here.
Students ....
3 Making a loud noise is prohibited here.
You ....
4 It is obligatory to wear a seat belt.
You ....
5 Copying is not allowed in exams.
You ....
6 It's essential for me to get a new passport.
I ....
7 My little brother has permission to ride his bike alone.
My little brother ....

WORKBOOK ▸ page 40 / 7 points

Should, shouldn't, ought to, 'd better

2 Are the sentences correct? If not, correct them.

1 My friends and I shouldn't to go out at the weekend.
2 You would better walk to school.
3 I think you ought go to the dentist.
4 What should I say when I see the headmaster?
5 We'd better leave now if we want to arrive on time.

WORKBOOK ▸ page 40 / 5 points

First and second conditional

3 Complete the sentences with the verbs in the correct tense.

1 If I were you, I .... (tell) Alex the truth.
2 Lewis .... (buy) me a souvenir if he goes to New York.
3 What .... you .... (say) if I told you I love you?
4 My mum will be angry if she .... (find) out where I was.
5 Connor wouldn't be angry if you .... (ask) him a favour.
6 If I .... (be) rich, I wouldn't have more than one car.
7 Where will your parents go on holiday if you .... (not go) with them?
8 If I .... (have) the time, I'd learn to play the guitar.

WORKBOOK ▸ page 43 / 8 points

Vocabulary revision

School and university subjects

1 In which school or university subject do you learn about …

1 the theories of Isaac Newton and Albert Einstein?
....
2 computers and the Internet? ....
3 TV, newspapers, magazines and radio?
....
4 different sports and games? ....
5 a country's legal system? ....
6 designing and building structures and machines?
....
7 stories, poems and plays? ....

WORKBOOK ▸ page 38 / 7 points

Words connected with school and university

2 Complete the sentences with words connected with school or university.

1 It's not right to .... in an exam.
2 After the course finished they sent me a .... through the post.
3 She didn't .... the exam – she got 80%.
4 Next week in history, I have to write an .... about the industrial revolution.
5 He only got 25% in the exam so he has to .... it.
6 Have you got your ....? Can you tell me what we have after maths on Friday morning?
7 I prefer .... It's not as stressful as doing an exam.

WORKBOOK ▸ page 38 / 7 points

Noun suffixes -er, -or, -ist, -ian, -ee

3 Make nouns for people by adding the suffixes *-er, -or, -ist, -ian, -ee* to these words.

1 scient............
2 instruct............
3 technic............
4 employ............
5 employ............
6 electric............

WORKBOOK ▸ page 41 / 6 points

Total / 40 points

6 Appliance of science

Grammar ▸ The passive ▸ *Have something done*
Vocabulary ▸ Everyday inventions ▸ Operating technology ▸ Prepositional phrases with adjectives
Speaking ▸ A debate
Writing ▸ A *for and against* essay

▸ Vocabulary

Everyday inventions

1 Work with a partner. Match the photos with some of these words. Check that you understand the meaning of the other words.

camcorder digital camera dishwasher
DVD player home cinema system
laptop microwave oven mobile phone
MP3 player remote control satnav
vacuum cleaner washing machine

2 What is the invention you use to …

1 wash clothes? ……………
2 clean the carpet? ……………
3 listen to music, especially when you are on the move? ……………
4 find the best way to get from one place to another? ……………
5 watch films at home? …………… and ……………

3 SPEAKING **Work with a partner. Write definitions for the other words from 1. Can your partner identify the words?**

You use it to send text messages.

A mobile phone.

Operating technology

4 Match the pictures with these words.

charge/recharge (a battery) connect X to Y insert plug in
select (a programme/a track/a function) switch/turn on/off
press a button (Power/Play/Stop/Fast Forward/Rewind)

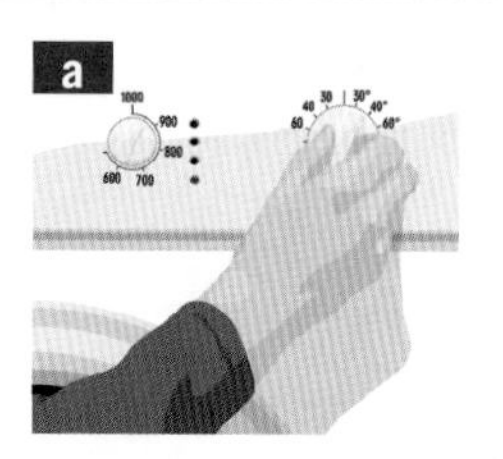

……………

……………

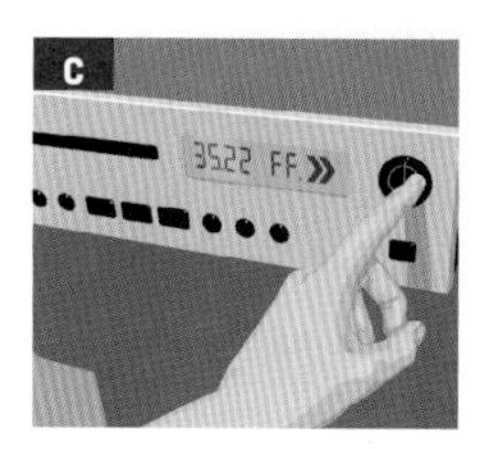

……………

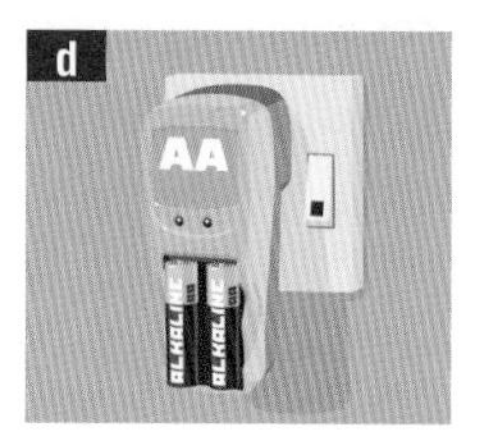

……………

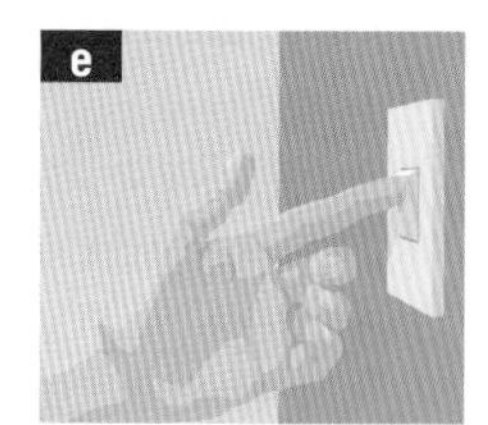

……………

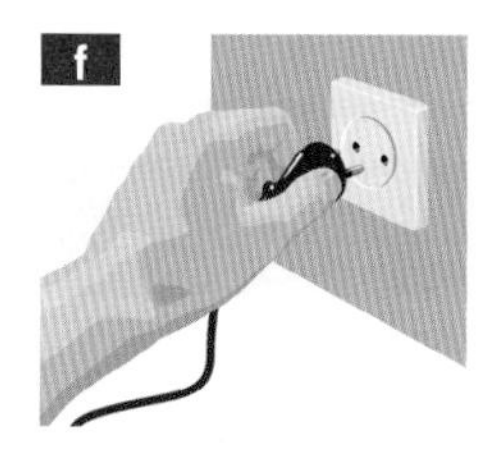

……………

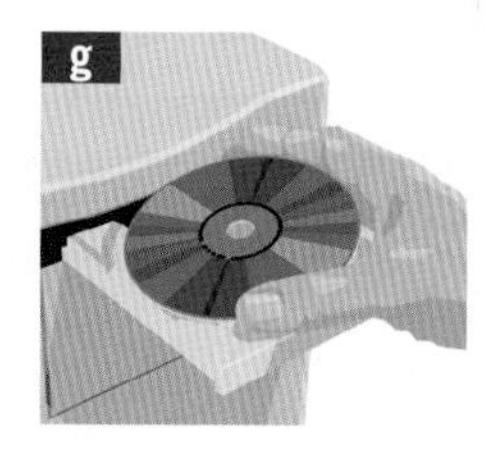

……………

5 2.01 **Listen and check your answers.**

6 LISTENING 2.02 **Listen. Which everyday invention are they talking about?**

1 ……………
2 ……………
3 ……………

7 Work with a partner. Write basic instructions for how to operate this equipment. Use as many words from 4 as possible.

1 a DVD player 2 a microwave oven 3 a mobile phone

8 SPEAKING **Work with a partner. Look at these questions and discuss your answers.**

1 Which of the inventions in 1 do you use the most? Why?
2 Which of the inventions do you never use? Why not?
3 If you were living alone and only had money for five of the inventions in 1, which would you buy and why?

Which of the inventions do you use the most?

Maybe my MP3 player because I use it to listen to music every day on my way to school. I also listen to it when I do my homework and when I'm in the car with my parents.

1 Work with a partner. Predict the answers to the questions.

1 When does sword-swallowing give you a sore throat?
2 What happens if you eat soup from a bowl that never gets empty?
3 Can rats understand languages when they are spoken backwards?

2 Read the text and check your answers.

The Ig Nobel Prizes

A Everybody knows about Nobel prizes. They are given every year to the best scientists and writers in the world. Not so many people are aware of Ig Nobel prizes though. These are also given annually to scientists. But they are organised by a group called Improbable Research. Their aim is to inform people of scientific investigation which 'makes people laugh, but then makes them think'.

B When we think of scientific research we usually think of practical projects which make a big difference to our everyday lives, like inventing smaller and better laptops, satnavs, and digital cameras. But not all scientific projects are like this. The Ig Nobel prizes go to scientists whose work is funny, unusual, and different. And to get a prize it is also essential that the work has been published in a serious scientific journal. Here are some examples of projects which have won the prize.

C In 2007 an Ig Nobel Prize was won by Brian Whitcombe and Dan Meyer. They wrote an article which was published in the British Medical Journal. The article was an analysis of the problems suffered by professional sword-swallowers.

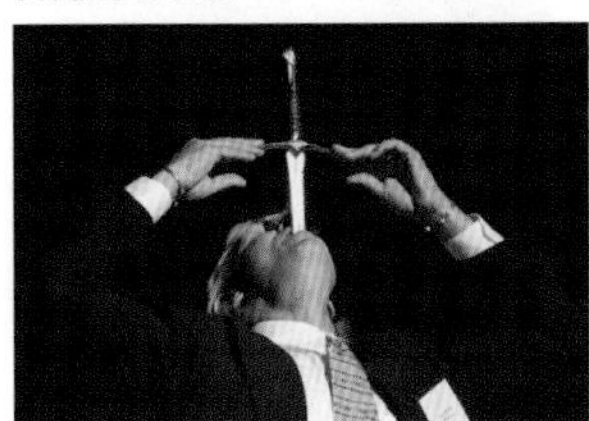

To do his research, Whitcombe interviewed nearly 50 sword-swallowers. He discovered that swallowing swords doesn't usually cause anything more serious than sore throats. Generally, these sore throats only occur in one of these four situations: when someone is learning to swallow swords, when the act of swallowing the sword is repeated frequently, when the sword has an unusual shape, or when more than one sword is swallowed at the same time.

D A Japanese scientist called Mayu Yamamoto won a prize a few years ago. She discovered a new way of extracting vanillin from cow excrement. Vanillin is the basis of vanilla flavouring and fragrance. It is used in the food industry and in cosmetics. A famous ice cream shop created a new ice cream in honour of Yamamoto's discovery and presented it at her prize ceremony. The ice cream contained no cow excrement. The Japanese scientist doesn't think that her discovery will ever be used in food. She reckons that if people know where the vanilla flavour comes from, they won't want to eat it!

E Another Ig Nobel Prize was won by neuroscientists at Barcelona University. They were interested in exploring the way in which languages are acquired by the brain. They discovered that rats cannot tell the difference between somebody speaking Dutch backwards and somebody speaking Japanese backwards.

64 rats were taught to press a button when they heard normal Dutch or Japanese. They could learn to do this. But when they heard the languages backwards they had no idea what was happening.

F Talking about food, a food psychologist from New York called Dr Brian Wansink won his Ig Nobel prize for an interesting experiment with soup. He invented a never-ending bowl. When people ate tomato soup from the bowl, the bowl was automatically filled again from a tube connected to the bottom of the bowl. He discovered that people ate 73% more than usual when they used this bowl. But they didn't feel full.

The conclusion was that we decide how much to eat with our eyes, not with the way our stomach feels.

G Other scientists have won prizes for thinking about questions like 'Why is the sound of fingernails on blackboards so awful?', 'Why does dry spaghetti break into three pieces, not two?', or 'How many photos do you need to take to be sure that nobody in a group has their eyes closed?'. Maybe these questions are different from the typical questions that scientists ask themselves, and maybe questions like this won't change the world. But they will make you laugh ... and then think.

EXAM SUCCESS

You are going to do a matching activity for this reading text. In this type of activity, you say which text or part of a text contains a specific piece of information. After reading the text once quickly to get a general idea, what should you do next?

EXAM SUCCESS ▸ page 152

3 Which paragraph (A–G) tells us about …

1 the philosophy behind the Ig Nobel prizes? ....
2 a work that appeared in a magazine for doctors? ....
3 a scientist who is not sure they will use her work? ....
4 a discovery about human mental processes? ....
5 the danger of doing one action too many times? ....
6 turning something bad into something good? ....
7 an invention that tricks people? ....
8 how to win an Ig Nobel prize? ....

4 Look at these words in the text and guess their meaning. Then use a dictionary to check your ideas.

1 aware of
2 journal
3 acquired
4 fingernails
5 research
6 sore
7 never-ending

5 SPEAKING What about *you*?

1 What do you think of the Ig Nobel prizes?
2 Which scientific research in the text did you like the most? Why?

I think they're all a bit silly! They're funny but I don't think they are useful.

I don't agree. I think some of the projects could be really useful.

GRAMMAR GUIDE

The passive

1a Look at the sentences. Which sentence is *not* in the passive?

1. The prizes are given to scientists.
2. The work has been published in a journal.
3. The prize was won by neuroscientists at Barcelona University.
4. A Japanese scientist won the prize.
5. Perhaps her discovery will be used.
6. Lots of interesting research is being done at the moment.

1b Choose the correct alternative.

1. We use the passive when we are interested mainly in the *action/person who does the action*.
2. We use the passive when we *know/don't know* the person who does the action.
3. We use the passive when it *is/isn't* obvious who does or did the action.

1c Look at the sentences in 1a and answer the questions.

1. Which tense is each sentence written in?
2. What changes in different tenses of the passive – the verb *to be* or the past participle?
3. What preposition do we use to introduce the agent (the person or thing which does the action)?

GRAMMAR REFERENCE ▸ page 80

2a PRONUNCIATION **Look at the sentences. Which words do you think are stressed in each sentence? Why?**

1. The gadget was invented last year.
2. The new phones are sold here.
3. Ten prizes were given.
4. The disc was inserted.
5. Emails are sent every day.

2b 2.03 Listen and check your answers. What happens to the pronunciation of the verb *to be*?

2c Listen again and repeat the sentences. Pay special attention to the stress in each sentence.

3 Choose the correct alternative.

1. The work *is/are* done by robots.
2. The president of the society *gave/was given* the prize to the scientist.
3. The prize *has/has been* won by a student.
4. The project *has been/was* finished last year.
5. An experienced scientist *discovered/was discovered* the solution.
6. The ceremony is *filming/being filmed* for television.
7. All of the money has *spent/been spent* on future investigation.
8. The results are *deciding/being decided* right now.

4 Add one word in each sentence to make a correct passive sentence. Then write which tense each sentence is in.

1. The Theory of Relativity was developed ^by Einstein. *past simple*
2. Many inventions been created by women. ....
3. A lot of people think most jobs be done by robots in a few years. ....
4. Velcro, penicillin and the microwave oven invented by accident. ....
5. Millions of dollars spent on CDs and DVDs every year. ....
6. Football is by thousands of professionals and amateurs each weekend. ....
7. *1984* written by George Orwell. ....
8. Walt Disney's creations have seen by millions of children around the world. ....

5 Change these sentences from active to passive.

1. Alfred Nobel invented dynamite in 1867.
2. They gave the first Nobel prizes in 1901.
3. The Hurley Machine Company of Chicago produced the first electric-powered washing machine in 1908.
4. People have used this invention since 1908.
5. People are using this invention right now.
6. Perhaps people won't use electricity in the future.
7. Joseph Niépce took the first photo in 1826.
8. People take lots of photos on holidays.

6 Complete the text with the passive or active form of the verbs.

Correction fluid is the name for a white fluid. The fluid **(a)** .... (use) to cover mistakes when they **(b)** .... (make) on paper. Now people also **(c)** .... (use) correction tape. Correction fluid **(d)** .... (invent) by a secretary called Bette Nesmith Graham in 1951. She **(e)** .... (invent) it when she was working in a bank. Before the invention of correction fluid, when a mistake **(f)** .... (make), usually the complete document **(g)** .... (throw) in the bin. Since its invention, millions of bottles of correction fluid **(h)** .... (sell). Students often **(i)** .... (buy) correction fluid. Maybe it **(j)** .... (use) at this very moment by somebody in your class! After use, don't forget to put the top back on. If the top **(k)** .... (not put) back on, the fluid goes dry. And don't get it on your fingers – it's very messy. I think something better than correction fluid **(l)** .... (invent) one day. But for me it's not important. I **(m)** .... (not make) ~~misteaks~~ *mistakes*.

Correction Fluid

7a SPEAKING Work with a partner and discuss the questions.

1 Who was penicillin invented by?
2 Who was *Don Quixote* written by?
3 Who was the film *Lord of the Rings* directed by?

7b Now prepare a quiz with this table.

Who	was were	X X and Y	invented discovered written sung composed directed drawn painted created won	by?

7c Ask another pair of students your questions.

Prepositional phrases with adjectives

1a What preposition do we usually use after these adjectives?

aware different interested

1b Find the adjectives and prepositions in the text on page 71 and check your answers.

2 Match the adjectives with the prepositions and check that you understand the meaning.

Adjective	Preposition
1 good	a of
2 bored	b of
3 worried	c for
4 tired	d with
5 afraid	e for
6 responsible	f at
7 similar	g with
8 ready	h about
9 pleased	i to

3 Complete the sentences with the correct prepositions.

1 Are you good .... science?
2 Are you interested .... technology?
3 Are you aware .... the latest stories in the news?
4 Are you tired .... hearing celebrity gossip?
5 Are you pleased .... your school marks this year?
6 Are you ready .... your next exam?
7 Are you afraid .... flying?
8 Are you similar .... anyone in your family or are you very different .... them all?
9 Are you worried .... global warming?
10 Are you ever responsible .... looking after anybody?
11 Are you bored .... today's TV?

4 SPEAKING Ask your partner the complete questions in 3. How many of your answers are the same?

Are you good at science?

Not too bad. And you?

I'm quite good at biology, but I'm not very good at physics. I think it's really difficult.

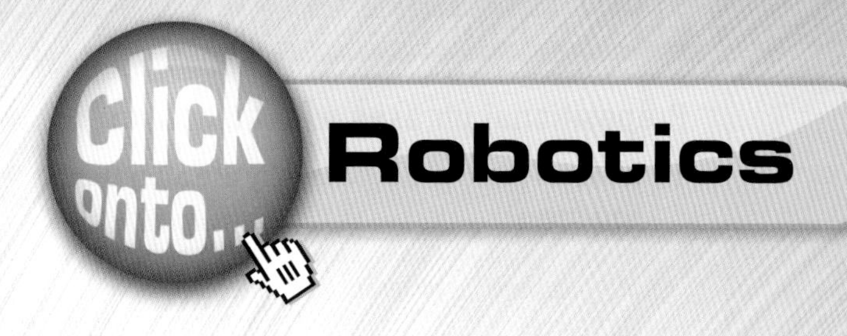

Robotics

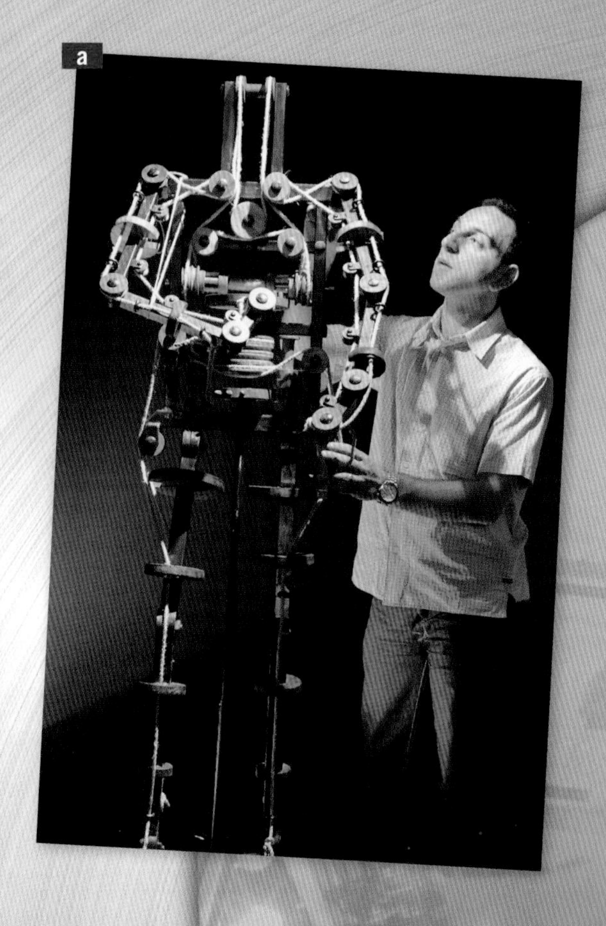

Cross-curricular – Science
The world of robots

1 Work with a partner. Write a definition of *robot*. Compare your definition with other students. Are they the same?

2 LISTENING 2.04 **Listen to a science documentary about robots. Match each speaker with one of the pictures.**

3 Listen again and decide if the sentences are true (T) or false (F).

1 The name 'robot' was invented by a scientist. T/F
2 The original 'robots' were very similar to machines. T/F
3 Leonardo Da Vinci designed a robot in around 1495. T/F
4 NASA's robots only need to carry heavy objects. T/F
5 War robots won't be able to take their own decisions. T/F
6 There are a lot of people who think that war with robots will be worse, not better. T/F

4 Can you explain why the false sentences in 3 are false?

5 What about *you*?
What do you think about robots being used as soldiers or police officers? Explain your opinion.

It could be good to use robots as soldiers because real people won't die.

They will die if robot soldiers fight against real people.

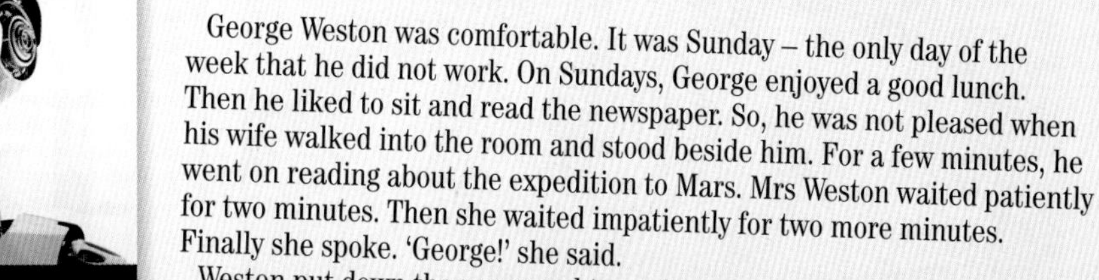

Literature
I, Robot by Isaac Asimov

6 Read this extract from *Robbie*, a short story from *I, Robot*. Find out what these three characters think of Robbie the robot.

1 Mr George Weston
2 Mrs Grace Weston
3 Gloria Weston

7 Read the text again and answer the questions.

1 Where and when does the story start?
2 Why doesn't Mr Weston really want to talk to Mrs Weston at that moment?
3 Why does Mr Weston feel the way he does about Robbie?
4 Why does Mrs Weston feel the way she does about Robbie?
5 Who wins the argument between Mr and Mrs Weston in the end?
6 What do you think is going to happen when Mr Weston and Gloria go to the visivox show?
7 Why couldn't Mr Weston look at his daughter's face?

8 What about *you*?

1 Would you like to have a robot living in your house? Why?
2 Do you like science-fiction stories generally? Why/Why not?

I'd like a robot at home because it could do all the housework.

That's true, but I think I'd be frightened.

▸ WORD BOOSTER

Match the words and definitions.

1 nanny
2 frowned
3 harm
4 get rid of
5 argued

a spoke to each other in an angry way
b showed that he was not happy with his face
c injure, damage, hurt
d throw away or give away
e a woman whose job is to look after children

I, Robot
Isaac Asimov
MACMILLAN READERS

George Weston was comfortable. It was Sunday – the only day of the week that he did not work. On Sundays, George enjoyed a good lunch. Then he liked to sit and read the newspaper. So, he was not pleased when his wife walked into the room and stood beside him. For a few minutes, he went on reading about the expedition to Mars. Mrs Weston waited patiently for two minutes. Then she waited impatiently for two more minutes. Finally she spoke. 'George!' she said.

Weston put down the paper and turned toward his wife.

'What is it, dear?' he asked.

'George! It's Gloria and that terrible machine,' she said. 'That … the robot that Gloria calls Robbie. He doesn't leave her for a minute.'

'Well, that's his job,' Mr Weston said. 'Robbie is Gloria's nanny. And he certainly isn't a terrible machine. He's the best robot there is.'

'Listen to me, George,' Mrs Weston went on angrily. 'I don't want a machine to take care of my daughter. Nobody knows what it's thinking.'

Weston frowned. He was feeling a little angry. And his face showed that he did not understand why there was a problem. 'Robbie has taken care of Gloria for two years,' he said. 'You haven't been worried before.'

'I wasn't worried at first,' said Grace. 'But –'

George interrupted his wife. 'Grace,' he said. 'Robbie was made to take care of a little child. He was made to be gentle and nice.'

'But something might happen and that … that thing will go crazy and …' Grace could not finish her sentence.

'That's impossible,' George said. 'We discussed the First Law of Robotics when we bought Robbie. You know that a robot cannot harm a human. Anyway, you can't take him away from Gloria. She loves Robbie.'

'But, George,' Grace said. 'Gloria won't play with other children. She only wants to be with that machine. We've got to get rid of that horrible thing. It frightens me. You can sell it back to U.S. Robots. I've asked someone at the company about this.'

George was much angrier now. 'No, Grace,' he said. 'We're keeping the robot until Gloria is older. I don't want to hear any more about it.'

Mr and Mrs Weston argued about Robbie for a week. And each time, Mr Weston said, 'Robbie stays!' But each time, his reply was weaker.

Finally, Weston went to speak to his daughter.

'Should we go to a visivox* show downtown?' he asked her.

'Oh, yes!' said Gloria. 'Can Robbie go too?'

'No, dear,' her father replied unhappily. 'But you can tell him about the show when you get home.' And he turned away. He could not look at his daughter's face.

* visivox – a word invented by Asimov, which means a type of cinema in the future

INSIDE INFORMATION

- Isaac Asimov (1920–1992) was born in Russia but moved to the USA when he was a child.
- Asimov studied chemistry and biochemistry at university and then taught science. But he had started writing and selling stories when he was just 19 and he decided he wanted to be a writer. He wrote lots of short stories about robots and published them in the book 'I, Robot'. (The film 'I, Robot' does not tell any of the stories in this book.)
- This text comes from the first short story in the book, 'Robbie'. It was written in 1941. The story mentions the First Law of Robotics. (Asimov invented the word 'robotics' but it is used by scientists now.) The First Law of Robotics says 'A robot must not harm a human. And it must not allow a human to be harmed.'
- In the story, Gloria is an eight-year-old girl. George and Grace Weston are their parents.

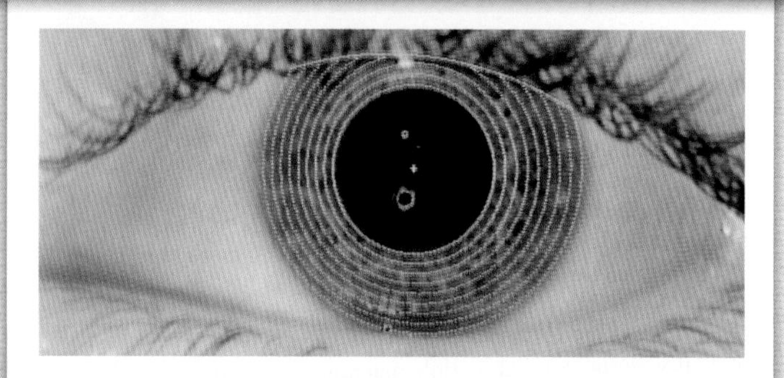

1 LISTENING 2.05 **You are going to listen to an expert talking about 'iris recognition'. Listen and answer the questions.**

1 What is iris recognition?
2 What objects will iris recognition make unnecessary?
3 Does the expert think it's a good thing? Why/Why not?

EXAM SUCCESS

You are going to do a multiple-choice listening activity. In this type of activity you have three or four answers and you choose the best answer. When should you read the answers for the first time? Do you think the questions are usually in the order that you hear them?

EXAM SUCCESS ▶ page 152

2 **Listen again and choose the best answers.**

1 People with blue eyes
  a have a lot of pigment in their iris.
  b don't have a lot of pigment in their iris.
  c have more pigment than people with brown eyes.

2 Your two irises are always
  a the same.
  b different.
  c coloured differently.

3 Iris recognition works with
  a just a photo of your iris.
  b your photo in a database.
  c a digital code made from a photo of your eye.

4 For it to work, the maximum distance your eye can be from the machine is
  a ten centimetres.
  b just less than a metre.
  c two metres.

5 The system
  a doesn't work with people who wear glasses or contact lenses.
  b works with people who wear contact lenses but not glasses.
  c works with people who wear contact lenses or glasses.

6 The system could be used at school
  a to operate computers.
  b to check who has come to school that day.
  c to check your identity.

3 **What about *you*?**

Do you think iris recognition is a good idea? Why/Why not?

Do you think iris recognition is a good idea?

I think it's a better idea than carrying an ID card.

GRAMMAR GUIDE

Have something done

1a Look at the sentences. Who does the action – the subject at the start of the sentence or somebody else?

1 You have your passport checked at the airport.
2 We had our photos taken by a journalist at school.
3 He got his glasses fixed at the optician's.

1b Look at the sentences again and answer the questions.

1 What comes after the verbs *have* or *get* – the subject or the object of the sentence?
2 What type of words are *checked, taken, fixed* in these sentences – verbs, nouns or adjectives?
3 Can we use *have* or *get* in different tenses in this type of sentence?
4 What does *by* introduce in these sentences?

GRAMMAR REFERENCE ▶ page 80

2 **What did these people have done last week? Write sentences using these verbs.**

cut make paint repair take out test

a
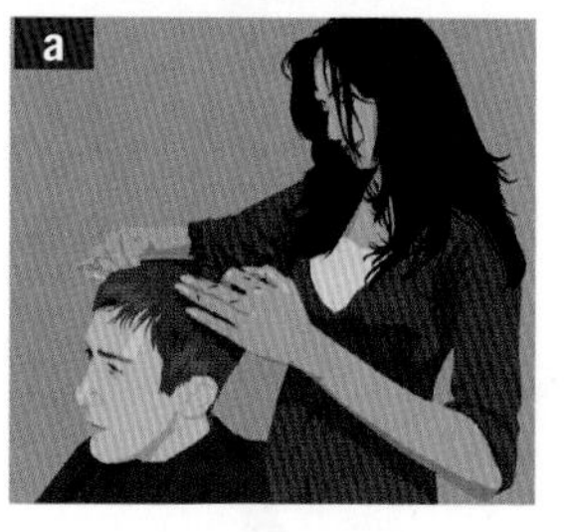
....

b

....

c
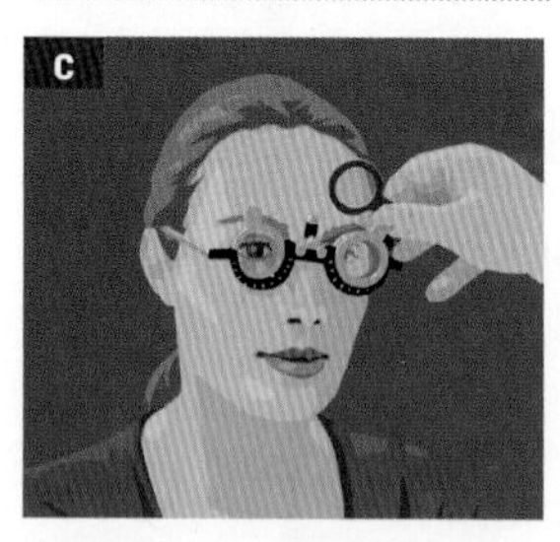
....

d

....

e

....

f
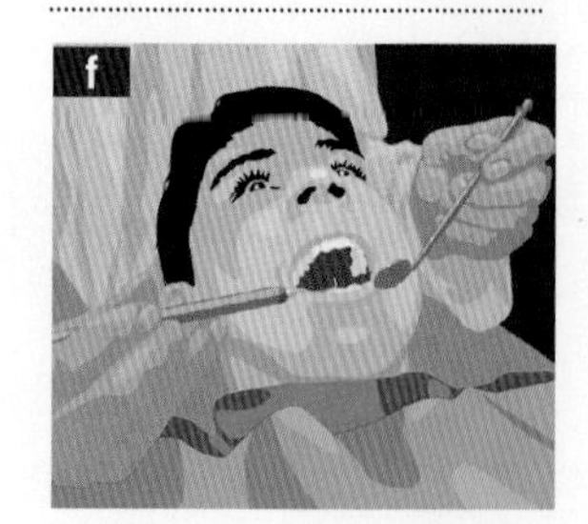
....

3 Complete the text by writing one word in each space.

Computers are **(a)** .... essential part of most of our lives nowadays. But computers are similar **(b)** .... cars. Many people can drive, but not many people know exactly **(c)** .... a car works. And that is why people usually **(d)** .... their cars serviced by a professional mechanic instead of **(e)** .... it themselves. Computers are the same for many people. They know how to **(f)** .... the 'start' button. But once something goes wrong, they have no idea how to fix it. Sometimes computers do strange things. They have a bug or crash and then they lose data because of the malfunction. But many problems are caused **(g)** .... human error. One type of problem is becoming more and more common. It's called 'computer rage'. People get so angry and stressed because of their computers, they're so tired **(h)** .... working with them all day, that they **(i)** .... something violent to them. One man was so angry with his laptop that he threw it down the toilet. And then he had to take the computer to a special company to get **(j)** .... fixed! Another laptop **(k)** .... destroyed by a woman who put it on top of her car when she was looking for her car keys. She got **(l)** .... the car but forgot that the laptop had **(m)** .... left on top of the car. She drove away and the computer fell onto the road. She then drove right over it! She tried to get the laptop examined **(n)** .... a specialist. But unfortunately computer specialists can't perform miracles.

4 Rewrite these sentences using the construction *have something done* in the correct tense. If we know who exactly did the action, introduce them with *by*.

1 They fixed our computer last week.
We ....
....
2 They've reinstalled the operating system on his computer.
He ....
....
3 A computer specialist rescued my files.
I ....
....
4 They're going to service my car next week.
I ....
....
5 Armani make all his suits.
He ....
....
6 They're knocking down our kitchen wall on Saturday.
We ....
....
7 Last summer they built a swimming pool in my friend's garden.
My friend ....
....
8 Her parents pay her telephone bills.
She ....
....

5 Put the words in the correct order to write questions.

1 cut often you do get How hair your?
....
2 yourself fix you Can computer your?
....
3 ever Have taken out tooth had you a?
....
4 When your you eyes time was last the had tested?
....
5 for Have ever had made clothes you you?
....
6 Do your photo you taken like having?
....
7 Have drawn had you ever picture your?
....

6a SPEAKING Ask your partner the questions in 5. Then ask more questions to find out extra information. Use these question words and your own ideas.

How often? What? When? Where? Who? Why?

6b Tell the class three interesting things you found out about your partner.

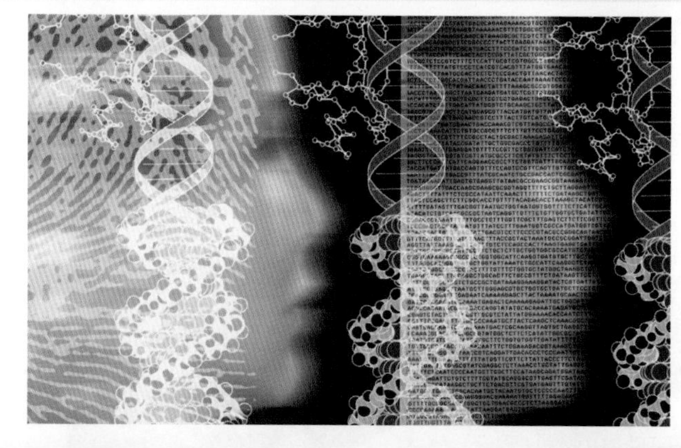

1 **Work in pairs. Look at these scientific inventions and discoveries.**
Student A: write down reasons why each one is good.
Student B: write down reasons why each one is bad.

antibiotics cars computers cloning mobile phones nuclear reactors oil tankers spaceships X-ray machines

2 SPEAKING **Tell your partner your ideas in 1.**

3 SPEAKING **Look at this statement. Do you agree or disagree with it? Think of reasons why.**

New technology doesn't make life better. It makes life worse.

4 LISTENING 2.06 **Listen to a boy and girl discussing the statement in 3. Whose opinion is closer to yours – the boy's or the girl's? Why?**

5 **Listen again. Complete the expressions in the second part of the Speaking Bank (Useful expressions for disagreeing or partially disagreeing).**

Speaking Bank

Useful expressions for agreeing or partially agreeing

- I (totally) agree (with you) (that ...)
- I agree to an extent (that ...)
- That's true.
- You're right.
- You've got a point.
- I take your point.
- I see what you mean.

Useful expressions for disagreeing or partially disagreeing

- I (totally) disagree (with you) (that ...)
- I agree to an extent, ...
- That's true, ...
- You've got a point, ...
- I take your point, ...
- I see what you mean, ...
- I'm not sure that's true.

6 **Individually, write down six statements. They can be about anything. You don't have to agree with the statements.**

Football is the best sport in the world.
Motorbikes are more dangerous than cars.

7 SPEAKING **Work in small groups. Listen to each other's statements. React to each statement with expressions from the Speaking Bank. You must say what you really think.**

Football is the best sport in the world.

I totally agree with you.

I agree to an extent, but basketball is really good too.

Practice makes perfect

8a **Look at the task. Half of the class must agree with the statement. The other half must disagree. Prepare a list of points to support your opinion.**

Today we have all the technology we need. There is nothing left to invent.

- Say if you agree or not.
- Give reasons for your opinion.

8b **Have a class debate with the expressions from the Speaking Bank.**

8c **When you finish, tell the class what you really think about the statement.**

STUDY SKILLS

What do the terms *accuracy* and *fluency* mean when we talk about speaking English? Which do you think is more important? **STUDY SKILLS ▸ page 148**

1 Work with a partner. Look at the statement and make a list of arguments for and against.

Life would be better without mobile phones.

2 Read this essay. Does it contain any of your ideas from 1?

Thirty years ago almost nobody had a mobile phone. Nowadays it seems everybody has one, from the youngest to the oldest. Is this a good thing or a bad thing?

Mobile phones can be useful for a number of reasons. Firstly, they allow us to communicate quickly in almost any situation. This can be really useful in emergencies, for example. Furthermore, they make it easy for people who are alone to be in contact with others. In this way, they do not feel so lonely. Finally, they are useful for other things, not just for making calls. For instance, we can use them to listen to music, play games and take photos.

However, mobile phones have disadvantages too. People depend on them too much and make calls which are not really necessary. What's more, their use can be dangerous, for example when they are used by people when they are driving. In addition, people often use them in public places and this can be very annoying, for example in cinemas, restaurants or on public transport.

To sum up, mobile phones have advantages but, on the other hand, they can also create problems. In my opinion, life would be worse without them because they often make our lives easier. However, we should limit their use because people often become addicted to them and use them for no real reason.

3 Read the essay again. Write a title or short description of each paragraph.

Paragraph 1: ....

Paragraph 2: ....

Paragraph 3: ....

Paragraph 4: ....

STUDY SKILLS

Why is it so important to divide texts into paragraphs when you are writing? STUDY SKILLS ▶ page 148

4 Complete the Writing Bank with these linkers.

As far as I'm concerned, However, In addition, Secondly, To sum up,

Writing Bank

Useful linkers in 'for and against' essays

Sequencing arguments
- Firstly,
- ....
- Finally,

Adding arguments
- Furthermore,
- What's more,
- ....

Making contrasts
- On the one hand … On the other hand …
- In contrast,
- ....

Expressing opinions
- In my opinion,
- Personally I think …
- ....

Concluding
- In conclusion,
- ....

Practice makes perfect

5a Look at the task and plan this essay with a partner. Remember to organise your ideas into paragraphs.

'The computer is the most important invention ever.'

Write an essay giving arguments for and against this statement and give your own opinion.

5b Write your essay individually. Use expressions from the Writing Bank.

Language reference and revision

Grammar reference

The passive

Form

Subject + **be** + **past participle** (+ **by** + **agent**)

The prizes are given at a ceremony. (present simple)

This invention is being used by millions of people. (present continuous)

These computers have been used by NASA. (present perfect)

The car wasn't invented in 1930. (past simple)

This type of energy will be used in the future. (will)

We make the passive with the correct tense and form of the verb *to be* and the past participle of the verb.

To make questions in the passive, we put the first auxiliary verb before the subject.

Is the ceremony being shown on TV?

Has the ceremony been filmed?

We use the preposition **by** to introduce the agent – the person or thing which does the action.

Use

We use the passive when:

1 we are more interested in the action than the people who do the action.
The bridge was built in 1866.
English is spoken here.

2 we do not know who exactly does the action.
My things have been moved.
His bag has been stolen.

3 it is obvious or understood who did the action.
The criminal was arrested at 5.30pm.
Smoking is not permitted.

In some languages, reflexive or impersonal forms are used instead of the passive.

Have something done

Form

Subject + **have** or **get** + object + **past participle** (**by** + agent)

I get my eyes tested once a year. (present simple)

She is having a dress made by Dolce and Gabbana. (present continuous)

We have had the house decorated. (present perfect)

He had his hair cut. (past simple)

They were getting the car serviced. (past continuous)

We'll get our photo taken. (will)

With this structure we make different tenses by changing the tense of **have** or **get**.

Use

1 We use **have something done** to talk about actions which we don't do ourselves; somebody or something does them for us. We often pay them to do this action. **Get** is slightly more informal.

I don't know anything about computers so when I have a problem I have my computer fixed by a friend who studied computers at university.
Son, you need to get your hair cut!
In this shop you can have shirts made specially for you.

2 We can use the preposition **by** to introduce the agent – the person or thing which does the action. We don't use **by** if it is not important who does the action.

Vocabulary

1 Everyday inventions

camcorder digital camera
dishwasher DVD player
home cinema system laptop
microwave oven mobile phone
MP3 player remote control
satnav vacuum cleaner
washing machine

2 Operating technology

charge/recharge (a battery)
connect X to Y insert plug in
press a button (Power/Play/Stop/Fast Forward/Rewind)
select (a programme/a track/a function) switch/turn on
switch/turn off

3 Prepositional phrases with adjectives

afraid of aware of bored with
different from good at interested in
pleased with ready for responsible for
similar to tired of worried about

4 Other words and phrases ▶ page 141

Grammar revision

The passive – present simple

1 Change the sentences from active to passive or from passive to active.

1 Robots make cars in this factory.
2 This programme is watched by millions of people.
3 They make SEAT cars in Spain.
4 They teach German in our school.
5 The dogs are looked after by my neighbour.
6 This comic is read by people of all ages.

WORKBOOK ▶ page 48

/6 points

The passive – other tenses

2 Complete the sentences with the verbs in the correct form of the passive.

1 His mobile phone .... (steal) last week.
2 A thousand copies of the DVD .... (sell) since it came out last week.
3 This museum .... (visit) by thousands of people each week.
4 Three new hospitals .... (build) next year.
5 The first portable stereo .... (invent) by Andreas Pavel more than thirty years ago.
6 Perhaps the final of next year's Champions League .... (play) in Poland.
7 Since its publication this book .... (translate) into over thirty languages..

WORKBOOK ▶ page 48

/7 points

Have something done

3 Complete the second sentences with the correct form of the expression *have something done*.

1 She didn't decorate the house herself. She .... by professionals.
2 He won't fix the car himself. He .... at a garage.
3 She doesn't do her own hair. She .... at the hairdresser's.
4 We didn't paint the room ourselves. We ....
5 They didn't build the garage themselves. They .... by a special company.
6 He didn't install the programme himself. He .... by a friend.
7 They haven't tested their son's eyesight themselves. They .... by an optician.

WORKBOOK ▶ page 51

/7 points

Vocabulary revision

Everyday inventions

1 Complete the names of these everyday inventions. Is each one usually used for pleasure (P) or for housework (H)?

1 dish...... ....
2 cam...... ....
3 vacuum ....
4 washing ....
5 MP3 ....
6 microwave ....
7 remote ....

WORKBOOK ▶ page 46

/7 points

Prepositional phrases with adjectives

3 Choose the correct alternative.

1 I'm really pleased of/with your work.
2 She isn't worried about/of her marks at school.
3 People say I look similar at/to my father.
4 Are you aware of/with the situation?
5 Some people are afraid of/with spiders.
6 Who is responsible for/of keeping this room tidy?
7 I'm bored at/with reality TV.

WORKBOOK ▶ page 49

/7 points

Operating technology

2 Complete the text with these words.

insert	press	plug … in
select	switch … off	turn … on

To play your favourite song from a CD

Your CD player doesn't have batteries so first you must **(a)** .... it .... Then you **(b)** .... the CD player .... You **(c)** .... the disc in the machine. You **(d)** .... the song you want to hear. You **(e)** .... 'play'. When you finish listening, you **(f)** .... the CD player ....

WORKBOOK ▶ page 46

/6 points

Total */40 points*

Gateway to exams *Units 5–6*

Reading

1 Work with a partner. Make a list of things that you have done with your hands so far today. How difficult would it be to do these things with only one hand?

2 Read the text. What do all the people in the text have in common?

Tip for Reading Exams

In matching activities, remember …

Read the text quickly to get a general understanding. Then read the piece(s) of information that you need to find. Are there are any special words that help you to find the text or part of the text which contains the information? Remember that the same information in the text could be expressed with different words. **EXAM SUCCESS ▸ page 152**

Becoming bionic

Many people think the word 'bionics' comes from two words – 'biology' and 'electronics'. Indeed those two words do help to explain bionics. The basic idea of bionics is to copy biological systems that are found in nature and apply them to engineering and technology. In the 1970s *The Six Million Dollar Man* was a popular TV series about an astronaut who is rebuilt after a terrible accident. His new bionic legs, arm and eye give him superhuman abilities. He can run incredibly fast, see in the dark, and his arm has incredible strength, as well as containing a Geiger counter to test for radioactivity! Before, bionics was just science fiction, but not now, as these people show us.

A Claudia Mitchell

In 2006 Claudia Mitchell became the first person to become bionic. She lost her arm in a motorbike accident. She couldn't do even simple tasks. At meal times, she had to have her food cut for her because she couldn't hold a knife and fork. But a bionic arm was created for her and was fitted to her body. When Claudia thinks about moving her bionic hand or arm, electrodes on her chest receive these brain signals from the nerves and send signals to operate the artificial arm. She practised four to five hours a day, five to six days a week, and was able to operate her hand in this way seven weeks after the arm was fitted.

B Donald McKillop

Donald McKillop lost his right hand in an industrial accident almost 30 years ago. But in 2006 he was given a bionic hand and says that it has transformed his life. The hand was made by Touch Bionics, a Scottish company which has succeeded in creating the world's most sophisticated bionic hand. Each finger on the hand has its own motor and can move independently. The hand can be bought for £8,500 in Britain. 'Every day it gets easier to use,' says Mr McKillop. 'I was amazed at how much I could do within the first hour of trying it. My wife used to cut up meat for me, and so when we went out for a meal I always tried to choose something that I could cut easily on my own. For the first time in 30 years I can have what I want from the menu.'

C Jason Henderson

American Independence Day celebrations in 2007 cost Jason both his hands. He was moving fireworks when they suddenly exploded in his hands. A family member told Jason about Touch Bionics and their bionic hands and almost two years later, Henderson is using two of these. 'It's definitely given me a lot of independence, more than I thought I was going to have.' Jason is in the unique position of using two bionic hands. One interesting consequence is that they both function equally so one hand is not 'better' than the other. Now Jason can write at about 80% of his speed before the accident and so he has been able to continue his university studies.

3 Which person (A–C) might say these things?

1 I didn't expect to have this much freedom.
2 I enjoy eating out more now.
3 I had an accident at work.
4 I had an accident while I was travelling.
5 I'm in a different situation to the other people in the texts.
6 I'm not right-handed or left-handed.
7 I'm a student.
8 It took me nearly two months to learn how to use my hand.

Writing

Tip for Writing Exams

In writing exams, remember…

Before you start writing you should know who you are writing to, how many words you need to write, and what information you need to include. **EXAM SUCCESS ▸ page 151**

4 Work with a partner. What do you think about school uniform? Do you think it's a good idea or not? Give reasons.

5 Do this task individually. Remember to use linkers and your ideas in 4.

> Your school magazine wants to know what students think about school uniform. Write an article for the magazine.
>
> Give reasons for and against school uniform.
>
> Finish the article with a conclusion giving your opinion. (Write 120–150 words.)

Listening

Tip for Listening Exams

In multiple-choice activities, remember …

Read the questions before you listen. The questions are usually in the order that you hear them in the recording. EXAM SUCCESS ▸ page 152

6 2.07 Listen to a programme about teenage students and choose the best answers.

1 Professor Foster discovered that teenage students

- **A** prefer studying in the afternoon.
- **B** remember more in the afternoon.
- **C** have more lessons in the afternoon.

2 Professor Foster thinks that teenagers

- **A** need more rest than young children and adults.
- **B** need alarm clocks more than younger and older people.
- **C** should sleep longer at least two days a week.

3 At his school, Dr Kelley wants to

- **A** change the school timetable.
- **B** have classes only in the afternoon.
- **C** have easy lessons between 9 and 11am.

4 Most students

- **A** like Dr Kelley's idea.
- **B** don't like Dr Kelley's idea.
- **C** don't mind getting up early.

7 What about *you*?

1 What do you think about Dr Kelley's idea?

2 When do you study better – in the morning, afternoon or evening?

Use of English

Tip for Use of English Exams

In cloze activities, remember …

The gaps in cloze activities will often be for prepositions, articles, pronouns, auxiliary verbs, modal verbs and conjunctions (*and, but, although*, etc.). EXAM SUCCESS ▸ page 151

8 Work with a partner. What do you know about Oxford University? Make notes and then exchange ideas.

9 Read the text. Do any of your ideas appear? Ignore the gaps in the text.

Oxford is the oldest university (a) .... the English-speaking world. It is difficult to give an exact date for when it began but teaching existed at Oxford in some form in 1096. Many people who are responsible (b) .... global affairs have studied at Oxford. Twenty-five British Prime Ministers have (c) .... educated at Oxford, but there have also been at least 30 international leaders, 47 Nobel Prize winners, 6 kings and 50 Olympic medal winners. Of course, there have been other famous people studying and teaching at Oxford. *The Lord of the Rings* (d) .... written by Professor JRR Tolkien while he was teaching English there.

To get a degree at Oxford, students usually only do two sets of examinations – the first at the end of the first year and the second at the end of the course. Students need to be good (e) .... organising their work themselves so they are ready (f) .... their exams when they finally come. Oxford is a modern and vibrant university, but it is also a place of old traditions and rules. To do exams, male students (g) .... wear a dark suit, black socks and shoes, a white shirt and a white bow tie. (h) .... they don't wear these clothes, they won't be allowed to take the exam.

Women usually wear a white blouse, black skirt and black tie. Nowadays, they (i) .... have to wear a skirt – they can wear trousers if they want. But all students have to wear a gown and a hat called a mortarboard. The good news is that they can take (j) .... their hats while they are actually doing their exams!

10 Complete each gap in the text with one word.

'Can Do' Progress Check

CEF

1 How well can you do these things in English now? Give yourself a mark from 1 to 4.

1 = I can do it very well.	2 = I can do it quite well.	3 = I have some problems.	4 = I can't do it.

- **a** I can talk about obligation, prohibition and advice using modal verbs. ☐
- **b** I can talk about possible and imaginary situations and their consequences using the first and second conditional. ☐
- **c** I can talk about different aspects of life at school and university. ☐
- **d** I can describe photos and pictures using expressions to talk about different parts. ☐
- **e** I can write a formal letter applying for a scholarship. ☐
- **f** I can talk about processes using different forms of the passive and *have something done*. ☐
- **g** I know which prepositions to use with certain adjectives. ☐
- **h** I can understand written and spoken texts about inventions and technology. ☐
- **i** I can take part in a debate expressing agreement and disagreement. ☐
- **j** I can write *for* and *against* essays. ☐

2 Now decide what you need to do to improve.

1 Look again at my book/notes.

2 Do more practice exercises. → WORKBOOK pages 38–55

3 Other: ....

7 Game on!

Grammar ‣ Defining relative clauses ‣ Non-defining relative clauses
Vocabulary ‣ Sports ‣ Sports venues and equipment
‣ Phrasal verbs connected with sport
Speaking ‣ Giving a presentation
Writing ‣ A film review

‣ Vocabulary

Sports

1 Work with a partner. Match the pictures with these words.

athletics basketball boxing diving football golf
gymnastics ice hockey judo sailing skiing snowboarding
swimming table tennis volleyball weightlifting

2a PRONUNCIATION **In the box in 1, there are seven sports with three syllables. Which are they?**

2b Put the words in the correct column, according to the stress.

●	●••	•●•	●•	●•••
golf				

2c 2.08 **Listen and check your answers. Then practise saying the words with the correct stress.**

> **‣ STUDY SKILLS**
>
> How important is correct word stress for good pronunciation?
>
> STUDY SKILLS ‣ page 148

3 Work with a partner. Match one sport in 1 to each of these categories. Then add another example of your own.

1 team sports ....
2 individual sports ....
3 ball sports ....
4 water sports ....
5 winter sports ....
6 martial arts ....

Sports venues and equipment

4 Complete the sentences with these words.

course court gym pitch
pool rink slope track

1 We go swimming and diving in a ....
2 We do gymnastics in a ....
3 You ski down a ....
4 You play tennis or basketball on a ....
5 You play football on a ....
6 You play ice hockey on a ....
7 You do athletics on a ....
8 You play golf on a ....

5 Look at the photo and find three of these pieces of equipment.

boots club goal goggles net
racket skates skis trainers

6 Work with a partner. How many sports can you think of that use each piece of equipment in 5?

You need a net to play tennis, table tennis, volleyball ...

7 LISTENING 2.09 **Which sport in 1 is the subject of each conversation?**

1 .... 3 ....
2 .... 4 ....

8 SPEAKING **Work in groups. Think of a sport. The others must find out what it is by asking questions. You can only answer *yes* or *no*. You can ask a maximum of twenty questions.**

Is it a team sport?

No, it isn't.

Do you do it in a gym?

No, you don't.

1 Work with a partner. Discuss these questions.

1 What is a superstition? 2 What superstitions exist in your country? 3 Do you have any superstitions? What are they?

Sports superstitions

To be a sports champion you have to have lots of skill and dedication. But a little bit of luck is always useful too. That may be why so many professional sportsmen and sportswomen have their little superstitions and rituals.

1 TOM DALEY

Tom Daley was only seven when he took up diving. In 2008 he became one of the youngest people ever to take part in an Olympic event, competing in the diving competition. The British diver has a lucky mascot which he takes with him every time he has a competition. He always puts the mascot on top of his sports bag where he can see him from up on the diving board. And in case you're wondering, the mascot is a monkey. It doesn't have a name. 'He's just my lucky monkey,' says Daley. 'I know he probably isn't lucky but I've been taking him with me for a long time and I don't want to stop doing it.'

2 CASSIE PATTEN

And he isn't the only sports personality with a special mascot. Cassie Patten is a British Olympic swimmer. Every time she goes away to a swimming competition, she has to put her teddy bear, Rainbow, and her clown, Sniffy, into bed at her home before she can leave.

3 BEN AINSLIE

Then take Ben Ainslie. He is one of Britain's best sailors ever. He has won an Olympic gold medal in three consecutive Olympic Games. It was quite natural that he should win a gold medal in Beijing in 2008. Ben's superstition was perfect for competing in China. His superstition is that before each race he always has to eat a Chinese meal.

4 MICHAEL JORDAN

Clothes are often important for sports stars too. Michael Jordan, one of the greatest American basketball players of all time, played many matches for the Chicago Bulls. But whenever he went on court to play a professional match he always wore a pair of blue shorts under his other shorts. These were the shorts that he wore at the University of North Carolina. The University of North Carolina was the place where Jordan started playing seriously. After winning lots of matches with them he felt that they gave him luck. Incidentally, this superstition started a fashion. Because he wore two pairs of shorts, the second pair had to be especially long to cover the others. People started copying him. That is one reason why basketball shorts are so long and baggy today.

5 PATRICK ROY

What about ice hockey? Well, even big strong ice hockey players have their superstitions. Patrick Roy was a great player who came from Canada. He was a goaltender. Goaltenders are the players whose job is to stop the other team from scoring. He used to talk to his goal posts during the game. 'They're my friends,' he explained. In the rink he never stood on the red or blue lines. Before a game, when he was warming up, he always skated out to the blue line and looked at the goal. He then started to visualise the goal getting smaller and smaller.

6 RAFAEL NADAL

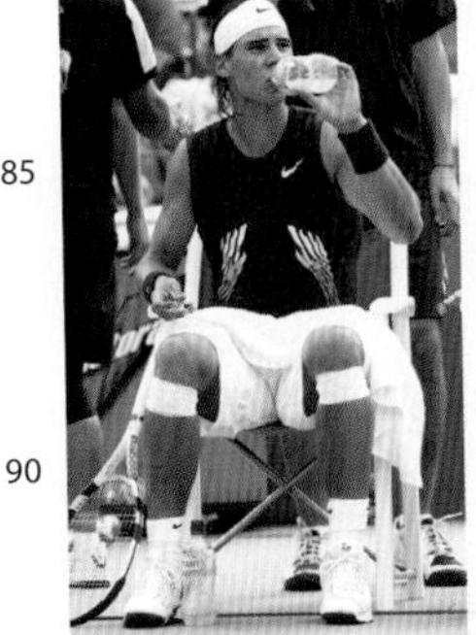

It's clear that many sports superstitions are a question of repetition. When things go right, many professionals try to do things the same way the next time they compete. Take the Spanish tennis superstar Rafael Nadal. He always has to have two bottles of water in front of his chair by the side of the court. When he drinks from them, he spends a long time putting the bottles back in exactly the position he wants. The labels must always be looking towards the side of the court where he is playing. Nadal's socks must always be in exactly the same position all through each match too. And he doesn't like wearing long shorts but he says he'll continue to wear them while he's winning matches. The funny thing is that when people ask Nadal if he's superstitious, he says 'No, no. Not at all!'

2 Read the text and complete the Sport column of the table.

Person	Sport	Nationality	Superstition(s)
1 Tom Daley			
2 Cassie Patten			
3 Ben Ainslie			
4 Michael Jordan			
5 Patrick Roy			
6 Rafael Nadal			

3 Read the text again and complete the rest of the table.

4 Are these statements true (T) or false (F)? Write the line where you find the answer.

1 Tom Daley isn't really a very superstitious person. T/F ....
2 Cassie Patten takes her lucky mascots with her to competitions. T/F ....
3 Ben Ainslie has never won two gold medals in the same Olympic Games. T/F ....
4 Lots of players started wearing two pairs of shorts like Michael Jordan. T/F ....
5 Patrick Roy imagined the goal helping him. T/F ....
6 Nadal does things he dislikes because of superstition. T/F ....

5 Find words in the text with similar meanings to these words and expressions.

1 asking yourself *(paragraph 2)*
2 every time *(paragraph 5)*
3 big, not tight *(paragraph 5)*
4 form a picture in your mind *(paragraph 6)*
5 a piece of paper giving information about a product *(paragraph 7)*

6 SPEAKING What about *you*?

1 Which superstition in the text do you think is the funniest or most unusual? Why?
2 Do you know anybody else who is very superstitious?

I think Patrick Roy talking to his goal posts is really funny!

GRAMMAR GUIDE

Defining relative clauses

1a Look at these sentences. The words in bold are relative pronouns. Use them to complete the rules a–e.

1 He was a great player **who** came from Canada.
2 He has a lucky mascot **which** he takes with him.
3 They are the players **whose** job it is to stop the other team from scoring.
4 2008 was the year **when** he won a gold medal.
5 These were the shorts **(that)** he wore.
6 She's the swimmer **that** has two lucky mascots.
7 Beijing is the place **where** the 2008 Olympics took place.

a We use .... and .... with people.
b We use .... and .... with things.
c We use .... to talk about possessions.
d We use .... with places.
e We use .... with times.

1b Why do you think we call these words 'defining' relative clauses? What do they define?

Why can we omit *that* in sentence 5 but not in 6?

GRAMMAR REFERENCE ▸ page 94

2 Choose the correct alternative. If you think both are correct, choose both.

1 Football is a game *which/-* many people play.
2 A stadium is a place *that/where* you can watch football matches.
3 The people *who/-* watch sports events are called spectators.
4 The leader of the Tour de France is the person *who/whose* shirt is yellow.
5 June is the month *when/which* Wimbledon starts.
6 A jockey is a person *who/that* rides a horse in a race.
7 Brazil is the country *where/which* has won the FIFA World Cup most times.
8 Ice hockey is a sport *-/that* is very popular in Canada.

3 Complete the text with relative pronouns.

Chess boxing is a very unusual sport **(a)** .... was invented by a Dutch artist **(b)** .... name is Iepe Rubingh. If you've never heard of it, the name chess boxing can help you to imagine it. Yes, you've guessed it. It's a mixture of chess and boxing! The Dutch man **(c)** .... invented the sport thinks that chess and boxing are two sports **(d)** .... have a lot in common. The rules are easy. First, there is a round of chess, and then there is a round of boxing. And then more chess and more boxing! They play in a boxing ring **(e)** .... they bring a table and chairs after each round of boxing. And, of course, they can take off their gloves when it's time to play chess. The winner is the person **(f)** .... gets checkmate or knocks out their opponent first. Berlin was the place **(g)** .... they had the first ever Chess Boxing World Championship, in 2007. An American and a German were in the final, and the one **(h)** .... won was German. Maybe that's why the sport has become so popular there. There is a school in Berlin **(i)** .... children can learn how to play the sport. What is the idea behind the sport? To show that boxers can be clever too. If you want to win chess boxing, you have to be strong *and* intelligent!

4 Match the sentence halves with a relative pronoun. Look up the words in *italics* in your dictionary if necessary.

1 The winner in a gymnastics competition is the person
2 A *referee* is the person
3 2020 is a year
4 A room with *tatami* mats is the place
5 *Time out* is a moment in a basketball match
6 A *black belt* is a thing
7 In football, *goalkeepers* are often the players
8 The *puck* is the thing

a you get when you are really good at judo or karate.
b shirt has a number 1 on the back.
c you hit in an ice hockey match.
d mark is the highest.
e there will be the Olympic Games.
f the players stop playing.
g job is to control football matches.
h you do judo.

STUDY SKILLS

What action can you take to improve your results in grammar exercises? **STUDY SKILLS ▶ page 148**

5 Write complete sentences with relative pronouns. You can give information or a personal opinion.

1 Torres is a football player
Torres is a football player who comes from Spain.
2 Basketball is a game
....
3 A racket is an object
....
4 The goal is the place
....
5 Synchronised swimming is a sport
....
6 Winter is the season
....
7 Physical Education is a subject
....
8 The beach is a place
....
9 Ice hockey is a sport
....
10 A gym is a place
....

6a SPEAKING Work with a partner. Look at the definitions. What are the words?

1 It's the name for a person who is walking, not driving a car or riding a bike.
2 It's a type of meat which comes from a cow.
3 It's a place where they make or produce things to sell.
4 It's usually the first thing that you do when you arrive at the airport to catch a plane.

6b Now prepare definitions for at least six words that you have learnt so far this year. Read out your definitions to other students. Can they identify your words?

It's an adjective which means the same as 'clever'.

It's a type of accommodation where you pay to stay in a room.

Phrasal verbs connected with sport

1 Look at the sentences and match the phrasal verbs in bold with their definitions a–g.

1 He **took up** diving when he was eight because he saw a competition and wanted to try it.
2 He was **warming up** before the race so that his legs were ready.
3 Italy have **knocked out** England in the World Cup so England will be on the plane home tomorrow.
4 Hey, you! Don't just sit there watching. Come and **join in**.
5 It's impossible to beat you. I **give in**!
6 She's really fit because she **works out** at the gym five times a week.
7 It's a difficult match but they're going to **go for** it.

Phrasal verbs	Definitions
1 take up	a prepare for a sport or another activity by doing gentle exercises
2 warm up	b stop competing and accept that you cannot win
3 knock out	c try very hard to win or get something
4 join in	d start doing an activity with other people who are already doing it
5 give in	e start a sport or hobby
6 go for	f do physical exercise
7 work out	g eliminate somebody from a competition by beating them/make somebody unconscious

2 Complete the sentences with the correct form of the phrasal verbs from 1.

1 I'm going to .... tennis. Tomorrow I'm going to buy a racket.
2 Yesterday we played in the semifinal. We aren't in the final because the other team .... us ....
3 A: Why don't you ....? B: Because I don't like team sports, I prefer individual ones.
4 She's got the right attitude to be a champion. When she's losing she never ....
5 It'll be a hard race but she's going to .... the gold medal.
6 He's hurt his leg because he didn't .... before running.
7 They're really strong. They .... in the gym, doing weightlifting.

3 SPEAKING Complete the sentences with the correct form of the phrasal verbs from 1. Then ask your partner the questions.

1 Do you ever .... out to keep fit? How often?
2 If there is a match or competition at school, do you .... in or do you just watch?
3 If something is difficult, do you usually .... for it and try hard to win, or do you .... in easily?
4 Have you ever been .... out of a competition?
5 When you do sport, do you usually .... up first or do you begin straight away?
6 What new sport or hobby would you like to .... up?

Click onto... Amazing runners

Cross-curricular – History
The first marathon runner

1 Work with a partner. Guess this information about marathons.

1 the length of a marathon
2 the origin of the marathon
3 where the name 'marathon' comes from

2 Work with a partner. Look at the pictures. What do you think is happening in the story?

3 Match the pictures with the texts.

4 🎧 2.10 Listen and check your answers.

5 Why …

1 was the Battle of Marathon so important in history?
2 did Phidippides run to Sparta?
3 was it difficult, in theory, for the Athenians to beat the Persians?
4 did the Athenians win?
5 do you think the sports company Nike chose that name?
6 is the distance of a marathon approximately 40 kilometres?

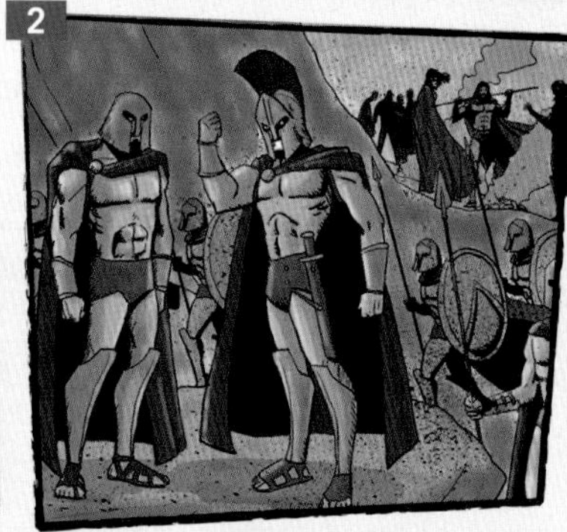

▸ WORD BOOSTER

Match the words and definitions.

1 plain
2 capture
3 massive, immense
4 increased

a very big
b take control of someone or something from your enemy in a war
c a large, flat area of land
d made bigger

A A VICTORY FOR THE POWERFUL PERSIAN EMPIRE COULD DESTROY THE INDEPENDENCE OF THE GREEK CITY-STATES AND END GREEK CIVILISATION AND CULTURE. THE PEOPLE OF ATHENS HAD TO PREPARE FOR A BATTLE THAT WAS TO MAKE AN ENORMOUS DIFFERENCE TO THE HISTORY OF THE WORLD.

B 600 SHIPS HAD BROUGHT AN IMMENSE ARMY OF 20,000 PERSIAN SOLDIERS. THERE WERE ONLY 10,000 MEN IN THE ATHENIAN ARMY. BUT THE ATHENIANS TRIED TO SURPRISE THE PERSIANS BY ATTACKING THEM WHILE THEY WERE STILL PREPARING FOR BATTLE. THE STRATEGY WORKED AND THE ATHENIANS WON.

C IN 490 BC, AN ARMY FROM PERSIA ARRIVED ON THE PLAIN OF MARATHON, ABOUT FORTY KILOMETRES FROM ATHENS. THEIR INTENTION WAS TO CAPTURE THE CITY OF ATHENS AND MAKE THE PEOPLE THEIR SLAVES.

D THE LEGEND SAYS THAT HE RAN THE 40 KILOMETRES FROM MARATHON TO ATHENS IN ABOUT THREE HOURS. HE GAVE THE MESSAGE (POSSIBLY JUST THE GREEK WORD 'NIKE', WHICH MEANS VICTORY), COLLAPSED AND DIED.

E WHEN PHIDIPPIDES GOT THERE, THE SPARTANS TOLD HIM THAT THEY COULDN'T HELP BECAUSE THEY WERE CELEBRATING A SPECIAL HOLIDAY AT THE TIME.

F WHILE THE MASSIVE PERSIAN ARMY WAS LANDING ON THE COAST, THE ATHENIANS SENT A MESSENGER NAMED PHIDIPPIDES (OR PHEIDIPPIDES) TO SPARTA. HIS MISSION WAS TO ASK THE SPARTANS TO HELP ATHENS IN THE BATTLE WHICH WAS ABOUT TO TAKE PLACE. THEY SAY HE RAN APPROXIMATELY 240 KILOMETRES IN LESS THAN TWO DAYS!

G AS SOON AS THE GREEKS WON THEY SENT A MESSENGER TO ATHENS TO ANNOUNCE THE GOOD NEWS TO THE PEOPLE OF THE CITY. ACCORDING TO LEGEND, THE RUNNER WAS PHIDIPPIDES, THE SAME RUNNER WHO HAD ALREADY GONE TO SPARTA.

Cross-curricular – Physical Education
Modern marathons

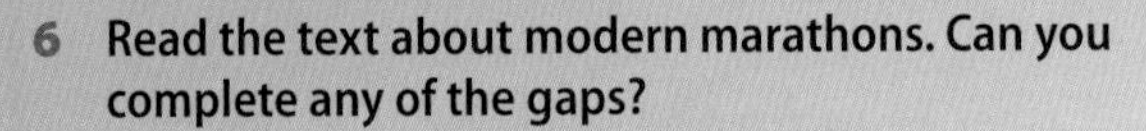

6 Read the text about modern marathons. Can you complete any of the gaps?

7 2.11 Listen and complete the gaps.

8 What about *you*?

1 Do you like watching the Olympic Games?
2 Which is your favourite event?
3 In general, which is your favourite sport to watch?

I like watching the Olympic Games.

Me too. I like watching the gymnastics.

I enjoy watching the swimming, but I never watch the running events.

The first modern marathon was run at the Olympic Games celebrated in **(a)** .... in **(b)** .... The race was from **(c)** .... to **(d)** .... There were **(e)** .... runners and the winner was a **(f)** .... man who carried water for a living. At the **(g)** .... Olympic Games the original distance of the marathon race was made a little bit longer so that the race finished just opposite the place where the **(h)** .... was sitting. This new distance of 26.2 miles, or 42.195 kilometres, became the official distance. Nowadays the world's largest marathon is in **(i)** .... More than **(j)** .... people finish the race each year!

Cross-curricular – Physical Education
Too young to run?

9 Work with a partner. In what ways do you think running can be good for your body? In what ways do you think it can be bad? Use these words to help you.

bones dehydration fit heart
impact knees muscles

10 2.12 Listen to a doctor speaking about children and long distance running. Which of these is the best summary of his opinions?

1 Young people can run any distance because their bodies are very resistant and prepared for anything.
2 A young person is better prepared to run shorter distances but running longer distances may be OK if a child really wants to do it.
3 Young people should be prohibited from running long distances because running in general is not so good for us.

11 Listen again and choose the correct alternative.

1 A four-year-old Indian boy called Budhia Singh once ran 65/70/75 kilometres.
2 He stopped because he collapsed/the police stopped him/a medical expert stopped him.
3 Usually you must be 16/18/21 years old to run a marathon.
4 The impact of running long distances can be very bad for children's bones/feet/muscles.
5 It's usual for kids to get too tired/nervous/hot when they run long distances.
6 It's good/impossible/possible to drink too much water when you run a long distance.
7 The doctor thinks running is good/OK/not good for all people.

12 What about *you*?

1 Do you like running? Why/Why not?
2 What is the longest distance you have ever run?

I don't enjoy running much. I prefer ball sports.

I like running. I sometimes run with my dad on Sundays.

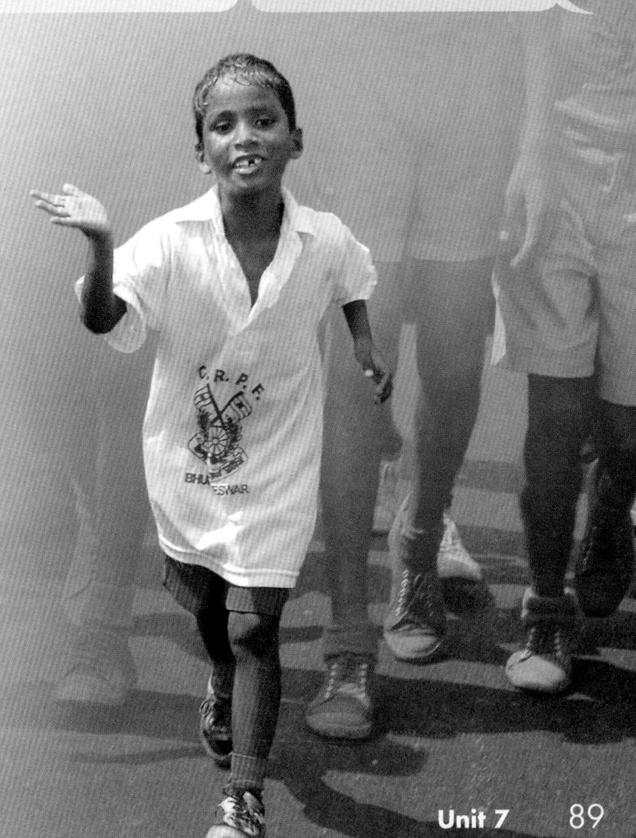

EXAM SUCCESS

You are going to do a true/false listening activity. What should you do if you miss the answer to a question?

EXAM SUCCESS ▸ page 152

1 Look at these statements about the origin of tennis. Work with a partner. Do you think they are true (T) or false (F)? Guess.

1 Tennis began in at least the 11th century. T/F ....
2 The first sport similar to modern tennis came from Germany. T/F ....
3 King Charles VIII of England played tennis. T/F ....
4 In 1858 an English man and a Scottish man helped to invent the modern sport of tennis. T/F ....
5 The first ever tennis championship was at Wimbledon. T/F ....

2 LISTENING 2.13 **Listen and check your guesses in 1.**

3 Listen again and answer the questions.

1 What are the two possible origins of the name 'tennis'?
2 In tennis, each point begins when the player 'serves' the ball. What is the possible origin of the word 'serve' in tennis?
3 In English we say 'love' instead of zero. What is the possible origin of the word 'love' in tennis?

4 SPEAKING **What about *you*?**

1 Do you like playing or watching tennis? Why/Why not?
2 Have you got a favourite tennis player? Who?

I don't like playing tennis but I like watching it.

Why?

It's really exciting seeing the best players, especially when it's a final.

GRAMMAR GUIDE

Non-defining relative clauses

1 Look at sentences 1–7 and answer the questions a–d.

1 The king, who was very big, loved playing tennis.
2 The rules, which were invented in 1858, are still quite similar today.
3 The first game that was similar to modern tennis came from Europe.
4 The servant, whose job was not very interesting, had to throw the ball up in the air.
5 The first English king who played tennis was Henry VII.
6 In the fifteenth century, when tennis was already popular, they only played indoors.
7 In 1877 there was a tennis championship at Wimbledon, where they still play today.

a Which sentences do you think are non-defining relative clauses – giving extra, non-essential information?
b Which clauses have commas; defining or non-defining relative clauses?
c Can we omit the relative pronouns in sentences with non-defining clauses?
d In sentence 2, we cannot use *that* because of what comes just before the relative pronoun. What comes just before it?

GRAMMAR REFERENCE ▸ page 94

2 Write sentences with non-defining relative clauses and the information given.

1 Tennis balls, *which are usually yellow for high visibility*, used to be white.
(They are usually yellow for high visibility.)

2 Adi Dassler, ... , began Adidas in the early 1920s.
(His younger brother was the owner of Puma.)

3 Formula 1, ... , has seen great technological progress.
(It is probably the world's most expensive sport.)

4 Scotland, ... , has lots of great golf courses.
(Golf began there.)

5 Paula Radcliffe, ... , is a great marathon runner.
(She won the New York marathon in 2007.)

6 In 1966, ... , the final was in London.
(England won the World Cup.)

7 Ana Ivanovic, ... , is a great tennis player.
(She is from Serbia.)

3 Read the text and decide which answer (A, B, C or D) best fits each space.

Oscar Pistorius, **(1)** .... was born in South Africa in 1986, is a great example for all of us. He was born with a congenital problem in both of his legs. **(2)** .... he was just eleven months old, both his legs were amputated below the knee. But Pistorius knew he wasn't going to spend the rest of his life in a wheelchair. He likes to tell people: 'You're not disabled by the disabilities you have, you are able by the abilities you have.' At primary school and secondary school, he played rugby, water polo and tennis. In January 2004, recovering from a rugby injury, Pistorius took **(3)** .... running. He loved it. Soon he was competing in the Paralympics. In China, **(4)** .... the 2008 Paralympics took place, he won three gold medals. But his times are so fast (he has run 100 metres in 10.91 seconds) that Pistorius wanted to compete in the Olympic Games. At first, the International Association of Athletics Federations (IAAF) said that Pistorius had an unfair advantage because of his artificial legs, **(5)** .... are called 'Cheetahs'. **(6)** .... then they changed their minds and let him try to classify for the Beijing Olympics. In the end, his times were not fast enough to represent his country. But Pistorius, **(7)** .... nicknames include 'Blade Runner' and 'the fastest man on no legs', is not going to give **(8)** .... He's going to continue training to see if he can compete in the next Olympics. The actor Tom Hanks, **(9)** .... is a fan of Pistorius, wants to make a film **(10)** .... his life.

1	A when	B that	C whose	D who
2	A When	B And	C But	D For
3	A in	B up	C after	D out
4	A that	B which	C when	D where
5	A that	B which	C –	D how
6	A And	B But	C When	D So
7	A which	B whose	C who	D that
8	A him	B surrender	C in	D on
9	A that	B –	C which	D who
10	A in	B about	C for	D with

4 Join the sentences with a relative clause.

1 The city is beautiful. I was born there. (Defining)
The city where I was born is beautiful.

2 The boys were really nice. I met them on holiday. (Non-defining)

3 Last year was great. I passed all my exams. (Non-defining)

4 The man is mad. He rang yesterday. (Defining)

5 This drink is my favourite drink. It's really healthy. (Non-defining)

6 My neighbours aren't very nice. Their dog makes a lot of noise. (Non-defining)

7 The hotel was beautiful. We stayed there in the summer. (Defining)

8 The singer is really good. His new CD is number one. (Non-defining)

5a SPEAKING Write short, simple sentences with information about people, places, things, activities and events in this book.

The Mini is a very popular car.
Isaac Asimov wrote 'I, Robot'.
Songjiang City is in Shanghai, China.

5b Read your sentences to your partner. He or she must add extra information to the sentences using non-defining relative clauses.

The Mini, which was invented in England, is a very popular car.

Isaac Asimov, who was American, wrote 'I, Robot'.

Songjiang City, where many people live, is in Shanghai, China.

1 SPEAKING **Work with a partner. Look at this question:**

Are top football players paid too much?

Make notes of arguments to justify your opinion.

2 **Organise your notes in 1 in a logical order. Add a short introduction and a conclusion.**

3 LISTENING 2.14 **Listen to a student giving a presentation on this subject. Does she generally agree or disagree that top football players are paid too much? Does she use any of the arguments in your notes?**

4 **Listen again and tick the expressions in the Speaking Bank which you hear.**

Speaking Bank

Useful expressions in presentations

Beginning a presentation

- I'd like to begin by saying …
- I'm going to talk about …

Introducing arguments

- Firstly,
- Secondly,
- It's also true that …
- What's more,
- First of all,
- Another thing is that …
- Furthermore,

Giving examples

- For example,
- Look at the case of …
- Finally,
- Last but not least
- For instance,
- Concluding,
- To sum up,
- In short,
- The point I'm trying to make is…

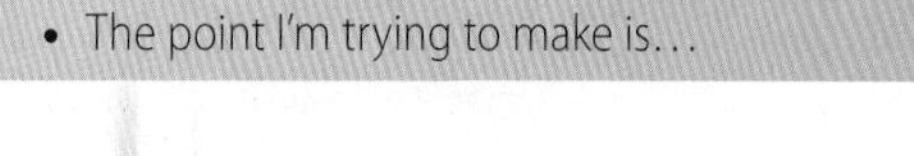

5 SPEAKING **Work with a partner. Put these stages of giving a presentation in the correct order.**

1. During your talk, use your notes to remember what comes next but don't just read things aloud. ....
2. Organise your notes in a logical way. ....
3. Finish your presentation at the right time. ....
4. Look at the question which you have to talk about. ....
5. Make notes with your ideas and arguments. ....
6. Begin your presentation and look up at the audience. ....
7. Think of a short introduction and a conclusion. ....

EXAM SUCCESS

What other advice would you give to somebody who is about to give a presentation to the class in English?

EXAM SUCCESS ▶ page 152

Practice makes perfect

6a **You have 5 minutes. Look at the task and make notes.**

> Prepare a presentation on this topic:
>
> Should sports people who are guilty of doping be banned for life?

6b **Give your presentation to the class. Use expressions from the Speaking Bank and the advice from the Study Skills box.**

1 **Look at these films, which are all about sports. Tell your partner anything you know about them. Do you know any other sports films?**

2 **Read the review about the film *Coach Carter* and answer the questions.**

1 Who is the main actor in the film?
2 What happens in the film? Do not write more than three sentences.
3 What did the writer like most about the film?
4 Who would the writer recommend the film to?

Film Coach Carter

128 of 130 people found the following review helpful:

More than just a sports film 27 March 2011
By S. Wilkinson (UK) – See all my reviews
This review is from: Coach Carter [DVD] [2005] (DVD)

1 'Coach Carter' is an American film that was released in 2005. It stars Samuel L. Jackson as the main character. It is a drama about basketball players at an American High School.

2 The plot is really interesting. A new basketball coach arrives at the high school. The team of students that he works with is not very good. There isn't much discipline in the team and so they usually lose. But Carter changes all this. He's very strict but the students start to respect him and win matches. However, Coach Carter has one important rule – if the students don't get good marks at school, they can't play basketball for the team. Carter finds out that some students never do their homework and fail all their exams. So he stops the team. Parents, teachers and students are all against him, but he doesn't give in. In the end, he wins. The players study harder and the team wins the cup. It's the typical happy ending!

3 I really liked the acting and the screenplay in this film. Samuel L. Jackson, who was in Pulp Fiction, plays the role of Carter brilliantly. There are no special effects and the soundtrack, which is basically hip-hop and soul, is nothing special. But the relationship between the teenagers and coach is very emotional, especially when you know that it's a true story.

4 To sum up, if you are a basketball fan, you'll love this film. If you aren't interested in basketball, you won't enjoy the match scenes. But I would still recommend you to see it because the message of the film is very inspiring.

3 **Match the paragraphs with the descriptions of their content.**

Paragraph 1 a recommendation to see the film
Paragraph 2 a summary of the plot or story
Paragraph 3 basic information about the film
Paragraph 4 the writer's opinion of the film

4 **Look at the review again and answer the questions.**

1 What tense does the writer use to summarise the plot?
2 Does the writer mix tenses to write the summary of the plot?
3 Is the text only a summary of the plot?
4 Does the writer give reasons and examples for his/her opinions?

5a **Read the review again and find the words in the Films section of the Writing Bank.**

5b **Use your dictionary to check the other useful words and expressions in the Writing Bank.**

Writing Bank

Useful words and expressions in film reviews

Films
happy ending, main character, play the role of, plot, scene, screenplay, soundtrack, special effects, the acting, to star

Adjectives to describe films
Positive: amazing, exciting, funny, hilarious, great, inspiring, interesting, spectacular
Negative: awful, boring, stupid, uninspiring

Types of film
action, animated film, comedy, drama, fantasy, horror, musical, science fiction, thriller, war, western

6a SPEAKING **Prepare notes about your favourite film or a film you have seen recently. Use words from the Writing Bank.**

6b **Use your notes to tell your partner about your film.**

Practice makes perfect

7 **Look at the task. Write a review of the film you chose in 6. Use the words and expressions in the Writing Bank and the paragraph plan in 3 to organise your ideas.**

Your school wants students to write film reviews for the school magazine. Write a review of your favourite film or a film you have seen recently.

Language reference and revision

Grammar reference

Defining relative clauses

Form

Major T H Gem and J B Perara were the people ***who/that*** *helped to invent modern tennis.*

That's the sport ***which/that*** *I play.*

That's the player ***whose*** *team is top of the league.*

Beijing is the place ***where*** *they held the 2008 Olympics.*

Sunday is the day ***when*** *I play tennis.*

We use **who** and **that** for people, **which** and **that** for things, **whose** for possessions, **where** for places, and **when** for times.

In defining relative clauses we can omit **who**, **which**, or **that** when a noun or pronoun comes immediately after.

That's the sport that I play. = That's the sport I play.
She's the tennis player that my brother likes. = She's the tennis player my brother likes.

but

That's the sport that is popular. = ~~That's the sport is popular.~~
She's the tennis player that won the cup. = ~~She's the tennis player won the cup.~~

We do not use commas in defining relative clauses.

Use

We use defining relative clauses to give essential information about the person, thing, place or time in the first half of the sentence.

The sentence does not usually make sense without the relative clause.

Rafael Nadal is the tennis player who won Wimbledon in 2008.

~~Rafael Nadal is the tennis player.~~

Non-defining relative clauses

Form

Major T H Gem and J B Perara, ***who*** *were English and Spanish, helped to invent modern tennis.*

Tennis, ***which*** *is my favourite sport, is a very old game.*

John, ***whose*** *team is top of the league, is a very good player.*

Beijing, ***where*** *they held the 2008 Olympics, is a fascinating place.*

Yesterday, ***when*** *I played tennis, was a really warm day.*

We use **who** for people, **which** for things, **whose** for possessions, **where** for places, and **when** for times.

We do not use **that** in non-defining relative clauses.
In non-defining relative clauses we cannot omit the relative pronoun.

We always use commas in non-defining relative clauses.

Use

We use non-defining relative clauses to give extra, non-essential information about the person, thing, place or time in the first half of the sentence. The commas work in a similar way to parentheses, showing that the information is not vital to the sentence.

Non-defining clauses are not so common in conversation and can seem formal.

This city, where I was born, is famous for its football teams.

Vocabulary

1 Sports

athletics basketball diving football golf gymnastics ice hockey judo sailing skiing swimming snowboarding table tennis volleyball weightlifting

2 Sports venues and equipment

boots club course court goal goggles gym net pitch pool racket rink skates skis slope track trainers

3 Phrasal verbs connected with sport

give in go for join in knock out take up warm up work out

4 Other words and phrases ▸ page 142

Grammar revision

Defining relative clauses

1 Complete the sentences with a relative pronoun. If you don't need a pronoun, put –.

1 The friends .... I made in primary school live near my house.
2 You're the teacher .... classes I like the most.
3 Jenny is the person .... has helped me the most.
4 This is the town .... I lived in when I was eight.
5 Autumn is the time of year .... the leaves fall off the trees.
6 This is the country .... football began.

WORKBOOK ▶ page 58 / 6 points

Non-defining relative clauses

2 Are the sentences correct or not? If not, correct them.

1 The driver, which car wasn't very fast, never won a race.
2 This sport, that was invented only a few years ago, is becoming really important.
3 Rafael Nadal, whose uncle was a professional football player, won Wimbledon in 2008.
4 My neighbours, are really nice, have got two kids of my age.
5 That house, that I lived in when I was small, now belongs to my uncle.
6 Last summer, when we went to the beach, we had a brilliant holiday.

WORKBOOK ▶ page 61 / 6 points

Defining and non-defining relative clauses

3 Write two sentences for each of these things, people, times or places. One must contain a defining relative clause and the other a non-defining relative clause.

Football
1 *Football is a game which is popular all over the world.*
2 *Football, which I always play on Sunday, is my favourite sport.*

Madonna
1 ....
2 ....

Hollywood
1 ....
2 ....

Last year
1 ....
2 ....

Chocolate
1 ....
2 ....

WORKBOOK ▶ pages 58 and 61 / 8 points

Vocabulary revision

Sports

1 What are these sports? Choose the correct alternative.

1 play/go/do ....
2 play/go/do ....
3 play/go/do ....
4 play/go/do ....

WORKBOOK ▶ page 56 / 8 points

Sports venues and equipment

2 Write the words.

1 The place where you play football: p ....
2 The place where you skate or play ice hockey: r ....
3 The thing you use to hit the ball in golf: c ....
4 The thing you hit the ball over in tennis or volleyball: n ....
5 The place where you ski, the thing you ski down: s ....
6 The place where you play basketball or tennis: c ....

WORKBOOK ▶ page 56 / 6 points

Phrasal verbs connected with sports

3 Match the columns.

Phrasal verb part 1	Phrasal verb part 2	Meaning
1 warm	out	a do an activity with other people who are already doing it
2 knock	in	b eliminate somebody from a competition
3 join	up	c do gentle exercises before doing sport
4 give	up	d stop competing and accept that you cannot win
5 go	for	e start a sport or hobby
6 take	in	f try very hard to win or get something

WORKBOOK ▶ page 59 / 6 points

Total / 40 points

8 Art attack

Grammar	‣ Reported speech – statements ‣ Reported speech – questions and commands
Vocabulary	‣ Art, theatre, music ‣ Artists ‣ Adjectives ending in *-ing* and *-ed*
Speaking	‣ Describing a past event
Writing	‣ An announcement

‣ Vocabulary

Art, theatre, music

1 Use these words to talk about this photo.

audience cast lighting performance play stage

2 Work with a partner. Look at the words in bold. Check that you understand them. Use your dictionary if necessary.

1 Pass me the pencil. I haven't finished the **drawing** yet. This is just a **sketch**.
2 Do you think this painting looks like me? It's a **self-portrait**.
3 After playing a lot of **gigs**, the band are in the **studio** again making a new album.
4 What is it? Is it a **still life** painting, with fruit and flowers? Ah! Now I understand. They aren't real objects. It's an **abstract painting**.
5 I like the music in this song but I hate the **lyrics**.
6 Let's go and see an **exhibition** of paintings at that new gallery in London. There are some **masterpieces** like Van Gogh's *Sunflowers*.
7 The British artist Constable was famous for his **landscapes**, the pictures he painted of the English countryside.
8 He uses a lot of different materials like stone and wood for his **sculptures**.

3 Put the words in 1 and 2 in the correct column. Some words can go in more than one column.

Art	Theatre	Music

Artists

4 Work with a partner. Look at the sentences. Complete the words in *italics* with *-or, -er, -ian* or *-ist*.

1 Will Smith is a famous Hollywood *act*..................... .
2 A *sculpt*.................... is a person who makes sculptures.
3 She's a great *music*.................... . She can play the guitar, the piano and the violin.
4 Leonardo da Vinci was a great *art*..................... .
5 It must be difficult being a *conduct*.................... and responsible for a whole orchestra.
6 My cousin wants to be a ballet *danc*..................... .
7 A *paint*.................... usually needs a brush and canvas.
8 She's a great *perform*.................... . She loves being on the stage.
9 Mozart is my favourite *compos*..................... .
10 Bob Dylan is a famous *sing*....................-*songwrit*..................... . He usually sings his own songs.

5a SPEAKING Work with a partner. Think of a person for each of the words in italics in 4. Write one or two pieces of information about them.

5b Read out your information to the class. Can they guess who it is?

He was a composer. He wrote lots of famous ballets. One of the most famous was Swan Lake.

Tchaikovsky.

6 LISTENING 2.15 Which of these people or things can you hear in each clip?

an actor performing an audience the cast of a play
a conductor a composer a gig a musician
an orchestra a portrait painter a sculptor

1 .... 6 ....
2 .... 7 ....
3 .... 8 ....
4 .... 9 ....
5 .... 10 ....

7 SPEAKING Work with a partner. Ask and answer these questions. For each question, think of a follow-up question to get more information.

1 Do you ever go to gigs?
2 Which is more important for you in a song – the music or the lyrics?
3 Do you ever go to the theatre?
4 Which plays have you seen or read?
5 Do you ever go to art exhibitions?
6 Which artists or paintings do you like?

Reading

1 **Work with a partner. Look at these photos. Take it in turns to describe what you can see.**

2 **Read the three newspaper articles and match them with the correct headlines and photos.**

1 **Danger! Artist at work**
2 Recycling art can be good for you
3 Mini-masterpieces

a

b

c

A Three women have been hurt by falling into the latest 'sculpture' at the Tate Modern gallery in London – a crack in the floor. The 152-metre crack runs along the floor in the Turbine Hall of the Tate Modern. Some people think the crack is painted and realise their mistake when they fall in! The work is by Colombian artist Doris Salcedo. It begins as a small crack but gets wider and wider. It's 152 metres long, but it's also nearly a metre deep in some places, although the artist said, 'It is bottomless. It is as deep as humanity.' A representative for the gallery said that three visitors had fallen in but that there hadn't been any serious injuries. 'Twelve thousand people visited the installation on the first day and there have been no other incidents,' said the representative. The installation cost £300,000 and took more than six months to complete. The artist told reporters that the work had needed delicate and intricate sculpting by artists on two continents. 'But what is important is the meaning of the piece. The making of it is not important.' She said that the crack represented the division of integrating immigrants into European society.

B Chinese artist Jing Ying Hua has just finished a portrait, the biggest he has ever done. Nothing too surprising, perhaps, for a professional artist. But you *may* be surprised to learn that it is on a single human hair and is only 6 millimetres long. It's a portrait of 42 US presidents. Each president's face has a diameter of less than 0.4mm. Once the artist took ten days to paint a giant panda on a tiny part of another human hair. He used a paintbrush made with a single rabbit hair. This type of painting is called 'micro-painting'. Even more amazing is 'micro-sculpture'. Willard Wigan is probably the world's best micro-sculptor. He once told an interviewer that the movement caused by traffic outside could affect his work. He said he had to control his breathing and heartbeat to keep the movement of his hands to a minimum. Obviously, mistakes are easy to make when you are sculpting grains of rice or sand. Once he accidentally inhaled one of his sculptures! The good thing is that you don't need a big gallery for micro-art. But a microscope is essential!

C A painting which was found in the street has just been sold for over *$1 million*. One morning in 2003 Elizabeth Gibson was taking her morning walk in Manhattan when she came across an abstract painting lying in a pile of rubbish. She said the painting had caught her attention so she decided to take it home. 'I know nothing about modern art but it didn't seem right for any piece of art to be thrown away like that,' she said. The painting turned out to be an interesting work by Mexican artist Rufino Tamayo, from 1970. It was on her wall for months when a friend told her that it might be valuable. Ms Gibson soon discovered that it was. It was worth over a million dollars! When Ms Gibson found out, she looked for the original owners and she gave the work back to them. The painting had been stolen from them in 1987 but it only reappeared when Ms Gibson found it in 2003. The owners were amazed to get their painting back and gave Ms Gibson a reward and a percentage of the sale of the painting.

3 **Choose the best answers.**

1 The crack in the floor of the Tate Modern gallery
  a doesn't really exist.
  b is so deep that there is no bottom.
  c is deep enough to cause injuries.

2 Doris Salcedo
  a doesn't know how the crack was made.
  b is most interested in the symbolic aspect of the crack.
  c is anti-European.

3 Jing Ying Hua paints normal things
  a in unusual periods of time.
  b with unusual materials.
  c for unusual reasons.

4 Micro-sculpture
  a is made by mistake.
  b is not shown in big galleries.
  c is very delicate.

5 For sixteen years the Rufino Tamayo painting was in
  a the possession of criminals.
  b Manhattan.
  c the owner's house.

4 **Why do these numbers appear in the texts?**

1 1 million
2 two
3 300,000
4 42
5 152
6 0.4
7 1970

5 **Find these words in the texts. Guess their meaning from the context. Then check your answers in your dictionary.**

Text A	Text B	Text C
1 deep	1 single	1 pile
2 bottomless	2 slightest	2 thrown away
3 incidents		3 valuable
4 intricate		

STUDY SKILLS

What strategies can help you to understand new words in a text? STUDY SKILLS ▸ page 148

6 **SPEAKING What about *you*?**

1 Which work of art in 2 do you like the most? Why?
2 Which work of art do you think is the most unusual? Why?

GRAMMAR GUIDE

Reported speech – Statements

1a Match the reported sentences 1–9 with the direct sentences a–i.

1 He said that some of his works took him a year to complete.
2 She told us that she knew nothing about modern art.
3 The artist said the work had needed delicate sculpting.
4 A friend told her that it might be valuable.
5 She said she was working on a new project.
6 He said he'd already painted lots of tiny pictures.
7 He told the reporter he could paint with a single rabbit hair.
8 He said he had to be very careful.
9 He said he would finish the work soon.

a 'It may be valuable'
b 'Some of my works take me a year to complete.'
c 'I can paint with a single rabbit hair.'
d 'I know nothing about modern art.'
e 'I will finish the work soon.'
f 'The work needed delicate sculpting.'
g 'I've already painted lots of tiny pictures.'
h 'I'm working on a new project.'
i 'I have to be very careful.'

1b Choose the correct alternative.

1 *Nouns/Pronouns* usually change when they go from direct to reported speech.
2 The tenses of most verbs *change/don't change* in reported speech.
3 With **say** we *need/don't need* to say the person we spoke to.
4 With **tell** we *need/don't need* to say the person we spoke to.
5 With **say** and **tell** we *always need/don't always need* to use **that.**

GRAMMAR REFERENCE ▸ page 106

2 How do these tenses change in reported speech? Look at the Grammar reference for help.

Direct speech	Reported speech
1 present simple →	*past simple*
2 present continuous →	
3 present perfect →	
4 past simple →	
5 *will* →	
6 *can* →	
7 *may* →	
8 *must/have to* →	

3 Complete the table with these words.

a (week/month/year) ago here the day before
the following (week/month/year) today
the previous (week/month/year) that that night

Direct speech	Reported speech
this	**(1)**
(2)	there
(3)	that day
yesterday	**(4)**
(5)	the next/following day
tonight	**(6)**
next (week/month/year)	**(7)**
last (week/month/year)	**(8)**
(9)	a (week/month/year) before

4 Rewrite the sentences with *told* and the words in brackets.

1 The musicians said they couldn't play because they didn't know the music. (the audience)
The musicians told the audience they couldn't play because they didn't know the music.
2 You said you wanted to be a dancer. (me)
3 Katie said she would never go on stage again. (her music teacher)
4 She said the concert had been fantastic. (us)
5 The artists said the exhibition was going to be a great success. (the reporters)
6 The singer said that she was recording new songs in her studio that day. (her fans)
7 The artist said he had to stop moving. (the model)
8 The conductor said they weren't good enough to be in his orchestra. (the two musicians)

5 Now put the reported speech in 4 into direct speech.
We can't play because we don't know the music.

6 **Look at the statements made by famous artists. Write them in reported speech.**

1 **Salvador Dali:** 'At the age of 6 I wanted to be a cook.'
2 **Grandma Moses:** 'Painting isn't important. The important thing is keeping busy.'
3 **Damien Hirst:** 'I wanted to be stopped but no one will stop me.'
4 **Claude Monet:** 'My garden is my most beautiful masterpiece.'
5 **Pablo Picasso:** 'I don't say everything, but I paint everything.'
6 **Vincent Van Gogh:** 'The only time I feel alive is when I'm painting.'
7 **Paul Klee:** 'Colour has taken possession of me.'
8 **Andy Warhol:** 'In the future everyone will be famous for fifteen minutes.'

7a SPEAKING **Write down things that your friends or family have said or told you recently.**

7b **Tell your partner the things that people have said. Can your partner guess who said these things?**

Someone told me that I had to get my hair cut.

Was it your dad?

Yes!

Adjectives ending in *-ing* and *-ed*

1 **Look at the two sentences.**

1 The owners were **amazed** to get their painting back.
2 It was **amazing** that somebody had returned the painting to the owners.

The words in bold are adjectives. Which adjective describes how somebody feels? Which adjective explains why they feel this way?

2 **Look at these adjectives. Which are positive (+) and which are negative (–)?**

amazed bored confused disappointed disgusted embarrassed excited frightened inspired interested relaxed surprised tired uninspired

3a PRONUNCIATION **Look at the adjectives in 2 again. In which adjectives do we pronounce *-ed* as /ɪd/?**

3b **Listen and check your answers. Which letter comes before *-ed* in all those adjectives?**

3c **Practise saying the adjectives in 2.**

4 **Choose the correct alternative.**

1 Artists are often inspiring/inspired by nature.
2 Yuck! This soup is disgusting/disgusted.
3 Working all day and studying at night is tiring/tired.
4 Many people are confusing/confused when they see modern art.
5 When artists explain their own work, it can be a bit boring/bored.
6 I would be embarrassing/embarrassed if I had to stand on a stage and sing.
7 In my opinion, that band's new CD is very disappointing/disappointed – the songs are awful.
8 We're really exciting/excited about going to see that play next week.

5a SPEAKING **Prepare things to say about the topics below.**

1 Two people you think are inspiring.
2 Two activities you think are boring.
3 A moment in your life when you were very surprised.
4 A time when something embarrassing happened to you.
5 The most exciting thing you have ever done.
6 A time when you were frightened.

5b **Talk about the topics with a partner. Ask questions to keep the conversation going.**

5c **Tell the class what your partner told you about one of the topics.**

Dana told me that she is inspired by her sister. Her sister works for a charity that helps children with family problems …

Click onto... The arts in Ireland

International cultural knowledge
Irish music and dance

1 Work with a partner. Choose the correct answers to the quiz. If you don't know, guess.

THE IRELAND QUIZ

1. What is a common name for Ireland?
   The Green Island/The Emerald Isle/The Shimmering Isle
2. Which is part of the United Kingdom?
   Ireland/Northern Ireland
3. What is the capital of Northern Ireland?
   Dublin/Belfast/Limerick
4. What appears on the Irish Euro coins?
   A plant/A harp/A church
5. What colour is the Republic of Ireland flag?
   Green, white and red/Green, white and orange/Green, white and blue
6. Why did so many Irish people emigrate in the nineteenth century?
   Because there was not enough food./Because of the plague./Because there was a flood.
7. Which famous rock band is from Ireland?
   U2/AC-DC/UB40
8. What is another name for traditional Irish dancing?
   River dancing/Step dancing/Line dancing

2 Read this text about music and dance in Ireland. Can you find any of the answers to the quiz?

3 Turn to page 150 for the rest of the answers to the Ireland quiz.

4 Answer the questions.

1. Who were harpers and why were they important?
2. Can you see Uilleann pipes or a Bodhran in one of the photos on this page? Which of the instruments do you hit and which needs air?
3. How do we know that traditional Irish music is alive now?
4. What are the special characteristics of Irish dancing?
5. What is Michael Flatley's nationality?
6. What types of music do modern Irish musicians play?

5 What about *you*?

1. Have you ever heard any traditional Irish music? What did you think of it?
2. Do you know any of the modern Irish musicians or bands in the text? Do you like them?

What do you think of traditional Irish music?

I heard some Irish folk music at a party once. It's good to dance to!

Anybody who has been to Ireland will know all about how important music and dance are for the Irish. And even if you've never been to the Emerald Isle you must know something about Irish song and dance because they are two of the country's best exports.

One of the most famous symbols of Ireland is the harp. This instrument has played an important part in Ireland's history. You can tell how important it is from the fact that the harp is present on all of Ireland's Euro coins. The importance is centuries old. Harpers (musicians who played the harp) were permanent companions to the ancient Irish kings and chieftains. They played in courts and the art of playing the harp passed from one generation to the next. The last of the great harpers was Turlogh Carolan, who died in 1738.

But the harp was not the only important traditional instrument in Ireland. Go to an Irish pub and you may well see a group sitting and playing the 'Uilleann' pipes (or Irish bagpipes), the fiddle (violin), the flute and the Bodhran (a type of drum). There are thousands of traditional songs, many of them hundreds of years old. But Irish music is about the past and the present. Lots of young people learn to play the old songs and they are still popular, in Ireland and all over the world. There are even groups that mix traditional Irish folk music with heavy metal or with African rhythms.

Once the music starts, it probably won't take long for the dancing to start too. Dance was an important part of social life in the past in Ireland. Irish dance is special because the feet and legs generally move very quickly but the arms and body almost don't move at all. Another name for it is 'step dancing'. The foot touches, or taps, the floor very fast. The record for the number of taps per second is forty! Recently stage shows like Riverdance and Lord of the Dance have renewed the popularity of Irish dance. Michael Flatley is one of the most famous Irish dancers in the world. In fact, Flatley is American. That's not surprising though. His Irish parents were just two of the millions of Irish immigrants in the USA

Today, Irish music is still going strong. There are rock bands like U2, singer-songwriters like Damien Rice, singers like Ronan Keating and 'boy bands' like Westlife. And more recently there have been 'indie' bands like Snow Patrol (with members from Northern Ireland and Scotland) whose CD *Eyes Open* from 2006 has sold nearly five million copies.

The Irish love their music and dance, and the rest of the world is glad that they do.

Literature
The Picture of Dorian Gray by Oscar Wilde

Look at the pictures from the story *The Picture of Dorian Gray*. What is the difference? What do you think the story is about?

6 **Read the text. Which picture illustrates the final scene of the book correctly?**

1

2

He looked round and saw the knife that had stabbed and killed Basil Hallward. He had cleaned it many times. It was bright, and shone. It had killed the painter, and now it would kill the painter's work. It would kill the past, and when the past was dead, he would be free, he would be at peace. He took the knife and stabbed the picture with it. (5)

There was a scream and then a crash. The scream was so horrible that the frightened servants woke up and crept slowly and nervously out of their rooms. Two gentlemen, who were passing in the square below, stopped and looked at the great house. They walked on till they met a policeman and brought him back. The man rang the bell several times, but there was no answer. Except for a light in one of the top windows, the house was completely dark. After a while, the policeman walked away, then turned and stood and watched. (10, 15)

'Whose house is that, Constable?' asked the older of the two gentlemen.

'Mr Dorian Gray's, sir,' answered the policeman.

The two gentlemen looked at each other and walked away.

Inside, the servants were talking in low whispers to each other. After about a quarter of an hour, three of the men went upstairs and knocked on the door but there was no reply. They called out. Everything was still. Finally, after trying to force the door without success, they went out onto the roof and tried to get in through the balcony. The windows opened easily. (20, 25)

When they entered, they found hanging upon the wall a splendid portrait of their master as they had last seen him. In the portrait he was incredibly young and handsome. Lying on the floor was a dead man wearing formal clothes with a knife in his heart. He was old and extremely ugly. It was only when they had examined the rings that they recognised who it was. (30)

7 **Read the text again and decide if the statements are true (T) or false (F). Write down the line(s) where you find the answer.**

1 Gray wanted to attack the painting with a knife. T/F
2 Gray knew that by attacking the painting he would die. T/F
3 Nobody heard Gray's cry. T/F
4 A policeman tried to help but couldn't. T/F
5 The servants in the house were very worried. T/F
6 The servants had to go outside the house to get into the room where Gray was. T/F
7 It was almost impossible for the servants to know who the dead man was. T/F

8 **What about *you*?**
Do you like reading horror stories and thrillers? Why/Why not?

I like horror stories.

Me too. But they don't make me frightened. They're exciting, though!

WORD BOOSTER

Match the words and definitions.

1 stabbed — a moved quietly and slowly
2 scream — b talking but making very little noise
3 crept — c attacked violently with a knife
4 in low whispers — d place where you can stand just outside a window
5 balcony — e noise you make when you are very frightened

INSIDE INFORMATION

- This story, which appeared in 1890, was the only novel written by Oscar Wilde. Wilde was born in Dublin, Ireland, in 1854.
- In this story, a painter called Basil Hallward paints a portrait of a handsome young man called Dorian Gray. One day, Gray says that he would like his portrait to grow old so that he can stay forever young and handsome. Gray leads an evil life, hurting many people. He realises one day that his face hasn't changed. But the face in the portrait is getting older and uglier. One day he has an argument with Basil Hallward and kills him with a knife. Gray continues with his evil life but then he tries to change. He goes to see if the face in the painting looks better but he sees that it is worse than ever. This is where the text begins.

1 **Look at these photos. What do you think the connection between them is? Guess.**

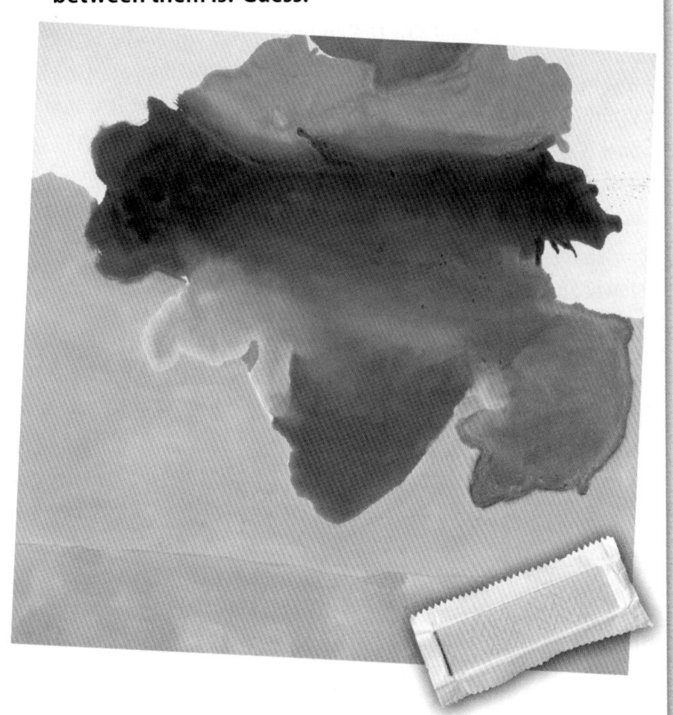

2 LISTENING 2.17 **Listen and check your ideas in 1.**

STUDY SKILLS

What should you do when you are listening to English and there is a section that you do not understand?

STUDY SKILLS ▸ page 148

3 **Listen again and choose the best answers.**

1 The boy was
 a on his own in the art gallery.
 b with other students in the gallery.
 c with his parents in the gallery.

2 The painting was
 a not worth much because it wasn't very old.
 b was worth between one and two million dollars.
 c should cost five million dollars.

3 Experts
 a couldn't restore the painting.
 b restored the painting easily.
 c took time finding the best way to restore the painting.

4 The boy
 a had to pay for the painting.
 b was punished twice.
 c didn't care about the punishment.

5 The two speakers think
 a the boy was completely responsible for his actions.
 b the teachers needed to make the boy behave.
 c the boy didn't realise what he had done.

4 **What about *you*?**

What would you say or do to the boy if you were his teacher or parent?

I would tell him that he couldn't go on any more school trips.

GRAMMAR GUIDE

Reported speech – Questions

1 **Look at the direct and reported questions. Then decide if rules a–e are true (T) or false (F).**

1 'Why did you do it?'
2 The people from the museum asked him why he'd done it.
3 'Do you realise the importance of your actions?'
4 They asked him if he realised the importance of his actions.

a Tenses and pronouns change in reported questions in the same way as in reported statements. T/F
b We do not use the auxiliary verb *do* in reported questions. T/F
c We put the subject before the verb in reported questions. T/F
d We use question marks in reported questions. T/F
e We use *if* or *whether* when there is no question word. T/F

GRAMMAR REFERENCE ▸ page 106

2 **Choose the correct alternative.**

1 'Where are you from?'
They asked the boy where was he from/where he was from.

2 'Do you like art?'
They asked the boy why/if he liked art.

3 'Did you come alone?'
They wanted to know whether he had come alone/had he come alone.

4 'Do you behave well in class?'
They asked him if he did behave/he behaved well in class.

5 'Have you touched any paintings?'
They asked if he has touched any paintings/had touched any paintings.

6 'Will you do it again?'
They asked him if he would do it again/would he do it again.

3a SPEAKING **Write five questions to ask a partner about art, theatre or music.**

3b **Work with a partner and ask your questions.**

3c **Change partners. Tell your new partner the five questions your first partner asked you, and your answers.**

She asked me if I liked going to the theatre. I told her that I didn't like it much.

4 Complete the reported questions.

1 'Did you like the exhibition?'
She asked him ……………………………………………

……………………………………………

2 'Who is your favourite artist?'
She wanted to know ……………………………………………

……………………………………………

3 'Do you often visit art galleries?'
She asked him ……………………………………………

……………………………………………

4 'Will you recommend the exhibition to other people?'
She asked him ……………………………………………

……………………………………………

5 'Why did you decide to see the exhibition?'
She wanted to know ……………………………………………

……………………………………………

6 'Are you going to buy anything in the shop?'
She wanted to know ……………………………………………

……………………………………………

7 'Have you ever bought an original painting?'
She asked ……………………………………………

……………………………………………

GRAMMAR GUIDE

Reported speech – Commands

5 Look at the direct and reported commands and answer the questions.

1 'Be good!'
2 The teachers told the children to be good.
3 'Please don't touch the paintings!'
4 They asked the children not to touch the paintings.

a Which verbs can we use to report commands?
b Do we change the tense of the verb from the direct command or use the infinitive in the reported command?
c Where does *not* come in reported commands that are negative?

GRAMMAR REFERENCE ▸ page 106

6 Report these commands.

1 'Pay attention!' the teacher told the class.
The teacher ……………………………………………

……………………………………………

2 'Give me your tickets, please,' the man at the entrance asked them.
The man at the entrance ……………………………………………

……………………………………………

3 'Don't shout!' his mum told him.
His mum ……………………………………………

……………………………………………

4 'Please don't take photos inside the museum,' the guide asked the visitors.
The guide ……………………………………………

……………………………………………

5 'Don't come home late!' Dad told me.
Dad ……………………………………………

……………………………………………

6 'Use a bigger brush,' the art teacher told Jake.
The art teacher ……………………………………………

……………………………………………

7 'Please write a description of the painting for homework,' the teacher asked the students.
The teacher ……………………………………………

……………………………………………

7 SPEAKING Play in two teams. Take it in turns to try and remember things that teachers asked or told you to do this week. You get one point for each correct sentence.

Our English teacher asked us to do this exercise.

She told us not to speak in our own language.

1 SPEAKING Work with a partner. Discuss these questions.

1 Do you ever go on school trips? If so, what type of places do you usually go to?

2 Did you go on school trips when you were at primary school? Where did you go?

2 SPEAKING Work with a partner. Look at the pictures. Take it in turns to describe what you can see.

3 LISTENING 2.18 Listen to a teenager talking about a school trip that was special for her. Which pictures are similar to her experience?

4 SPEAKING Work with a partner. Are these sentences true (T) or false (F)? Correct the false sentences.

1 The school trip was when the girl was at primary school. T/F

2 The play was really good. T/F

3 The girl really wanted to go on stage because she had a good voice. T/F

4 The girl was very embarrassed at first, but later she really enjoyed herself. T/F

5 She only sang one song. T/F

5 Listen again and tick the words and expressions that you hear in the Speaking Bank.

Speaking Bank

Useful words and expressions for reporting past events

- At first
- Next
- Later
- First
- Then
- A few seconds/minutes/hours/days later
- After ten minutes/half an hour/a while
- After that
- Finally
- In the end

EXAM SUCCESS

What can you do to prepare for a speaking exam where you have to talk about a past event?

EXAM SUCCESS ▶ page 153

6 Think about a memorable school trip or a trip to a concert, play or exhibition that you went on. Individually, make notes on these questions.

1 Where did you go?
2 When was it?
3 How old were you?
4 Who did you go with?
5 What happened first? And later?
6 How did you feel?
7 What happened in the end?

Practice makes perfect

7a Work with a partner. Take it in turns to do this task. When you are listening, ask your partner questions to find out details and to help him or her to continue talking. Use words and expressions from the Speaking Bank.

Tell an English-speaking friend about a memorable school trip, or a memorable trip to a concert, play or exhibition. Say:

- where and when you went, and who you went with.
- what happened first.
- how you felt and how the trip ended.

7b Change partners and talk about your trip again.

1 Look at the school announcement and find this information.

1 What is the event?
2 What exactly do the organisers want?
3 When do they want it?
4 Can you win anything if you participate?
5 When is the event?
6 Who can be in the event?
7 What should you do if you want to know more?

Let the artist inside you come out!

We want *you* to participate in the school's *first ever* art exhibition.

Everyone is welcome to join in!

We need paintings, photos and sculptures. You can do anything you want.

Surprise us!

We need to receive you work by **20th October**. All art will be displayed in the hall for one week, starting **1st November**.

There will be prizes for students in each year for three different categories:

- best painting
- best photo
- best sculpture.

So what are you waiting for? Start your art today!

For further information speak to Lily Merchant, 10B.

2 Put the questions in 1 in the order that the answers appear in the announcement.

3 Look at the advice in the Writing Bank. Does the announcement in 1 follow the advice?

Writing Bank

Useful advice for writing announcements

- Use short, clear sentences.
- Have a slogan or a title which attracts attention.
- Make the announcement easy to understand and interesting to read.
- Include all the practical information and details that a reader needs to know.

4 Work with a partner. Choose one of these events below.

1 A school play
2 A school magazine
3 A school concert

Complete a diagram with information that you would need to include in an announcement for the event.

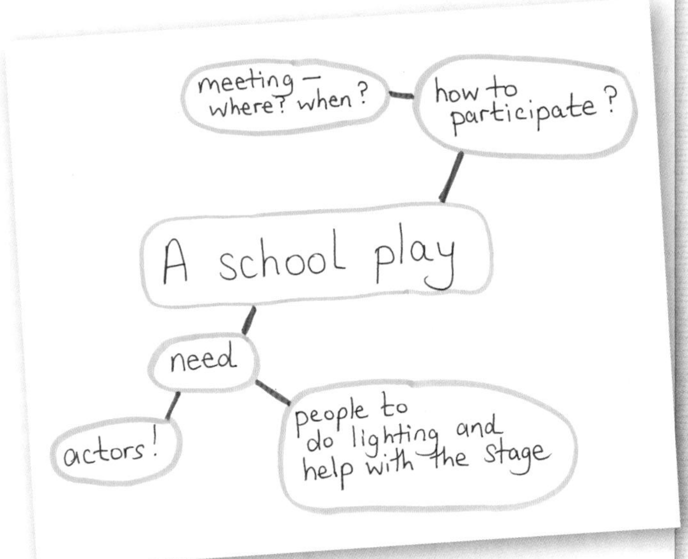

Practice makes perfect

5 Look at the task and write an announcement following the advice in the Writing Bank.

Write an announcement to ask people to participate in a school play, a school magazine, or a school concert. Include information about:

- what the event is
- what you need
- when you need it.

EXAM SUCCESS

Who are you writing to in this task? Why is it important to know who you are writing to?

EXAM SUCCESS ▶ page 153

Language reference and revision

Grammar reference

Reported speech – Statements

In reported speech, when the reporting verb (**say, tell**) is in the past, the tense of the other verb usually changes going one tense 'back'.

Direct speech tenses	Reported speech tenses
'I work at home.' **present simple**	She said she worked at home. **past simple**
'I'm working.' **present continuous**	She said she was working. **past continuous**
'I have worked.' **present perfect**	She said she had worked. **past perfect**
'I worked.' **past simple**	She said she had worked. **past perfect**
'I had worked.' **past perfect**	She said she had worked. **past perfect**
'I will work.' **will**	She said she would work. **would**
'I can work.' **can**	She said she could work. **could**
'I may work.' **may**	She said she might work. **might**
'I must/have to work.' **must/have to**	She said she had to work. **had to**

Could, **would**, **should** and **might** do not change.

'You should see his new exhibition.' → He said I should see his new exhibition.

When the reporting verb is in the present simple, the tense of the verb in reported speech can stay the same.

'I enjoy painting.' → He says he enjoys painting.

When the reporting verb is in the past but the statement is something which is still true, or is and will always be true, the tense of the verb in reported speech usually stays the same.

'Museums are usually free.' → The guide told us that museums are usually free.

In reported speech, pronouns and possessive adjectives also change. *'I've got your pen.' → Mark said he had my pen.*

We use reported speech to report the words spoken by another person.

'I painted that picture in 1990,' said the artist.
The artist said that she had painted that picture in 1990.

Reported speech – say and tell

With **say** you do not need to use a personal object.

He said he needed help. ~~*He said the teacher he needed help.*~~

With **tell** you must use a personal object.

He told the teacher he needed help. ~~*He told he needed help.*~~

Reported speech – Questions

We do not use the auxiliary verb **do** in reported questions.
'Do you know my sister?' → She asked me if I knew her sister.
There is no inversion of subject and verb in reported questions.
'Who are you?' → He asked me who I was.

Reported questions are not real questions so they do not need question marks. ~~*She asked me what I needed?*~~

When there is no question word (*who, what, how, why*, etc), we use *if* or *whether*. *'Can you do it?' → They asked me if I could do it.*

Reported speech – Commands

Direct Speech	Reported Speech
'Stand up!'	She told them **to stand** up.
'Don't write on the table!'	They told him **not to write** on the table.
'Please **write** your name here.'	He asked me **to write** my name there.

For reported commands we use **to + infinitive** or **not to + infinitive.**

If necessary we change pronouns and other words in the same way as in reported statements.

We use **told** to report stronger commands and **asked** for more polite requests.

Vocabulary

1 Art, theatre, music

abstract painting audience cast drawing exhibition gallery gig landscape lighting lyrics masterpiece orchestra performance play sculpture (self-)portrait sketch stage still life studio

2 Artists

actor artist composer conductor dancer musician painter performer sculptor singer-songwriter

3 Adjectives ending in *-ing* and *-ed*

amazed/amazing bored/boring confused/confusing disappointed/disappointing disgusted/disgusting embarrassed/embarrassing excited/exciting frightened/frightening inspired/inspiring interested/interesting relaxed/relaxing surprised/surprising tired/tiring uninspired/uninspiring

4 Other words and phrases ▸ page 143

Grammar revision

Reported speech – Statements

1 Look at what this pop star said to a reporter and rewrite the sentences in reported speech.

1 I'm happy to be here today.
2 I'm writing a lot of new songs.
3 I'll go to a studio to record them next month.
4 I was very inspired after travelling to Morocco last week.
5 I may go again with my band next year.
6 I've never played on stage outside Europe.
7 I must go now because my fans are waiting for me.

a She said ....
b She told ....
c She said ....
d She said ....
e She told ....
f She said ....
g She said ....

WORKBOOK ▶ page 66 | /7 points

Reported speech – Questions

2 Rewrite these reported questions in direct speech.

1 She asked me what I was doing there.
'................................?'
2 They asked me when I had arrived.
'................................?'
3 The teacher asked him if he knew what the answer was.
'................................?'
4 The interviewer wanted to know if she had ever written a love song.
'................................?'
5 I asked him what he would do with the money.?
'................................?'
6 I asked him how many pages the book had.
'................................?'
7 I asked her if that bag was hers.
'................................?'

WORKBOOK ▶ page 69 | /7 points

Reported speech – Commands

3 Write the direct commands.

1 The police officer told him to get out of the car.
....
2 They told me not to panic.
....
3 She told him to do the exercise carefully.
....
4 I asked her not to sing that song.
....
5 They told me to turn round slowly.
....
6 She asked him not to interrupt her.
....

WORKBOOK ▶ page 69 | /6 points

Vocabulary revision

Art, theatre, music

1 Complete the definitions.

1 A *still life* is a painting of ....
2 A *masterpiece* is a work by an artist which ....
3 The *lyrics* are the part of the song which ....
4 The *audience* are the people who ....
5 The *lighting* is important because without it ....
6 A *sketch* is a picture which ....
7 At a *gig* you ....
8 A *portrait* is a picture of ....

WORKBOOK ▶ page 64 | /8 points

Artists

2 Complete the names of these people.

1 The person in charge of an orchestra:
c .... d .... r
2 Someone who plays music or acts on stage:
p ...... r f .... r
3 Someone who plays music: m ...... s .... a ......
4 Someone who writes classical music: c .... o ...... e ......
5 Someone who makes sculptures: s .... l ....

WORKBOOK ▶ page 64 | /5 points

Adjectives ending in -ing and -ed

3 Complete the sentences with the *-ing* or *-ed* form of the words given.

1 Aren't you ....? You've been studying all day. **TIRE**
2 It's .... when an actor can't remember their words in a play. **EMBARRASS**
3 I'm .... I just don't know what to think. **CONFUSE**
4 The result of the match was .... for us because we lost 6-0. **DISAPPOINT**
5 We were .... because we thought we were going to win. **SURPRISE**
6 This meal is .... There's a dead insect in it! **DISGUST**
7 She's a very .... teacher because she makes you feel like you can do anything well. **INSPIRE**

WORKBOOK ▶ page 67 | /7 points

Total /40 points

Gateway to exams *Units 7–8*

Speaking

Tip for Speaking Exams

In activities where you have to report a past event, remember …

Before the exam, make sure you know as many regular and irregular past forms and tenses as possible. Revise words and expressions to explain the order of events – *First; Then; Next; In the end.*

EXAM SUCCESS ▸ page 153

1 Look at the three sentences. Which tense is used in each one and why?

1 We were all waiting for the start of the match.

2 They had already won the match.

3 We put our trainers on and went outside.

2 Write down a list of short sentences saying what you did this morning. Write them in the order you did them.

I woke up.

I got out of bed.

I went to the bathroom.

3 Work with a partner. Tell your partner what you did this morning. Introduce each sentence with a different word or expression to explain the sequence.

***First** I woke up. **Then** I got out of bed.*
***A few seconds later** I went to the bathroom.*

4 Look at the task and, individually, prepare what you are going to say.

> Tell an English-speaking friend about a sports event that you took part in or watched and that was special to you. Say:
> - what the event was
> - where and when the event took place
> - what happened first
> - what happened in the end
> - why it was special.

5 Work with a partner. Take it in turns to do the task.

Listening

Tip for Listening Exams

In true/false activities, remember …

Do not panic if you do not understand information the first time. If you don't hear the answer to one question, start listening immediately for the answer to the next question. Use the second listening to find the answers you didn't hear the first time.

EXAM SUCCESS ▸ page 152

6 Work with a partner. Take it in turns to describe the photo. What do you think it shows?

7 2.19 Listen to two people who are at the scene of the photograph. Find out what is happening in the scene.

8 Listen again. Are these statements true (T) or false (F)?

1 The title of the work is a number. T/F

2 The runners participate in the work of art for money. T/F

3 The runners bring their own sports equipment. T/F

4 The work of art has a message. T/F

5 The athletes can choose which speed they run at. T/F

6 The inspiration for the work came from an experience which the artist had in Italy. T/F

7 Visitors can participate in the work of art. T/F

8 The artist designed the work but he doesn't run in it. T/F

9 Work with a partner. Say why the sentences are true or false.

Sentence 1 is true because the title is Number ...

10 What about *you*? What do you think of this work of art?

Speaking

Tip for Speaking Exams

In presentations, remember …

Make notes with your ideas and arguments before your presentation. During the presentation, use your notes to remember what comes next but don't just read your notes aloud.

EXAM SUCCESS ▸ page 152

11 Complete the expressions 1-8 with these words.

instance what's sum of by least in case

Beginning a presentation
I'd like to begin (**1**) .... saying …
I'm going to talk about …

Introducing ideas and arguments
Firstly,
First (**2**) .... all,
Secondly,
Another thing is that …
It's also true that …
Furthermore,
(**3**) .... more,

Giving examples
For example,
For (**4**) ....,
Look at the (**5**) .... of …

Concluding
Finally,
To (**6**) .... up,
Last but not (**7**) ....
The point I'm trying to make is …
(**8**) .... short …

12 Look at the task. You have five minutes to prepare. Then give your presentation to the class.

> Prepare a presentation on this topic:
> *Modern art is rubbish.*

Writing

Tip for Writing Exams

In writing exams, remember …

Always read the instructions carefully and check that you know exactly who you are writing to. Write in the correct style for that reader. You will usually get more marks if you write in an appropriate way for the task.

EXAM SUCCESS ▸ page 153

13 Look at this advice for writing an announcement. Decide which are DOs (you should do them) and which are DON'Ts (you shouldn't do them).

1 Write long sentences.
2 Be clear.
3 Think of a slogan or title.
4 Give lots of detailed description.
5 Include all the necessary practical information.
6 Write long paragraphs.
7 Make the reader interested.

14 Look at the task and write the announcement.

> Write an announcement to ask students at your school to participate in a race which will raise money for a charity. Include information about:
> - the date, time and place
> - the distance
> - the prizes (everybody who participates gets something!)
> - the charity you are collecting money for
> - what you can do if you don't want to/can't run, e.g. help with the organisation, etc.

'Can Do' Progress Check

CEF

1 How well can you do these things in English now? Give yourself a mark from 1 to 4.

1 = I can do it very well. 2 = I can do it quite well. 3 = I have some problems. 4 = I can't do it.

a I can describe or give extra information about people, things or places using defining or non-defining relative clauses. ☐
b I can talk about sports and use phrasal verbs connected with sport. ☐
c I can understand written and spoken texts about sports. ☐
d I can give simple oral presentations. ☐
e I can write a simple film review. ☐
f I can report what other people have said, asked or ordered using reported speech. ☐
g I can discuss art, theatre and music. ☐
h I can describe people and things using adjectives ending in *-ing* and *-ed*. ☐
i I can describe past events and explain what order they happened in. ☐
j I can write an announcement. ☐

2 Now decide what you need to do to improve.

1 Look again at my book/notes.
2 Do more practice exercises. → WORKBOOK pages 56–73
3 Other: ....

9 History's mysteries

Grammar ▸ Modal verbs of speculation and deduction – Present and Past ▸ Third conditional
Vocabulary ▸ Nations ▸ State and politics ▸ Adjective suffixes
Speaking ▸ Describing photos 2
Writing ▸ A story

▸ Vocabulary

Nations

1 Work with a partner. Match these words with the photos of the USA. Which word or set of words has no photo? Why not?

capital city currency flag king/queen/prince/princess national anthem prime minister/president

a

b

c

d

2 Work with a partner. Talk about the United Kingdom using the words from 1.

I know that the capital city is London.

I'm not sure who the prime minister is.

State and politics

3 Match these types of government with the explanations below.

constitutional monarchy democracy monarchy republic

1 A country that is ruled by a president or other leader, not by a king or queen.
2 A system of government where people vote in elections to choose the people who will govern them.
3 A type of government where a country is ruled by a king or queen.
4 A country ruled by a king or queen whose powers are limited by a set of basic laws.

4 Work with a partner. Can you think of a country, in the past or present, for each type of government?

5 Read the text about the United Kingdom. Match the underlined words with the definitions 1–9.

The United Kingdom is a constitutional monarchy. The head of state is the King or Queen but power is in the hands of the Prime Minister. The Prime Minister is the leader of the political party which wins the general elections. They have general elections at least every five years. You have to be 18 to vote in a general election.
The three biggest political parties are the Labour Party (traditionally left-wing), the Conservative Party (traditionally right-wing), and the Liberal Democrat Party (traditionally more or less in the centre). In fact, nowadays the distinction between the three parties is not always so clear. The Prime Minister has approximately 22 senior ministers who help him or her to run the country. For example, there are ministers for Health, Justice and Foreign Affairs. The United Kingdom is a member of the European Union and the United Nations.

1 Occasions when you can vote for a government: ....
2 With socialist ideas and objectives: ....
3 A part of an organisation or group: ....
4 A group of people with similar ideas about politics: ....
5 With conservative ideas or objectives: ....
6 Not socialist or conservative: ....
7 Control, organise: ....
8 Things which happen in other countries: ....
9 People in control of government departments: ....

▸ STUDY SKILLS

Close your book and write down as many new words as possible from this page. Why do you think we remember some words and not others? How can you remember more words? STUDY SKILLS ▸ page 149

6 SPEAKING Work with a partner. Discuss the questions.

1 How often do you have general elections in your country?
2 How old do you have to be to be able to vote?
3 Which are the most important political parties in your country?
4 How interested in politics and voting are young people in your country? Why do you think that is?

1 **Work with a partner. Look at the picture. What do you know about this historical event? Where did it happen? Who were the protagonists? What happened afterwards? If you don't know the answers, guess.**

2 **Read the text and answer these questions**

1 Who was Louis XVII?
2 What was the mystery of Louis XVII?

The mystery of Louis XVII

1789 saw the start of the French Revolution, and the start of a nightmare for a four-year-old boy called Louis Charles. Louis Charles was the handsome son of Louis XVI, King of France, and of the infamous Marie Antoinette. Louis XVI and Marie Antoinette had very public executions, killed by the guillotine in January and October 1793. But what happened to little Louis Charles?

When Louis XVI died, Louis Charles became the uncrowned King of France, Louis XVII. Up until that time he had been imprisoned with his mother and sister. But on 3rd July 1793, guards came in the middle of the night to take him away. Louis Charles was now a dangerous person because officially he would become the new king. His captors were nervous.

At first, Marie Antoinette did not let the guards take her little son, who cried and screamed to stay with her and his sister. But finally the soldiers told her that they would kill both her and the boy if he didn't come immediately. She had to let him go.

Louis Charles was taken to a small, dark room in a tower of the Temple prison. He must have suffered enormously in his new 'home'. People said that the boy was continually hit, insulted and tortured. He couldn't see his mother or sister. He shared his room with rats, he was always hungry and he received almost no medical care.

The official records say that Louis Charles died soon after from tuberculosis. The date was 8th June 1795. He was just 10. A tradition of the time was to take the heart of the king and preserve it. A doctor who examined the body of Louis Charles was a monarchist. He secretly cut out the boy's heart and took it away when he left the prison. He put it in alcohol and kept it in his house.

Immediately after the boy's death, the rumours and speculation began. The royal child might have been murdered by his guards to stop him from becoming the king. Or he may have escaped. People loyal to the royal family could have helped him to get out of the prison, putting another boy in his place. This was the most popular rumour.

If he escaped, where did he go and what happened to him?

When the monarchy was restored in France in 1814, suddenly hundreds of people said that they were Louis Charles. A surprising candidate was a German clockmaker called Karl Wilhelm Naundorff. It seems amazing that this German man, who could hardly speak a word of French, might convince people that he was the son of the King of France. But he met servants who knew Louis Charles as an infant in the palace at Versailles. They were all 100% sure that Naundorff must be Louis Charles. This was because of some special marks on his face and because he knew details about life at the palace that nobody else could know. After some years, Naundorff changed his name to Louis Charles de Bourbon. His latest descendant still uses this aristocratic name. Might he be the true descendant of Louis XVII?

3 **SPEAKING** **Work in groups and discuss the questions.**

1 Do you think Naundorff was the true descendant of Louis XVII? Why/Why not?
2 What do you think was the solution to the mystery?
3 How do you think they discovered the solution?

4 **Read the last part of the mystery. What was the solution?**

After 200 years, a curious tradition helped modern scientists to solve the mystery at last. Remember that a doctor took Louis Charles' heart when he died? The heart went from place to place for two hundred years. It was stolen, given back, given as a present and returned again. In 1999 it was in a church in Paris, safe in a crystal jar. To solve the mystery, they decided to do DNA tests on the heart. The tests proved that the heart must belong to a relative of Marie Antoinette. Doctors also agreed that the heart must have belonged to a boy of approximately ten years of age. The terrible truth was that the boy who died ill, hungry and alone in a dark room in the prison tower, was indeed Louis Charles, the lost King of France.

5 **Read the text again and answer the questions.**

1 Why did the revolutionaries put Louis Charles in prison?
2 What was life like for Louis Charles in prison?
3 Why did a doctor take Louis Charles' heart?
4 What were the two main theories after the events of 8th June 1795?
5 Why did people take Karl Wilhelm Naundorff seriously?
6 Why was the heart so important in solving the mystery?
7 When and where did Louis XVII of France die?

6 **Match the underlined words in the text with the definitions.**

1 people who catch somebody and keep them in prison
2 put back into the original situation or condition
3 a relative of a person who lived in the past
4 not officially the king or queen yet
5 serious illness which makes it difficult to breathe
6 unofficial stories that may or may not be true

GRAMMAR GUIDE

Modal verbs of speculation and deduction – Present

1 Look at the sentences and and answer the questions.

1 He **may** be a descendant of King Louis XVI.
2 He **can't** be a member of the royal family.
3 He **must** be the King.
4 He **might** have royal blood.
5 He **could** come from an aristocratic family.
6 He **might not** be a descendant of King Louis XVI.

a Which verb do we use when we are 90% certain that something is true?
b Which verb do we use when we are 90% certain that something is *not* true?
c Which verbs do we use when there is a 50% possibility that something is true (or not)?
d What form of the verb comes after the verbs in bold?

GRAMMAR REFERENCE ▸ page 120

2 Choose the correct alternative.

Country 1

1 **It's a constitutional monarchy.**
It *must/can't* be the USA because they don't have kings or queens.
2 **The national anthem doesn't have words.**
It *must/might* be Spain because Spain is one country whose national anthem doesn't have words.
3 **The capital city is Madrid.**
It *must/may* be Spain.

Country 2

1 **The currency is the Euro.**
It *could/can't* be lots of countries because 14 countries or more use Euros.
2 **It's a republic which has a president and a prime minister.**
It *may/can't* be France or Ireland because they both have a president and a prime minister.
3 **Their national anthem is La Marseillaise.**
It *could/must* be France.

3 Make deductions about these flags using *may, might, must,* and *can't*.

Flag 1

1 **This flag has stars on it.**
It .... be the US flag because that has stars.
2 **It has six stars on it.**
It .... be the US flag because that has 50 stars.
3 **Five of the stars show the Southern Cross, the brightest constellation from Australia, and the top corner of the flag contains the British flag.**
It .... be the Australian flag.

Flag 2

1 **This flag has a red background.**
It .... be the Irish flag because that is green, white and orange.
2 **There is a white cross on the flag.**
It .... be the Swiss flag, or it .... the Danish flag because they both have white crosses.
3 **The cross is in the centre of the flag, it doesn't divide all the flag.**
It .... be the Swiss flag because the cross on the Danish flag covers the whole flag.

4 SPEAKING **Work with a partner. Look at the picture and talk about where you think this place is. Use *can't, may, might, could* and *must* to make speculations and deductions.**

It must be a big city like New York or Paris.

It can't be Paris because the signs are in English.

GRAMMAR GUIDE

Modal verbs of speculation and deduction – Past

5 Look at the sentences and answer the questions.

1 He **may** have escaped.
2 They **might** have killed him.
3 They **may** not have killed him.
4 The heart **must** have belonged to Louis XVII.
5 He **could** have died on a different day.
6 Naundorff **can't** have been Louis Charles.
7 He **couldn't** have escaped.

a Which verb do we use when we are 90% certain that something was true?
b Which verbs do we use when we are 90% certain that something was not true?
c Which verbs do we use when there is a 50% possibility that something was true (or not)?
d What comes after the modal verbs – *have* + ...?

GRAMMAR REFERENCE ▸ page 120

6a PRONUNCIATION 2.20 **Listen to the two sentences. Do we pronounce *have* in the same way in both sentences?**

You have to go now. You must have known.

6b 2.21 **Listen to the sentences. Do you hear /hæv/ or /əv/?**

1 She might have gone.
2 It couldn't have been me.
3 They can't have done it.
4 You must have heard it.

6c Listen again and repeat the sentences.

7 Complete the sentences with past modals of speculation and deduction and the verbs given.

Did Shakespeare really write all of his plays?

1 Some people say Shakespeare .... (write) the plays because, from what we know, he never travelled or studied at university.
2 They say that the real author .... (be) another writer called Francis Bacon, or perhaps somebody called Christopher Marlowe, or possibly even Queen Elizabeth!
3 They think a very educated person .... (create) the works because they are so clever and contain so much historical information.
4 They say Shakespeare .... (have) much skill as a writer because his handwriting was bad and he spelt his name differently every time he wrote it!
5 If Shakespeare wrote all his plays, he .... (work) quickly and hard, because he wrote approximately 38 plays in 26 years.
6 Some people think that Shakespeare .... (be) only an actor, but nobody really knows. All we know is that the works are immortal, whoever wrote them!

8 Choose the best answers.

Who shot JFK?

Dallas. November 22, 1963. The US president John F Kennedy was shot as his car was **1** .... through the city. Lee Harvey Oswald was arrested. The police said he must **2** .... been the assassin because the bullet came from his gun. They said there was only one bullet, so he **3** .... have had any help with the assassination. But many people **4** .... were there say that they saw bullets coming from at least two different directions. If that was true, Oswald can't have **5** .... it alone. It must have been a conspiracy. Oswald **6** .... killed two days after the assassination by a man called Jack Ruby, while Oswald was in police custody. This convinced **7** .... people that there was something suspicious about the assassination – something which powerful and influential people wanted to keep quiet. So who killed Kennedy? Some people say it **8** .... have been the Mafia, others say it might have been the CIA! The truth is … we'll probably never know!

	A	B	C	D
1	**A** passing	**B** passed	**C** pass	**D** passes
2	**A** was	**B** has	**C** have	**D** had
3	**A** can	**B** might	**C** can't	**D** mustn't
4	**A** which	**B** where	**C** when	**D** who
5	**A** did	**B** done	**C** do	**D** been
6	**A** was	**B** has	**C** did	**D** have
7	**A** a	**B** any	**C** some	**D** much
8	**A** may	**B** can	**C** can't	**D** not

Adjective suffixes

1 Write these words in two columns: noun or adjective.

aristocracy aristocratic care careful comfort comfortable danger dangerous help helpless hunger hungry office official terrible terror uncomfortable

2 For each adjective in 1, underline the suffix which makes it an adjective.

aristocrat<u>ic</u>

3 Turn these words into adjectives and write them in the correct column(s).

~~artist~~ enjoy fame mystery nature sense thirst use

-y	-ous	-able	-ible

-ful	-less	-al	-ic
			artistic

EXAM SUCCESS

You are going to do a word formation cloze test. Read the instructions for the activity. How do you know if you need to add a suffix, a prefix, or both to the word given?

EXAM SUCCESS ▶ page 153

4 Look at the text. Use the words in capitals to form a word that fits in the gap.

My parents love visiting stately homes, so last year we decided to go to an old mansion near our house. It used to belong to an **(a)** .... **(ARISTOCRACY)** family who left it during the war. The house was big and dark and very **(b)** .... **(MYSTERY)**. My dad had already bought the **(c)** .... **(OFFICE)** guidebook but it was **(d)** .... **(USE)** because it didn't give any information. After looking at the rooms downstairs, we went to see the bedrooms. The stairs were in very bad condition so we had to be very **(e)** .... **(CARE)**. We were surprised when we saw the main bedroom because it didn't look very **(f)** .... **(COMFORT)** for such a big and important house. Suddenly it got very cold and windy, even though the window was closed. We were already **(g)** .... **(HUNGER)** by now and so we left the mansion. We found we had been very **(h)** .... **(SENSE)** to leave at that moment. People told us later that there had been a ghost in the bedroom ever since the family left during the war.

The commonwealth of nations

Cross-curricular – Geography
A family of nations

1 Work with a partner. Look at the Frequently Asked Questions (FAQs) on the right from a website on the Commonwealth. Can you answer any of them?

2 Read the text to check your answers. Match the paragraphs to the questions in 1.

1 .... 2 .... 3 ....
4 .... 5 ....

3 Are these statements true (T) or false (F)? In which section(s) did you find the answer?

1 Britain is in charge of the Commonwealth. T/F
2 The Commonwealth Games are more frequent than the Olympic Games. T/F
3 No empire has ever been bigger than the British Empire. T/F
4 The United Kingdom is divided into four teams for the Olympic Games. T/F
5 The Queen of England decides what happens in the Commonwealth meetings. T/F
6 There are Commonwealth countries in nearly every continent. T/F
7 The Commonwealth allows and accepts any democratic decisions taken by a country. T/F
8 The Commonwealth is bigger in terms of population than the British Empire was. T/F
9 The Commonwealth heads of state meet twice a year. T/F
10 Not all of the sports in the Olympic Games are in the Commonwealth Games. T/F

P PROJECT

4a Work in groups. Each group should choose a different Commonwealth country. In your group, make notes about these areas for the country you chose.

- Nation (capital city, flag, currency, national anthem, population)
- State and politics (prime minister/ president, monarch, type of government, main political parties)
- Customs (food, drink, sports, celebrations, music, clothes)

4b Each person in the group should choose one of the areas and find out more information about it. Look for pictures too.

4c In your group, decide how to present your information to the rest of the class. Prepare it and present it.

FAQs

1 What is the Commonwealth?
2 How does the Commonwealth work?
3 Which countries are in the Commonwealth?
4 What were the origins of the Commonwealth?
5 What are the Commonwealth Games?

a There is no set of rules or fixed constitution for the Commonwealth. There are some basic principles, for example the use of the English language, democracy and human rights. The King or Queen of England is the head of the Commonwealth but the monarch is a symbol. They have no power to tell countries what to do. The heads of government of the Commonwealth countries meet once every two years to discuss matters of common interest. If a country stops being democratic, it has to leave the Commonwealth. This is why the Commonwealth often sends observers to different countries, to check that their elections are fair and democratic.

b In the 16th and 17th centuries, British sailors started to travel outside Europe. They were looking for profitable trade in exotic products. They began colonising many different countries for many different reasons. Many British people went to these colonies to settle and start a new life. Gradually, these colonies, which were all part of the British Empire, gained their independence. In 1931, the British government gave many of these countries their independence but they remained as part of this new, equal commonwealth.

c It is a group of 53 countries. Almost all of the countries were once part of the British Empire. Queen Victoria (1819-1901) was once in charge of the biggest empire in the world. It covered a quarter of the world's land mass and a quarter of the world's population. Today, Britain is just another member of the Commonwealth, with no special powers or extra responsibilities. The main office for the Commonwealth is in London, but the people who work there are from all over the Commonwealth.

d Generally they are former British colonies which later became independent countries. They include the United Kingdom, Australia, Canada, New Zealand, India, Jamaica, Pakistan, Bangladesh, and Malaysia. At the moment, there are three members in Europe, twelve in North America, one in South America, eighteen in Africa, eight in Asia, and eleven in Oceania. Nearly one third of the world's population lives in Commonwealth countries.

e They began in 1930 and the idea was to be similar to the Olympic Games. But the idea from the beginning was that they should be 'happier'. There is a spirit of unity and friendship at these games, and their unofficial name is 'the friendly games'. They happen every four years, the same as the Olympics. There are between ten and twenty sports in the Commonwealth Games. Another interesting difference between the Olympics and the Commonwealth Games is that at the Olympics, the United Kingdom has just one team, but for the Commonwealth Games there is an English team, a Scottish team, a Welsh team and a Northern Irish team.

Cross-curricular – History
The SS Empire Windrush

5 2.22 Listen to a radio history programme and answer the questions.

1 What was the SS Empire Windrush?
2 Why was it so important in modern British history?

6 Listen again and complete the notes on the right.

SS Empire Windrush sailed from (a) .... to (b) ....

It carried (c) .... men and women.

Most of these people wanted to (d) ....

The biggest surprise at first was (e) ....

In the 1950s and 1960s many people came to Britain from (f) ....

Approximately (g) .... of the British population are from different ethnic backgrounds.

Literature
Small Island by Andrea Levy

7 Read the text and answer the questions.

1 Where is the narrator, Hortense, in this scene?
2 Why is she remembering Celia Langley at this moment?

It brought it all back to me. Celia Langley. Celia Langley standing in front of me, her hands on her hips and her head in a cloud. And she is saying: 'Oh, Hortense, when I am older …' all her dreaming began with 'when I am older…' 'When I am older, Hortense, I will be leaving Jamaica and I will be going to live in England.' This is when her voice became high-class and her nose pointed into the air – well, as far as her round, flat nose could – and she swayed as she brought the picture to her mind's eye. 'Hortense, in England I will have a big house with a bell at the front door and I will ring the bell.' And she made the sound, ding-a-ling, ding-a-ling. 'I will ring the bell in this house when I am in England. That is what will happen to me when I am older.'

I said nothing at the time. I just nodded and said, 'You surely will, Celia Langley, you surely will.' I did not dare to dream that it would one day be I who would sail on a ship as big as a world and feel the sun's heat on my face gradually change from roasting to caressing. But there was I! Standing at the door of a house in London and ringing the bell. Pushing my finger to hear the ding-a-ling, ding-a-ling. Oh, Celia Langley, where were you then with your big ideas and your nose in the air? Could you see me? Could you see me there in London? Hortense Roberts married with a gold ring and a wedding dress in a trunk. Mrs Joseph. Mrs Gilbert Joseph. What you think of that, Celia Langley? There was I in England ringing the doorbell on one of the tallest houses I had ever seen.

But when I pressed this doorbell I did not hear a ring. No ding-a-ling, ding-a-ling. I pressed once more in case the bell was not operational. The house, I could see, was shabby. Mark you, shabby in a grand sort of way. I was sure this house could once have been home to a doctor or a lawyer or perhaps a friend of a friend of the King. Only the house of someone high-class would have pillars at the doorway. Ornate pillars that twisted with elaborate design. The glass stained with coloured pictures as a church would have. It was true that some were missing, replaced by cardboard and strips of white tape.

8 Read the text again. Choose the best alternative and complete these sentences in your own words.

1 Celia Langley seems/doesn't seem to be a very nice person because ....
2 Hortense, the narrator, seems/doesn't seem happy now because ....
3 The house must/can't be in very good condition now because ....

9 At the time when this story happens the British Empire had finished. Read the last paragraph again. In what ways do you think the house in the text could be similar to the British Empire?

10 What about *you*?

1 What type of life do you think Hortense will have in England? Why?
2 Do you like reading stories that are based on real events? Why/Why not?

I think her life will be difficult because she has just arrived in a new country.

INSIDE INFORMATION

- Andrea Levy's mother and father were Jamaican passengers on the SS Empire Windrush, arriving in London in 1948.
- The novel, written in 2004, is about the experience of Jamaicans like her mother and father, and about how Britain changed during this period.
- The book won three important literary prizes, including the Commonwealth Writer's Prize.
- This text is from the start of the novel. Hortense is the female narrator of this section of the story.

WORD BOOSTER

Match the words and definitions.

1 hips	a moved her head to say yes
2 nodded	b big suitcase
3 dare	c old and in bad condition
4 caressing	d parts of the body between your waist and the top of your legs
5 trunk	e be brave enough to do something
6 shabby	f touching softly and gently

▶ Listening

1 This picture shows lifeboats from the Titanic. Work with a partner and guess the answers to these questions.

1. How many people were travelling on the Titanic when it sank?
2. How many lifeboats were there?
3. Who decided the number of lifeboats?
4. What was the most important factor for deciding the number of lifeboats?
5. Why was the Titanic travelling so fast when it hit the iceberg?

2 LISTENING 2.23 Listen to two people talking about the Titanic and find the answers to the questions in 1.

3 Listen again. Are these sentences true (T) or false (F)? Correct the false sentences.

1. They needed at least thirty lifeboats on the Titanic. T/F
2. Ismay died when the Titanic sank. T/F
3. They say it was Ismay's decision to sail as fast as possible. T/F
4. They didn't know there were icebergs in the area where they were sailing. T/F
5. There was nothing nice to say about Ismay. T/F

4 SPEAKING What about *you?*

At the time, many people thought it was Ismay's duty to stay on the Titanic to the very end. What do you think? Give reasons.

▶ Grammar in context

GRAMMAR GUIDE

Third conditional

1 Look at these sentences in the third conditional and answer the questions.

1. If Ismay **had allowed** more lifeboats, a lot more people **would have survived**.
2. If the ship **hadn't travelled** so fast, the iceberg **wouldn't have caused** so much damage.
3. I **would have done** the same if **I'd been** in his place.

1. What tense do we use in the half of the sentence with *if?*
2. What form of the verb do we use in the other half of the sentence?
3. Does the half of the sentence with *if* always come first?
4. How do we know when *'d* is *had* or *would*?
5. Do we use the third conditional for imaginary situations in the present or the past?

GRAMMAR REFERENCE ▶ page 120

2 Complete the sentences with the correct forms of the verbs.

Integer vitae scelerisque purus
Exegi monumentum aere perennius
Permitte divis cetera
Brevis esse laboro obscurus fio
Credite posteri

1. If the Roman Empire .... (continue), Latin would probably have remained the most universal language.
2. If the Titanic hadn't hit an iceberg, it .... (arrive) in New York safely.
3. Perhaps dinosaurs .... (survive) if an asteroid hadn't hit the Earth.
4. Perhaps Sir Isaac Newton wouldn't have thought about gravity if an apple .... (not fall) on his head.
5. If John Lennon and Paul McCartney .... (not meet), The Beatles would never have existed.
6. If Christopher Columbus had sailed east, he .... (not find out) that America existed.
7. The world would have evolved in a totally different way if somebody .... (invent) the computer two hundred years ago.
8. If aliens had landed on the earth, somebody .... (find) some physical evidence to prove it by now.

3 Read the text and choose the correct alternative.

In 1859, a British farmer called Thomas Austin wanted to organise a rabbit hunt on his land in Australia. Because rabbits didn't exist in Australia, he asked his nephew to send him 24 grey rabbits from England. But the rabbits quickly multiplied and by 1866 thousands of rabbits were living on Austin's land. By the 1940s, hundreds of millions of rabbits had spread across Australia. The environment in Australia was perfect for rabbits and they had no natural predators there. The rabbits destroyed over 1.5 million square miles of land and reduced the amount of food available to other animals. In the 1950s, they released myxomatosis to reduce the number of rabbits. It killed 99% of the rabbit population in Australia, but the other 1% have continued reproducing and are still a problem today.

1 If rabbits had *existed/exist* in Australia, Austin wouldn't *has/have* asked his nephew to send them.
2 If the environment in Australia hadn't *be/been* so good for the rabbits, the rabbit population *wouldn't/hadn't* have increased so quickly.
3 If there *had/have* been natural predators in Australia, they *would/had* have killed the rabbits.
4 If the rabbits *haven't/hadn't* destroyed so much land, they *would/wouldn't* have reduced the amount of food available to other animals.
5 If they hadn't *release/released* myxomatosis, the problem would have *been/being* much worse.
6 If they *killed/had* killed 100% of the rabbits in the 1950s, the problem would *have/had* stopped.

4 Read the situations and write sentences in the third conditional.

It was raining and we got wet because we didn't take an umbrella.

If we had taken an umbrella we wouldn't have got wet.

1 My friend was able to fix my computer because she did a course in computer science.
2 My brother had enough money to buy the tickets because they'd paid him his salary that morning.
3 I got 90% in the exam because I studied a lot.
4 The road was wet because it was raining.
5 I didn't buy you a present because I didn't have any money.
6 I only knew her secret because you told me.
7 We didn't know they were such horrible people when we became their friends.
8 He did really badly in the race because he hadn't trained.

5 Complete each sentence in the third conditional.

1 If it had snowed last summer,
....
2 If I'd been born in the USA,
....
3 If I'd been able to play the guitar when I was five,
....
4 If my parents had called me Englebert,
....
5 If the sun hadn't come up this morning,
....
6 If we hadn't been hungry yesterday,
....

6a SPEAKING Work with a partner. Ask and answer these questions.

What would you have done if …

1 you had met the Black Eyed Peas on your way to school?
2 aliens had stolen your homework?
3 you had been born a millionaire?
4 the teacher had given you a surprise exam yesterday?
5 your parents hadn't come home at the usual time yesterday?

6b Individually, write five similar questions. Then ask your partner your questions.

What would you have done if you had lost your mobile phone and you found it in your friend's bag?

I would have asked my friend why it was there!

1 SPEAKING **Work with a partner. Look at this photo and think of questions to ask about it. Write them down.**

Who can you see in the picture?
Where do you think they are?

2 LISTENING 2.24 **Listen to a student talking about the photo. Does she answer any of your questions? If so, make a note of her answers.**

3 SPEAKING **Work with a partner. Do you agree with what the speaker says about the picture? Why/Why not?**

The speaker says that the picture is of a city but I think it is a town because …

4 **Listen again. Tick any of the expressions in the Speaking Bank that you hear.**

▶ Speaking Bank

Making speculations and deductions

- I think
- I imagine
- (It) must be
- (It) may/might/could be
- (It) can't be
- (He/She/It/They) is/are probably
- (It) is probably
- It seems that
- (It) looks as if/like
- I'm not sure but
- (It) must have been
- (It) may/might/could have been
- (It) can't/couldn't have been

Practice makes perfect

5a **Work with a partner and look at the task. Each choose a photo and, individually, spend three minutes preparing to talk about it.**

Choose one of the photos and describe it.
- Say what you think is happening.
- Have you ever seen or been in a situation like the one in the picture? When? What happened?

5b **Take it in turns to do the task. Use the expressions in the Speaking Bank and the advice from Study Skills. If your partner stops, ask questions to help them.**

▶ STUDY SKILLS

What should you do if it's your turn to speak and you can't think of anything to say?

STUDY SKILLS ▶ page 149

1 Read the story about a bad day and answer the questions.

1 When did the story happen?
2 Who are the characters in the story?
3 Why was the day so bad for the person telling the story?

My Bad Day

If I'd known it was going to be such a bad day, I probably would have stayed in bed. It was the last day of the summer holidays. My friends and I had decided to spend our last day of freedom at a new indoor ski slope before school started again.

My friends were both really good at skiing because they used to go to the mountains when they were small. I'd only been once or twice. I wasn't very good but I really enjoyed it.

When we arrived at the indoor ski slope, the sun was shining so it was strange to go inside with all the snow and ice. First, we went to hire boots and skis and then we got changed. When we were all ready, we went onto the snow.

After an hour, I was really enjoying myself. I hadn't fallen once and I was starting to ski quite well. That was when it all went wrong. I was skiing down the slope fast when suddenly a man came out of nowhere just in front of me. I couldn't change direction and I hit him and went flying through the air. When I came back down, my knee smacked into the ice. I knew straight away that I must have done something serious. They carried me down and told me to go to hospital.

Later, when we arrived at my local hospital, all the nurses were laughing at me. They couldn't understand how anybody could have had a skiing accident in the summer. I wasn't laughing when, finally, they told me that I needed an operation on my knee. I wish I'd just stayed in bed!

2 Read the story again and underline any words or expressions which help you to understand when or in what order the events in the story happened.

3 In this story, what is the function of each paragraph?

4 Look at the Writing Bank. Match the tenses and verbs (1–5) with their uses in a story (a–e).

Writing Bank

Narrative tenses

1 past simple
2 past continuous
3 past perfect
4 *used to*
5 *must/may/might/can't have*

a We use it for the background of a story – to talk about actions that happened before other actions in the past.
b We use it to talk about past habits.
c We use these to make speculations or deductions about what happened.
d We use it to tell the main events and actions in a story.
e We use it to describe scenes; to say what activity was in progress when another interrupted it.

5 Look at the story. Find an example of each of the narrative tenses in the Writing Bank.

Practice makes perfect

6a Look at the task, then write your story. Use narrative tenses carefully and include words and expressions that explain when or in what order events happened.

> Write a story which begins:
> If I'd known it was going to be such a bad day, I probably would have stayed in bed.

EXAM SUCCESS

How should you organise your time in writing exams?

EXAM SUCCESS ▸ page 153

6b Read other students' stories. Who do you think had the worst day?

Language reference and revision

Grammar reference

Modal verbs of speculation and deduction – Present

Form

She **must** be good at maths because she always gets very good marks.
She **may** be good at maths but I don't really know.
She **might** do well in maths exams but I don't really know.
She **may not** be good at maths but I don't really know.
She **mightn't (might not)** know how to do maths exercises but I don't really know.
She **could** be good at maths but I don't really know.
She **can't** be good at maths because her marks are always bad.

After these modal verbs we use an infinitive without *to*.

Use

We use **must** when we are 90% certain that something is true.

We use **may, might, could, may not, mightn't** when there is a 50% possibility that something is true (or not).

We use **can't** when we are 90% certain that something is not true.

When we are 100% certain that something is or isn't true, we do not use modal verbs of speculation and deduction.

I know she's good at maths.

Modal verbs of speculation and deduction – Past

Form

She **must have done** well in her last exam because she was really happy afterwards.
She **may have passed** her exam but I don't really know.
She **might have failed** her exam but I don't really know.
She **may not have had** time to finish the exam but I don't really know.
She **mightn't (might not) have known** the answers but I don't really know.
She **could have copied** in the exam but I don't really know.
She **can't have passed** her exam because she was really sad afterwards.
She **couldn't have done** well in her exam because she was really sad afterwards.
To make sentences in the past using modal verbs we use this form:
must/may/might/could/can't/couldn't + **have** + past participle

Use

We use **must have** when we are 90% certain that something was true.

We use **may have, might have, could have, may not have, mightn't have** when there is a 50% possibility that something was true (or not).

We use **can't have, couldn't have** when we are 90% certain that something was not true.

When we are 100% certain that something was or wasn't true, we do not use modal verbs of speculation and deduction.

She didn't pass her exam.

Third conditional

Form

If + **past perfect, ... would/wouldn't have** + past participle

If I had seen him, I'd have spoken to him.
If we hadn't studied, we wouldn't have passed our exams.

The part of the sentence with **if** can go at the start of the sentence or at the end. There is no difference in meaning. However, if the part with **if** goes at the start of the sentence we must use a comma before the second half of the sentence.

If we had had more free time, we would have done more sport.
We'd have done more sport if we'd had more free time.

Use

We use the third conditional to talk about imaginary or impossible situations in the past and their consequences. The situations are impossible because we cannot change them now that they have happened.

If I had won the lottery last year (imaginary past situation – it didn't happen), *I would have bought a house.* (the consequence of this situation)

Vocabulary

1 Nations

capital city currency flag king/queen/prince/princess national anthem population prime minister/president

2 State and politics

affairs constitutional monarchy democracy foreign general election in the centre left-wing member minister monarchy political party republic right-wing run a country

3 Adjective suffixes *-er, -or, -ist, -ian, -ee*

aristocratic artistic careful careless dangerous enjoyable famous helpful helpless hungry mysterious natural official sensible terrible thirsty useful useless (un)comfortable

4 Other words and phrases page 144

Grammar revision

Modal verbs of speculation and deduction – Present and past

1 Complete the sentences with *must*, *may* or *can't*.

1 Sarah .... be Toby's sister because she looks totally different.

2 She .... be German because she's got a German passport.

3 That .... be my notebook because it's red and mine's yellow.

4 He .... play tennis really well but I don't know. I've never seen him play.

5 They .... like cats because they've got ten in their house!

6 Irene is very happy today. It .... be her birthday, or perhaps she's had some good news.

WORKBOOK ▶ page 76 / 6 points

2 Complete the sentences with the correct form of the verbs and *must*, *might* or *can't*.

1 You .... (see) Mike yesterday because he wasn't here; he was away on a trip.

2 Somebody called you this morning. It .... (be) Jack but I'm not sure. I didn't recognise the voice.

3 The postman .... (come) early because there are letters in the box already.

4 It .... (rain) last night because the roads are wet this morning.

5 It .... (snow) in the night because it isn't cold enough for snow.

6 Somebody in that class broke the window. Josh .... (do) it because he's in that class, but I don't know.

7 That man .... (kill) her because he was in a different city at the time of the murder.

WORKBOOK ▶ page 76 / 7 points

Third conditional

3 Complete the third conditional sentences with the correct form of these verbs.

buy cook die pass play send shine

1 If I .... my driving test, my parents would have bought me a car.

2 They .... me a present if they had known it was my birthday.

3 If her dog ...., she would have been really sad.

4 The meal would have been better if my mum .... it.

5 If the sun .... yesterday, we would have gone out for the day.

6 She .... him an email if she had known his address.

7 They would have won if they .... a bit better.

WORKBOOK ▶ page 79 / 7 points

Vocabulary revision

Nations

1 Complete the sentences about Germany with the correct words.

1 The .... is Berlin.

2 The unofficial title of the .... is 'Deutschland, über Alles'.

3 The .... has three colours: black, red and yellow.

4 The .... in 2010 was Christian Wulff.

5 The .... is over 82 million people.

6 The .... is the Euro.

WORKBOOK ▶ page 74 / 6 points

Adjective suffixes

2 Complete the sentences with the adjective form of these words.

artist care comfort enjoy mystery nature sense thirst

1 I'm really .... I haven't drunk anything all day.

2 He's very .... when he writes. He makes lots of mistakes.

3 My sister's very .... She's good at drawing.

4 It isn't very .... to go out in the rain without a coat.

5 I love sitting on this sofa. It's so ....

6 In this safari park, the animals live in a more .... environment than in a zoo.

7 We spent a very .... day in the country. I loved it.

8 He just disappeared. Nobody knows where he went. It was all very ....

WORKBOOK ▶ page 77 / 8 points

State and politics

3 Match the words and the definitions.

1	general	wing	a country ruled by a king or queen whose powers are limited by a set of basic laws
2	right	affairs	with conservative ideas or objectives
3	political	monarchy	things which happen in other countries
4	foreign	wing	occasions when you can vote for a government
5	constitutional	elections	with socialist ideas and objectives
6	left	party	a group of people with similar political ideas

/ 6 points

Total / 40 points

10 Shop until you drop

Grammar ‣ Indeterminate pronouns: *some-*, *any-*, *no-*, *every-* ‣ *So* and *such* ‣ *I wish* and *If only*
Vocabulary ‣ Shops ‣ Shopping ‣ Collocations with *money*
Speaking ‣ At a clothes shop
Writing ‣ A formal letter of complaint

‣ Vocabulary

Shops

1 Work with a partner. Match some of these places to the photos. What can you buy or do in each of the places in the box?

bakery   bank   butcher's   chemist's
clothes shop   department store
electrical goods store   greengrocer's
jeweller's   music and DVD store
newsagent's   post office   shoe shop
sports shop   stationery shop   supermarket

2 LISTENING 2.25 **Listen to these short conversations. Where are the people? What do they want to buy or do?**

1 ....
2 ....
3 ....
4 ....
5 ....

Shopping

3 Match these words to the definitions 1–14. Use your dictionary if necessary.

afford   bargain   cash   cashier   changing room
checkout   credit/debit card   discount   gift
queue   receipt   refund   shelves   trolley

1 A small plastic card that you use to buy things. ....
2 The person who takes the money in a shop. ....
3 Money in the form of notes and coins. ....
4 The place where you pay in a supermarket or a big shop. ....
5 The place where they put the products in a shop, particularly in a supermarket. ....
6 A line of people waiting, for example to pay in a shop. ....
7 Have enough money to buy something. ....
8 A reduction in the price of something. ....
9 Something that you buy which is much cheaper than usual. ....
10 Piece of paper that they give you to show that you've paid for something. ....
11 Money that a shop gives you when you return a product that you don't want. ....
12 A large container with wheels that you use to put products in, in a supermarket for example. ....
13 A present. ....
14 A place where you can try clothes on before you buy them. ....

4 Complete the text with words from 3.

The other day I was in my local supermarket, pushing the **(a)** .... and filling it with food for the week. I was bored with looking at the food, so I went to the CD section and looked at the CDs they had on the **(b)** .... I saw that they had a new CD by my favourite group. There was a 50% **(c)** .... on the CD. It was a real **(d)** .... so I bought it. There was a really long **(e)** ....with people waiting to pay at the **(f)** .... That was because the **(g)** .... (a young man who was new, I think) was really slow. Anyway, I didn't have any money with me so when it was finally my turn, I paid for everything with my **(h)** .... When I got home, I listened to the CD but I couldn't hear anything. The CD was blank. I went straight back to the supermarket with the CD and asked for a **(i)** .... I wanted my money back, obviously. They asked if I'd paid by **(j)** .... and I told them I hadn't. I had to show them my card to get my money back. But then they asked me for the **(k)** .... too, to show them that I'd bought it at that shop. I didn't have it. I'd thrown it away. In the end, the CD was a total waste of money!

5 SPEAKING **Work with a partner. Discuss the questions.**

1 Do you enjoy going shopping? How often do you go?
2 Who do you usually go shopping with?
3 Which type of shops do you like or hate? Why?
4 Which is your favourite shop and why?

Reading

1 Read the text and think of a good title. Be prepared to explain your title.

Title: ....

The next time you're in a shop or department store and you suddenly feel a strong need to get out your cash or credit card and buy something you can't really afford, stop and smell the air. It may be that you are under the influence of 'scent marketing'. Scent marketing is the use of fragrances, perfumes and smells to make you want to buy something.

1 ....

For a long time, many estate agents in the USA have used a special trick when they show people around a house or flat that they want to sell or let. Before the customers arrive, they make or bring freshly made cookies or bread. Straight away this makes the house seem more like a real home. It makes no difference if the flat is empty and unfurnished. The smell immediately brings to mind memories of childhood, happiness, safety and comfort.

2 ....

Of the five senses, smell is perhaps the most emotional and the one which can instantaneously bring back many memories.

Supermarkets have also known about the power of scent for some time. Traditionally, they have used the smell of freshly baked bread to attract customers. Often the smell is sent through the air conditioning so that the whole supermarket smells like a good old traditional bakery. And anybody who walks past the

entrance and smells warm bread will naturally want to go in. Once they're in, they find a trolley and fill it up.

3 ....

Some clothes shops have discovered that they can double their sales with women shoppers when they spray soft, 'feminine' fragrances such as vanilla. The same thing happens with men when they use more 'masculine' scents.

4 ....

They must design scents with the perfect balance. For example, experiments have shown that most men won't stay for long in a shop where the smell is too feminine. Meanwhile, some companies are taking these ideas further. Sony, for example, is experimenting with electrical goods. They are trying to add fragrances to the hard plastics that they use to make their gadgets.

5 ....

The interesting thing here is that nobody wants to give details about what scents they are using in their shops or in their goods. The experts and professionals prefer the smells to remain mysterious and to influence us subconsciously.

6 ....

In California, the Milk Processor Board started an advertising campaign in the streets using scent marketing. They had milk adverts at bus stops, and the adverts smelled, once again, of freshly made chocolate chip cookies.

7 ....

However, after a short time, the local authorities made the Milk Board remove all the adverts. They didn't think it was fair to force everybody at a bus stop to smell cookies. And, meanwhile, some members of the public had protested because of the possibility of allergic reactions.

On the evidence of the California milk advert, it's going to be a long time before scent adverts are everywhere. But try to remember – before you waste your money buying things you don't really want, be sure your nose knows what it's doing.

EXAM SUCCESS

The next exercise is a typical task that can appear in English reading exams. Do you know what type of tasks will appear in your next exam?

EXAM SUCCESS ▶ page 153

2 Read the article again and complete the text by putting sentences a–h into gaps 1–7 in the text. There is one sentence you do not need.

a But not everybody is happy about scent marketing, as this American experiment shows us.

b One reason why scent marketing is so powerful is precisely because of this.

c The idea, of course, was to make the public think of buying milk to go with their cookies.

d That's why many people think scent marketing can be dangerous in some circumstances.

e In this way, the product itself will have such an attractive smell that shoppers will want to buy it.

f Nowadays, however, scent marketing can happen anywhere, not just in a house or a supermarket.

g Here it is important for professional scent companies to get it just right.

h Scent marketing is not particularly new.

3 Complete the sentences in your own words but using information from the text.

1 Scent marketing is ....

2 Scent marketing is very effective because ....

3 Experts have to get the scents just right because ....

4 Experts don't want us to know the ingredients of their scents because ....

5 The milk advert in California wasn't a success because ....

4 Match the words in the text with these definitions.

1 rent a flat, house or room to somebody
2 take away
3 with no furniture
4 immediately
5 people who help you to buy and sell a house or flat
6 push liquid out of a container through a small hole into the air
7 without people realising or knowing

5 SPEAKING What about *you*?

1 What's your opinion of scent marketing?
2 What are your favourite fragrances or smells?

GRAMMAR GUIDE

Indeterminate pronouns: some-, any-, no-, every-

1a Look at the sentences.

1 You suddenly feel a strong need to buy **something**.
2 There isn't **anyone** in the shop.
3 Is there **anything** interesting in that shop?
4 **Anybody** who walks past the entrance smells warm bread.
5 **Nobody** wants to give details about what scents they are using.
6 **Everybody** likes cookies.
7 Scent marketing can happen **anywhere**.
8 These adverts aren't **everywhere** yet.

1b Now match the sentence halves to make rules.

1 We use pronouns with *some* ....
2 We use pronouns with *any* ....
3 We use pronouns with *no* ....
4 We use pronouns with *every* ....

a in negative sentences, questions, and in affirmative sentences when it means it doesn't matter who, what, where.
b with affirmative verbs because the meaning of the pronouns is already negative.
c in affirmative sentences and in offers and requests.
d in all types of sentences and in questions.

1c Complete the table.

some-	any-	no-	every-
something			
	anybody/ anyone	nobody/ no-one	everybody/ everyone
	anywhere		everywhere

GRAMMAR REFERENCE ▸ page 132

2 Choose the correct alternative.

1 I've finished my homework. I've done *anything/everything*.
2 Who's upstairs? I can hear *somebody/anybody*.
3 Where are my keys? I can't find them *somewhere/anywhere*.
4 The teacher's really angry. *No-one/Anyone* knows the answer.
5 Why are you so serious? Is *nothing/anything* wrong?
6 The party is a real success. *Everybody/Anybody* is having a great time.
7 I don't really want to go to that restaurant tomorrow. I want to go *somewhere/anywhere* different.
8 That's strange. There isn't *nobody/anybody* here.
9 I think I know that girl! There's *something/anything* about her that is really familiar.
10 Excuse me *everyone/no-one*! Does *anyone/everybody* know why all the computers have crashed?

3 Complete the dialogue with the indeterminate pronouns in 1c.

HOLLY: Would you like to go out **(a)** .... this weekend?
MEGAN: OK, but where?
HOLLY: **(b)** .... I don't mind. I just want to go out.
MEGAN: Well, how about going to the shops? I have to buy **(c)** .... for my sister. It's her birthday next week.
HOLLY: What are you going to buy her?
MEGAN: Clothes. She always says she can't go out because she hasn't got **(d)** .... to wear. So then she wears all my clothes – **(e)** ....! And, in the end, I've got **(f)** .... to wear and I can't go out.
HOLLY: **(g)** .... should speak to her.
MEGAN: Who? Me? My mum? My sister never listens to **(h)** ....!

4a SPEAKING Complete the questions with *anybody*, *anywhere* or *anything*.

1 If you could go .... in the world for your holidays, where would you go?
2 If you could have .... you liked for your birthday, what would you ask for?
3 If you could meet .... in the world, who would you meet?
4 If you could be .... in the world apart from yourself, who would you be?
5 If you could live .... in the world, where would you live?
6 If you could change .... in the world, what would you change?

4b Work with a partner. Ask and answer the questions. Are any of your answers similar?

GRAMMAR GUIDE

So and such

5 Look at the sentences and choose the correct alternative.

1 Scent marketing is **so** powerful.
2 They do it **so** well.
3 It's **so** effective that they now sell 50% more.
4 This is **such** a bargain.
5 The product will have **such** an attractive smell that shoppers will want to buy it.

a We use *so* to intensify the meaning of *adjectives and adverbs/nouns*.
b We use *such* to intensify the meaning of *adjectives only/nouns (with or without adjectives)*.
c After sentences with *so* or *such* we can continue the sentence with *that/than*.

GRAMMAR REFERENCE ▸ page 132

6a PRONUNCIATION 2.26 **Listen to the sentences. What do you notice about the pronunciation of *so* and *such*?**

1 That dress is so expensive.
2 It's such an amazing shop.
3 I'm so happy that you're here.
4 It's such a pity that you can't come.

6b Listen again and repeat.

7 Complete the sentences with *so* or *such*.

1 That's .... a good shop.
2 Those jeans are .... cheap.
3 I find shopping .... tiring.
4 It was .... a problem to get here.
5 You and I are .... good friends.
6 We did .... well in that competition.
7 I was .... sorry to hear the news.
8 The queue at the checkout was .... long.

8 Complete these sentences in a logical way. Use your imagination!

1 Everything was so expensive in the shop that ...
2 The customer was so angry that ...
3 It was so late that ...
4 It was such a rainy day that ...
5 The TV programme was so bad that ...
6 She was such a clever student that ...
7 The music was so loud that ...
8 He was such a strange person that ...

9 Work with a partner. Compare your sentences in 8.

Collocations with *money*

1 Look at these verbs. They frequently go with the word *money*. Use the verbs to complete the definitions.

borrow donate earn lend make
save spend waste win

When you:

1 .... money, you get it in a competition.
2 .... money, you use more than you should, or you use it in a silly way.
3 .... money, somebody gives it to you but you have to pay it back later.
4 .... money, you give it as a present to a charity, organisation or institution.
5 .... money, you get it for working.
6 .... money, you give it to somebody but they have to pay you back later.
7 .... money, you use it to buy something.
8 .... money, you don't spend it, you put it in a bank for example.
9 .... money, you get it for working or by investing it or through a business plan or transaction.

2 Complete the sentences with the correct form of the verbs in 1.

1 How much money do shop assistants usually .... when they work full time?
2 I .... £30 a month on CDs and books.
3 Can I .... some money? I forgot to bring any when I left home this morning.
4 My friend .... £1,000 on the lottery last week.
5 A lot of famous actors .... money to charities and organisations that help the poor.
6 Hey, where's my money? I .... you ten pounds last week and you still haven't given it back.
7 Bill Gates .... a lot of money from Microsoft.
8 I'm .... £20 a week because next year I want to buy a new computer.
9 You .... your money when you bought that exercise bike. You never use it!

The consumer society

International cultural knowledge
A British shopping centre

1 Work with a partner. Ask and answer the questions.
1 When you go shopping, do you prefer going to small, local shops or to big shopping centres? Why?
2 Which is the biggest shopping centre you have been to? What can you do there apart from shop?

2 Look at the picture in this leaflet for a British shopping centre called Bluewater. What do you think you can do there? Guess.

Bluewater

From clothes to stationery, electrical goods to travel, music and DVDs to jewellery, there are 330 stores and restaurants at Bluewater. You can buy gifts for family and friends at prices you can really afford and save money by looking out for the hundreds of discounts on offer.

Bluewater is so much more than just a shopping destination.

We offer a fantastic variety of leisure facilities for all ages, so next time you need ideas on how to entertain the family, why not:

Take in a movie?
Our 12-screen multiplex Cinema shows all the latest blockbuster films. You can save money by booking before 5pm. For tickets and information plus this week's show times, visit www.showcasecinemas.co.uk or call 0871 220 1000.

Book a session at Treejumpers Sky Park?
Located outside the Winter Garden, it's a great adventure activity for children and adults from 7 to 70! Fly across the lake at 30mph or climb our Aerial Trek with bridges, ropes and nets. We even offer a two hour 'Drop and Shop' session for children aged from 7 and up. So you can shop in peace while we make sure your kids have a great time. To find out more, call 0800 056 0474.

Climb the Big Blue Rock?
Adventurers from just six years old can climb our 36ft climbing wall in the Yellow Hall. Opening times are Monday to Friday 3pm until 8pm, Saturday 12 noon until 8pm, and Sunday 12.30pm til 5pm. For more information and prices, call 07870 194695.

Explore one of our six lakes?
We offer two and five-seater pedaloes and traditional rowing boats. Open every weekend and weekdays during the school holidays from 11am-6pm. Prices start at £8 per half hour. For bookings, call 01732 360630.

Hire a bike and explore the park?
It's a great way to get some exercise and with 50 acres to discover, there's plenty to see. Choose from a huge variety of bikes including tandems, family four-wheelers and even pedal-powered go-karts for kids. Cycles and tandems are only available at weekends, on bank holidays and during the school holidays. Call 07891 406038 for details.

Experience our free Wild Explorer Discovery Trail?
Bluewater is home to hundreds of species of animals, birds and insects. Get closer to them by going on our Wild Explorer Discovery Trail. The trail will take you on a 1,500m circular walk around the lakes, offering fascinating information on Kent wildlife and animals from around the globe.

Opening times
Monday–Friday 10.00am–9.00pm
Saturday 9.00am–9.00pm
Sunday 11.00am–5.00pm
Bank Holiday Monday 10.00am–7.00pm

How to get here
Bluewater is located at Greenhithe. This is between Dartford and Gravesend on the A2 London to Canterbury road.

How are you travelling to Bluewater?
- By car: With over 13,000 car parking spaces and just 2 miles from the M25, travelling by car couldn't be easier.
- By bus: Over 60 buses visit Bluewater every hour, connecting with all major routes in the area.
- By coach: There is a special Bluewater coach park which can accommodate over 50 coaches at any time.
- By train: Trains arrive at Greenhithe station every 15 minutes from London and other towns.
- By bicycle: Bluewater has over 4km of cycle paths and it has convenient places to leave your bike.

INSIDE INFORMATION
Bluewater is one of the biggest indoor shopping centres in Europe. It opened in 1999 and is visited by 27 million people a year.

3 Read the leaflet and answer the questions.
1 Can you go on the lakes on Wednesday morning during the school year?
2 Can parents leave a ten-year-old child at the Treejumpers Sky Park while they do their shopping?
3 Where is Bluewater?
4 What are the names of the two places where you can climb at Bluewater?
5 Do you have to take your own bike to explore the park?
6 How can you find out what films are on at Bluewater?
7 How many hours is Bluewater open each weekend?
8 How does Bluewater help people who want to cycle to the shopping centre?

4 Work with a partner. You are going to Bluewater to spend a Saturday there. Decide on a plan for the whole day. Compare your plan with other students. Vote for the most interesting plan!

WORD BOOSTER

Match the words and definitions.

1 leisure facilities
2 screen
3 blockbuster
4 pedalo
5 tandem
6 species
7 route
8 path

a a bicycle for two people
b a small boat that you move by pushing pedals with your feet
c a very successful film
d the way that you go to get from one place to another
e a way from one place to another that you can walk along
f places or things you can do to relax
g the place at the cinema where you see the pictures
h groups of animals or plants that are similar

Cross-curricular – Economics
Buy Nothing Day

5 You are going to listen to a radio programme about 'Buy Nothing Day'. Before you listen, work with a partner and predict what Buy Nothing Day is and why it exists.

6 2.27 Listen to the programme and check your predictions.

7 Listen again. Are these statements true (T) or false (F)?

1 Amanda thinks that it's easy to buy nothing. T/F
2 She says that the problem with going to the supermarket is that it makes us waste money. T/F
3 She is worried because a small part of the world is using a large part of its resources. T/F
4 She wants supermarkets to sell products from all over the world. T/F
5 The whole world celebrates Buy Nothing Day on the same day. T/F

8 What about *you*?

1 Do you think Buy Nothing Day is a good idea or not? Why?
2 Do you think you, or people in general, buy too many (unnecessary) products?

I think it's a good idea.

I agree. For some people, shopping is their only hobby.

Popular culture
If I had a million dollars

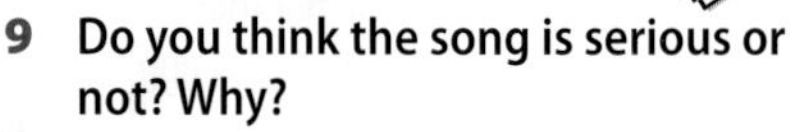

9 Do you think the song is serious or not? Why?

10 Put these words in the correct place in the song.

art automobile fridge
furniture help pasta
pet rich store

11 2.28 Listen and check your answers.

12 What about *you*?

1 What would you do if you had a million dollars?
2 Do you like this song? Why/Why not?

INSIDE INFORMATION

- This song is by a Canadian rock group. They often include elements of comedy in their songs and concerts. This is one of their most popular songs. When they sing this song in concert they change the words and add lots of other things that they would buy if they had a million dollars.
- This song includes various cultural references:
  A *chesterfield* is a type of sofa.
  An *ottoman* is a piece of furniture which you can put your feet on.
  K-cars and *Reliants* are old types of car made by Chrysler.
  John (Joseph) *Merrick* lived in Victorian times and was known as the Elephant Man because of his physical appearance.
  Kraft Dinners are famous pre-cooked meals.
  Garfunkel is a singer; his first name is Art.

1 If I had a million dollars (If I had a million dollars)
I'd buy you a house (I would buy you a house)
If I had a million dollars (If I had a million dollars)
I'd buy you **(a)** .... for your house
(Maybe a nice chesterfield or an ottoman)
If I had a million dollars (If I had a million dollars)
I'd buy you a K-Car (a nice Reliant **(b)** ....)
If I had a million dollars I'd buy your love.

2 If I had a million dollars
I'd build a tree fort in our yard.
If I had a million dollars
You could **(c)** ...., it wouldn't be that hard.
If I had a million dollars
Maybe we could put a little tiny **(d)** .... in there somewhere
(We could just go up there and hang out.
Like open the fridge and stuff, and there'd be foods laid out for us
With little pre-wrapped pizza and things. Mmmmm.
They have pre-wrapped pizza but they don't have pre-wrapped **(e)** ....
Well, can you blame them? Yeah)

3 If I had a million dollars (If I had a million dollars)
I'd buy you a fur coat (but not a real fur coat, that's cruel)
If I had a million dollars a million dollars (If I had a million dollars)
I'd buy you an exotic **(f)** ...., yeah (like a llama or an emu)
If I had a million dollars (If I had a million dollars)
I'd buy you John Merrick's remains
(All them crazy elephant bones)
If I had a million dollars I'd buy your love.

4 If I had a million dollars
We wouldn't have to walk to the **(g)** ....
If I had a million dollars
We'd take a limousine 'cause it costs more
If I had a million dollars
We wouldn't have to eat Kraft Dinner.
(But we would eat Kraft Dinner. Of course we would, we'd just eat more.
And buy really expensive ketchups with it.
That's right, all the fanciest Dijon ketchup. Mmmmmm.)

5 If I had a million dollars (If I had a million dollars)
I'd buy you a green dress (but not a real green dress, that's cruel)
If I had a million dollars (If I had a million dollars)
I'd buy you some **(h)** ....
(a Picasso or a Garfunkel)
If I had a million dollars (If I had a million dollars)
I'd buy you a monkey (Haven't you always wanted a monkey?)
If I had a million dollars I'd buy your love.

If I had a million dollars, If I had a million dollars
If I had a million dollars, If I had a million dollars
I'd be **(i)** ....

Listening

1 **Work with a partner. Look at the photo. Describe what you can see. Do you think people spend too much money on mobile phones? Why/Why not?**

2 **LISTENING 2.29 Listen to four conversations. Which conversation is about somebody who:**

a	doesn't like other people buying things for them?	1
b	wants to buy something they don't need?	2
c	bought something and regrets it?	3
d	doesn't like shopping?	4

3 **Listen again. Who …**

	A speaker in 1	2	3	4
1 doesn't believe what magazines or TV say?				
2 hasn't got enough money to pay to use a phone?				
3 has been lying to their friend to avoid going shopping with them?				
4 wants to go out but can't?				
5 doesn't need new things?				
6 needs to borrow money from a friend?				
7 would like to go shopping with their friend?				
8 wants to buy something that they don't use a lot?				

4 **SPEAKING What about *you*?**

Which speaker in the four conversations are you most similar to? Why?

I'm most similar to the boy in conversation 3 because I hate going shopping!

Grammar in context

GRAMMAR GUIDE

I wish and *If only*

1 **Look at the sentences and choose the correct alternative.**

1 I wish I **had** enough money to buy it.
2 If only I **knew** more people like you.
3 I wish I **hadn't bought** those shoes.
4 If only you'**d told** me it was your birthday.
5 I wish you **wouldn't** do that!

a Sentences 1 and 2 use *I wish/If only* + the present simple/past simple to talk about present/past situations. They express imaginary wishes.

b Sentences 3 and 4 use *I wish/If only* + the past simple/past perfect to talk about present/past situations that we would like to be different. They express regrets.

c Sentence 5 uses *I wish/If only* with the past simple/would to talk about habitual behaviour that the speaker wants/doesn't want to criticise and change.

GRAMMAR REFERENCE ▸ page 132

2 **Look at the situations. Use the word(s) to write what you think these people wish was different about their present situation.**

1 Joe's office is 10 kilometres away and there is no public transport to get there. (car)
He wishes he had a car.

2 Paul is short but he wants to be a basketball player. (taller)
....

3 Mary really loves animals but her parents won't let her have a pet. (cat or dog)
....

4 It's a cold winter's day but Lisa is thinking of the summer holidays. (on a beach)
....

5 Daniel is bald and he doesn't like it. (long hair)
....

6 Robert wants to have powers like Superman. (fly)
....

7 This is Mike's first skiing lesson and he keeps falling over. (ski well) ....

8 William works in an office but his passion is football. (professional football player)
....

3 **SPEAKING Work with a partner and look at these ideas. Tell your partner if you wish they were true for you, or not. Give reasons why.**

be a millionaire
have a famous boy/girlfriend
know what people are thinking
be famous
have X-ray vision
speak five languages

4 Complete the regrets with the verbs in the correct tense.

1 If only I .... (not tell) him my secrets yesterday.
2 I wish I .... (choose) to study something different last year.
3 I wish I .... (treat) my little sister better when we were younger.
4 If only I .... (study) more for our last exam.
5 I wish I .... (learn) to play the guitar when I was younger.
6 If only I .... (not listen) to my friend yesterday.
7 I wish I .... (not say) that to my dad last night.
8 If only I .... (pay) more attention to my last maths teacher.

5 Look at the pictures. What do you think the people are saying? Use *I wish you would/wouldn't…*

6a SPEAKING **Work with a partner. Decide what the people in the photos are wishing. You can use *wish/if only* + past simple, past perfect or *would*.**

6b Read out your ideas. Can other students match them to the correct pictures?

▶ STUDY SKILLS

Now that you have almost finished the course, think back on what you have studied. In which areas of English do you think you have made the most progress? What do you think you need to work on most to improve?

STUDY SKILLS ▶ page 149

1 SPEAKING **Work with a partner. Look at the photo and describe it. What clothes can you see?**

2 LISTENING 2.30 **Listen to a conversation in a shop. What does the girl buy?**

1 Type of clothing: .... 3 Colour: ....
2 Size: .... 4 For: ....

3 Put the lines in order to make a logical conversation.

1 *g* 2 ...... 3 ...... 4 ...... 5 ...... 6 ...... 7 ...... 8 ...... 9 ......

a Customer: It isn't for me. It's for **my brother**.
b Customer: Yes, I'm looking for **a jumper**.
c Shop assistant: No problem. Just remember to bring the receipt.
d Shop assistant: What size are you?
e Shop assistant: Oh, I see. What size is he?
f Shop assistant: These are new. We've got them in **black** or **grey**.
g Shop assistant: Can I help you?
h Customer: I like the **black** one. I'll take it. Can I bring it back if it doesn't fit or if he doesn't like it?
i Customer: **Medium**.

4 SPEAKING **Work with a partner. Use the lines in 3 to make and practise a conversation in a shop. Change the words in bold to make your conversation different.**

5 LISTENING 2.31 **Read and listen to a conversation with the same customer in the shop a week later. Answer the questions.**

1 What is the customer's problem?
2 What does the shop assistant offer her?
3 What does she get in the end?

SHOP ASSISTANT: Good morning. Can I help you?
LILY: Yes, I'd like to make a complaint.
SHOP ASSISTANT: Oh dear. I'm sorry. What seems to be the problem?
LILY: Well, I bought this hoodie here last week as a present for a friend.
SHOP ASSISTANT: Oh, didn't he like it? He can choose another one if he wants.
LILY: No, that's not the problem. He liked it but it shrank the first time he washed it. It was a large but now it's more like a small.
SHOP ASSISTANT: Oh dear. I am sorry. We haven't had anybody else with that problem. Are you sure he followed the washing instructions?
LILY: Yes!
SHOP ASSISTANT: I see. Well, we can either replace it for you straight away or we could give you a refund. Which would you prefer?
LILY: I'll take the refund.
SHOP ASSISTANT: Fine. Have you got the receipt?
LILY: Yes, here it is.
SHOP ASSISTANT: Thank you. £30. There you are. Sorry about that.

6 Look at the expressions in the Speaking Bank. Use your dictionary to check any new words. Which expressions can be used for:

1 making a complaint?
2 apologising?
3 offering help?
4 accepting help?
5 asking for information or an opinion?
6 giving information or an opinion?

Speaking Bank

Useful expressions in a shop

Shop assistant

- Can I help you?
- What size are you?
- How about this/these?
- What seems to be the problem?
- We can replace it.
- Sorry about that.

Customer

- Yes, I'm looking for …
- No, thanks. I'm just looking.
- Have you got anything in blue/green/medium/large?
- I like it/them.
- I'll take this one/these ones.
- Can I bring it back?
- I'd like to make a complaint.
- It shrank the first time I washed it.
- It's the wrong size.
- It's faulty.
- It's got a hole.
- Can I have a refund?

Practice makes perfect

7 Look at the task. Work with a partner.

Student A: Choose a type of clothing, a problem with it, and the solution you would like.

Student B: You are a shop assistant. Find out what the customer wants and try to keep them happy. Use the dialogue in 5 and the Speaking Bank to help you.

You are in a clothes shop. Last week you bought an item of clothing in the shop but there is a problem with it.

- Tell the shop assistant what the problem is.
- Say what solution you would like from the shop.

EXAM SUCCESS

What do you need to do to get a good mark in a speaking exam? Think of good advice.

EXAM SUCCESS ▸ page 153

1 Have you ever bought anything that didn't work or had a defect? What happened?

2 Read the letter of complaint and answer the questions.

1 What did Stephanie buy?
2 What was the problem with it?
3 What did she do?
4 What problems came next and what did she do about them?
5 What solution does she want?

Dear Sir or Madam,

I am writing to complain about the goods and service in your store.

On 16th March I bought an MP3 player at your store on Kings Road in Bath. When I arrived home, I removed the MP3 player from its box and discovered that it did not work. As a result, I took it back to the store the following day. However, the shop assistant told me that I could only have a refund if I returned the MP3 player in its original box.

The next day I went back again with the MP3 player in its original packaging. This time a new shop assistant told me that I could not have a refund, only a replacement. When I told him what his colleague had said the day before, he accused me of lying.

In the end, I left the store with a replacement MP3 player but I once again discovered that it was faulty. I will not go back to the store since your shop assistants are so rude. I demand a full refund immediately. Furthermore, I would like an apology from the shop assistant who treated me so badly. If I do not hear from you in the next two weeks, I will take my complaint to a Consumer Advice Centre.

I look forward to hearing from you soon.

Yours faithfully,

Stephanie Rothfuss

Stephanie Rothfuss

3 Put the pieces of information in the order that they appear in Stephanie's letter.

a Details of the complaint.
b Action to be taken if there is no solution.
c An explanation of the reason for writing.
d A demand for a solution.
e Where and when the problem began.

1 .... 2 .... 3 .... 4 .... 5 ....

4 Read the letter again and underline any expressions that you think are useful for a letter of complaint.

5 Look at these words from the letter and put them in the correct list in the Writing Bank.

As a result Furthermore However In the end since

Writing Bank

Useful linkers

- Consequence: *Therefore... and so...* ....
- Time and sequence: *Next... Then...* ....
- Contrast: *but... although...* ....
- Reason: *because... as...* ....
- Addition: *In addition... What is more...* ....

6 Complete these sentences in a logical way.

1 I am very disappointed with your shop. As a result, ...
2 The shop assistant was very unhelpful. Furthermore, ...
3 I am usually very happy with the service in your store. However, ...
4 I would like a refund since ....
5 I went back to the shop three times. In the end ....

Practice makes perfect

7a Look at the task, then write your letter of complaint. Use the letter in 2 and linkers from the Writing Bank to help you.

In March you ordered two tickets on the Internet for a concert by your favourite band, Muse. The tickets were very expensive. The concert was on 1st April, but the tickets didn't arrive until 3rd April. You rang the ticket company three times before 1st April and they promised the tickets would arrive on time. Write a letter of complaint to the manager of the ticket company.

- Explain what the problem is.
- Ask for a solution and explain what you will do if there is no solution.

7b Give your letter to another student. Now write a reply.

STUDY SKILLS

How can you improve your writing? Think of good advice.

STUDY SKILLS ▶ page 149

Language reference and revision

Grammar reference

Indeterminate pronouns: some-, any-, no-, every-

Form

some-	*any-*	*no-*	*every-*
something	anything	nothing	everything
somebody/ someone	anybody/ anyone	nobody/ no-one	everybody/ everyone
somewhere	anywhere	nowhere	everywhere

Use

We use **-thing** for objects, **-body** and **-one** for people, and **-where** for places.

We use pronouns with **some-** in affirmative sentences and in offers and requests.

Somebody is in the living room.

Would you like something to eat?

We use pronouns with **any-** in negative sentences, questions, and in affirmative sentences when it means it doesn't matter who, what, where.

I haven't got anything to wear.

Is there anybody there?

This is easy. Anybody can do it.

We use pronouns with **no-** with affirmative verbs because the meaning of the pronoun is already negative.

There's nobody here.

Is there nothing I can do?

We use pronouns with **every-** in all types of sentences and in questions.

I like everything in this restaurant.

You can't be everywhere at the same time.

Has everybody understood?

So and *such*

Use

We use **so** to intensify the meaning of adjectives and adverbs.

It's so hot.

She sings so well.

We use **such** to intensify the meaning of nouns, with or without adjectives. We use **a/an** after **such** when we continue with a singular countable noun, but not with uncountable or plural nouns.

It's such a hot day.

It's such a pity.

He sings such beautiful songs.

This is such good bread.

After sentences with **so** or **such** we can continue the sentence with **that**.

It's so hot that I can't concentrate.

I wish and *If only*

Use

We use **I wish/If only** + **the past** to talk about imaginary situations in the present. It expresses wishes for things to be different in the present.

I wish I was on a desert island right now.

If only I had a million dollars.

We use **I wish/If only** + **the past perfect** to talk about past situations that we regret or would like to be different.

I wish I had listened to the teacher last year.

If only I hadn't shouted at Liam.

We use **I wish/If only** with **would/wouldn't** + **infinitive** to talk about somebody's habitual behaviour that we want to criticise and change.

My dad smokes. I wish he wouldn't do it.

I wish you would listen to me.

Vocabulary

1 Shops

bakery bank butcher's chemist's clothes shop department store electrical goods store greengrocer's jeweller's music and DVD store newsagent's post office shoe shop sports shop stationery shop supermarket

2 Shopping

afford bargain cash cashier changing room checkout credit/debit card discount gift queue receipt refund shelves trolley

3 Collocations with *money*

borrow donate earn lend make save spend waste win

4 Other words and phrases ▶ page 145

Grammar revision

Indeterminate pronouns: some-, any-, no-, every-

1 Complete the sentences with the correct indeterminate pronoun.

1 I haven't got ………… in my bag.
2 Homeless people haven't got ………… to go at night.
3 She's got ………… important to tell you.
4 Can you come to the phone, Sam? ………… wants to talk to you.
5 ………… needs to drink water.
6 I can hear people talking but I can't see ………….

WORKBOOK ▸ page 84 / 6 points

So and *such*

2 Rewrite the *so* sentences with *such* and vice-versa.

1 This country is so big. …………
2 They're such good students. …………
3 The exam was so difficult. …………
4 The weather was so bad that we stayed at home.
…………
5 It was such a loud concert that my ears hurt. …………
…………
6 I've got such a bad headache. …………
…………
7 That road is so dangerous that there are always lots of accidents. …………
8 The experience was so painful. …………

WORKBOOK ▸ page 84 / 8 points

I wish and *If only*

3 Choose the correct alternative.

1 I wish I *have/had* a pen with me now.
2 If only you *had/would* pay more attention in class.
3 If only I *understood/had understood* what you're saying.
4 I wish I *met/had met* you last year.
5 I wish you *would stop/had stopped* interrupting me when I'm talking.
6 If only I *didn't fail/hadn't failed* my driving test last week.

WORKBOOK ▸ page 87 / 6 points

Vocabulary revision

Shops

1 In which shops can you buy these things?

1 meat: b … … … … … …' …
2 fruit and vegetables: g … … … … … … … … … … …' …
3 MP3 players, vacuum cleaners, dishwashers:
e … … … … … … … … … g … … … …
s … … … …
4 almost anything, not just food:
d … … … … … … … … … s … … … …
5 paper and pens: s … … … … … … … … …
s … … …
6 bread and cakes: b … … … … …
7 stamps for letters or packages: p … … …
o … … … … …

WORKBOOK ▸ page 82 / 7 points

Shopping

2 Write the words.

1 

c … … … … … c … … …

2 
t … … … … … …

3 
q … … … …

4 
c … … … … … …

5 
c … … … … … … …

6 

b … … … … … …

7 
g … … …

WORKBOOK ▸ page 82 / 7 points

Collocations with money

3 Are the sentences correct or not? If not, change the word in italics.

1 When you *lend* money, you get money but then you have to give it back.
2 You *win* money when you do professional work.
3 When you *donate* money you give it to a charity or an organisation.
4 When you *save* money, you use it to buy things you don't need.
5 When you *make* money, you get money by working, selling things, or making investments.
6 When you *spend* money, you give it to somebody for a time but then they have to give it back to you.

WORKBOOK ▸ page 85 / 6 points

Total / 40 points

Gateway to exams *Units 9–10*

Reading

1 Work with a partner. In March 2002, a 51-year-old British man went canoeing in the sea but didn't come back. What do you think might have happened to him?

2 Read the text. Were your ideas in 1 correct?

Tip for Reading Exams

In general, remember…

Make sure you know what type of tasks and exercises will appear in your exams. If you are familiar with these types of exercises, they will become easier. If you have problems with a type of exercise, practise. EXAM SUCCESS ▸ page 153

The mystery of the 'dead' canoeist

22nd March 2002: Pieces of a canoe were found on a beach in Seaton Carew, near the city of Hartlepool in north-east England. The canoe belonged to 51-year-old John Darwin, who was married with two children. Somebody said they had seen Darwin enter the sea with his canoe at 8 or 9am the day before. It was only later in the evening, when he did not arrive for work, that a colleague reported his disappearance. An expensive rescue operation began. Five boats, two rescue teams and a plane were used to try and find Darwin's body, but without any luck. Experts concluded that he must have died at sea. Six months after her husband's disappearance, Darwin's wife, Anne, told reporters how difficult it was to live in limbo, without finding her husband's dead body.

1st December 2007: Five years later, John Darwin walked into a police station in London and told the police 'I think I'm a missing person.' He gave the police officers his name, date of birth and details of his wife and two sons, but said that he was suffering from amnesia. Darwin was reunited with his two sons but his wife was not there because she had moved to Panama a year before. The police admitted that they had no idea what might have happened during those five years but said that they would interview him and make a full investigation.

5th December 2007: John Darwin was arrested by the police. In the following weeks, an incredible story came to light. The police were helped by a member of the public who found an interesting photo on the Internet and sent it to a British newspaper. The photo was of John Darwin on holiday in Panama with his wife Anne. They were both happy and smiling, but the photo was taken four years after Darwin's 'death'. After a long investigation, the police said that Anne had known about her husband's plan right from the start. On the day of the disappearance, she had even driven him to the local train station so that he could disappear. Afterwards, John had lived in a secret room in the family's house for three years. He had grown a long beard and always entered the house through a secret door. But, during all this time, John and Anne's sons had no idea what was going on. The couple had planned the whole thing to get insurance money. John had had financial problems and pretended to die so that his wife got thousands of pounds from his insurance policy. With this money they were planning to buy land in Panama and set up a holiday resort. So why did John Darwin go to the police station in London when their plan was working so well? Some people thought he might have had an argument with Anne. Others say that he must have wanted to see his sons again after so many years. But the police think that it was because his false passport was about to expire. He needed to come back to the UK to get a new, real passport. Darwin thought that the police would believe his story about suffering amnesia. But they didn't, and now John and Anne have to spend more than six years in prison.

3 Read the text again and choose the best answers.

1 John Darwin's disappearance was reported when
   A they found some pieces of his canoe.
   B the people at his place of work hadn't seen him.
   C somebody saw him go into the water.

2 When Darwin reappeared, he
   A couldn't remember who he was.
   B met up with his wife and children.
   C said he didn't know where he'd been.

3 The police knew both John and Anne were lying because
   A their story wasn't convincing.
   B they had physical evidence.
   C newspaper reporters wrote an article about them.

4 John went to the police station in London because he
   A was confident everything would be OK.
   B had to get a visa to go back to Panama.
   C needed to see his kids again.

Writing

Tip for Writing Exams

In writing exams, remember …

Make sure you know how many pieces of writing you have to do in the exam, and how much time you have to do them. Decide if you have time to write a rough version first.

EXAM SUCCESS ▸ page 153

4 Look at the task. Prepare your story and then write it. Remember to use narrative tenses carefully and include words and expressions to explain the sequence of events.

Write a story for your school magazine which begins:

I couldn't believe what I read in the newspaper that morning.

Speaking

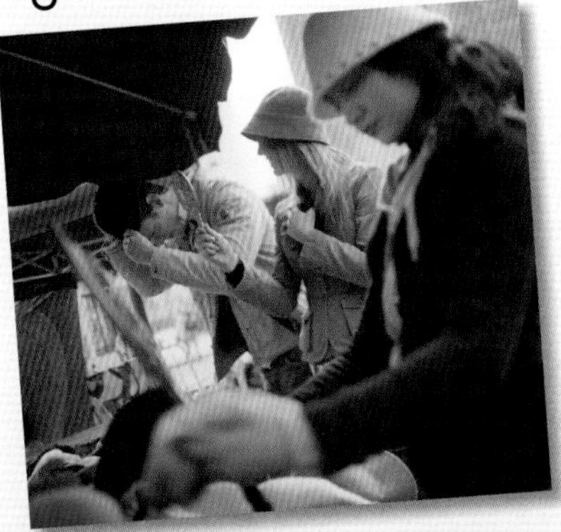

5 Work with a partner. Look at the task. Each choose a photo and then, individually, spend three minutes preparing to talk about it.

> Choose one of the photos and describe it.
> - Say what you can see. Make speculations about where it is, who the people are, etc.
> - Say if you would like to be with the people in the photo and explain why/why not.

6 Take it in turns to do the task.

Tip for Speaking Exams

In speaking exams, remember ...

Speak loudly and clearly and speak as much as possible. If you don't speak much the examiner won't be able to give you a good mark. Remember that the examiner is on your side.

EXAM SUCCESS ▸ page 153

Use of English

Tip for Use of English Exams

In word formation cloze activities, remember ...

Look at the words just before and after the gap and make sure you understand the whole sentence. To change the **type** of word you will usually need a **suffix** (e.g. *-ion* to make a noun, *-ly* to make an adverb). To change the **meaning** of the word you will usually need a **prefix** (e.g. *im-*, *re-*).

EXAM SUCCESS ▸ page 153

7 Read the text below. Use the words in capitals to form a word that fits in the gap.

When he was young, my brother always wanted to have a (a) .... (**DANGER**) job, like being an explorer. Then, when he was older he was (b) .... (**INTEREST**) in becoming a professional (c) .... (**HISTORY**) because he loved reading about the past. But now that he's started working, he doesn't think his job is very (d) .... (**INSPIRE**). He's (e) .... (**EMPLOY**) at a local department store where he has to work long hours. It's a (f) .... (**TIRE**) job and he doesn't earn much. Sometimes he works in (g) .... (**COMFORT**) conditions, for example, standing for hours and hours in the same position. But my brother is very (h) .... (**HELP**) and kind to the customers. The store he works for is part of a big (i) .... (**NATION**) group and so they might send him to work in a different country if he wants. My brother studies English in the evenings and he wants to get some type of certificate in English. So he's (j) .... (**EXCITE**) about the idea of going to an English-speaking country. My brother is clever and ambitious. It wouldn't be so (k) .... (**SURPRISE**) if one day he became the (l) .... (**DIRECT**) of the company!

'Can Do' Progress Check

CEF

1 How well can you do these things in English now? Give yourself a mark from 1 to 4.

1 = I can do it very well.	2 = I can do it quite well.	3 = I have some problems.	4 = I can't do it.

- **a** I can make speculations and deductions in the present and past using modal verbs. ☐
- **b** I can talk about imaginary situations in the past and their consequences using the third conditional. ☐
- **c** I can make adjectives by adding suffixes. ☐
- **d** I can describe pictures and make speculations and deductions about them. ☐
- **e** I can write a simple story using different narrative tenses. ☐
- **f** I can use indeterminate pronouns (*some-*, *any-*, *no-*) correctly. ☐
- **g** I can talk about imaginary wishes using I wish and If only. ☐
- **h** I can understand written and spoken texts about shopping and money. ☐
- **i** I can ask for things and explain problems in a clothes shop. ☐
- **j** I can write a formal letter of complaint. ☐

2 Now decide what you need to do to improve.

1 Look again at my book/notes.
2 Do more practice exercises. → WORKBOOK pages 74–91
3 Other: ....

Wordlists

(adj) = adjective (adv) = adverb (conj) = conjunction (n) = noun (pron) = pronoun (v) = verb	The most common and useful words in English are marked according to the Macmillan Essential Dictionary 'star rating'. This is so that you can easily recognise the vocabulary you need to know especially well. ★★★ = very common words ★★ = common words ★ = fairly common words If there is no star next to the word, this means that it is not very common.

Unit 1

Appearance

bald (adj) /bɔːld/
blonde (adj) ★ /blɒnd/
curly (adj) /'kɜːli/
dark (adj) ★★★ /dɑːk/
fair (adj) ★★★ /feə/
good-looking (adj) /ˌgʊd 'lʊkɪŋ/
handsome (adj) ★★ /'hæns(ə)m/
long (adj) ★★★ /lɒŋ/
medium-height (adj) /miːdiəm'haɪt/
overweight (adj) /ˌəʊvə'weɪt/
plain (adj) ★ /pleɪn/
pretty (adj) ★ /'prɪti/
short (adj) ★★★ /ʃɔːt/
straight (adj) ★★ /streɪt/
tall (adj) ★★★ /tɔːl/
thin (adj) ★★★ /θɪn/
ugly (adj) ★ /'ʌgli/
well-built (adj) /ˌwel 'bɪlt/

Personality

arrogant (adj) /'ærəgənt/
bossy (adj) /'bɒsi/
cheerful (adj) /'tʃɪəf(ə)l/
clever (adj) ★★ /'klevə/
friendly (adj) ★★ /'fren(d)li/
funny (adj) ★★★ /'fʌni/
hard-working (adj) ★ /hɑːd'wɜːkɪŋ/
impatient (adj) ★ /ɪm'peɪʃ(ə)nt/
lazy (adj) ★ /'leɪzi/
nice (adj) ★★★ /naɪs/
patient (adj) ★★ /'peɪʃ(ə)nt/
quiet (adj) ★★★ /'kwaɪət/
reliable (adj) ★ /rɪ'laɪəb(ə)l/
selfish (adj) /'selfɪʃ/
serious (adj) ★★★ /'sɪəriəs/
shy (adj) ★ /ʃaɪ/
talkative (adj) /'tɔːkətɪv/
tidy (adj) ★ /'taɪdi/
unfriendly (adj) /ʌn'fren(d)li/
untidy (adj) /ʌn'taɪdi/

Synonyms and partial synonyms

attractive (adj) ★★ /ə'træktɪv/
beautiful (adj) ★★★ /'bjuːtəf(ə)l/
bright (adj) ★★★ /braɪt/
difficult (adj) ★★★ /'dɪfɪk(ə)lt/
elderly (adj) ★★ /'eldəli/
fat (adj) ★★ /fæt/
glad (adj) ★★ /glæd/
happy (adj) ★★★ /'hæpi/
hard (adj) ★★★ /hɑːd/
intelligent (adj) ★★ /ɪn'telɪdʒ(ə)nt/
old (adj) ★★★ /əʊld/
outgoing (adj) /ˌaʊt'gəʊɪŋ/
skinny (adj) /'skɪni/
slim (adj) ★★ /slɪm/
sociable (adj) /'səʊʃəb(ə)l/

Other words and phrases

active (adj) ★★★ /'æktɪv/
actually (adv) ★★★ /'æktʃuəli/
annoy (v) /ə'nɔɪ/
apart from (prep) /ə'pɑːt frəm/
appointment (n) ★★★ /ə'pɔɪntmənt/
attach (v) ★ /ə'tætʃ/
avatar (n) /'ævəˌtɑː(r)/
barbarian (n) /bɑː'beəriən/
barrier (n) ★ /'bæriə/
believe (v) ★★★ /bɪ'liːv/
belt (n) ★ /belt/
bowler hat (n) /ˌbəʊlə 'hæt/
break down (= destroy) (v) /ˌbreɪk 'daʊn/
breathe (v) ★★ /briːð/
care about (v) /'keə(r) əˌbaʊt/
chips (n) /tʃɪps/
clear (adj) ★★★ /klɪə/
clutch (v) /klʌtʃ/
coast (n) ★★★ /kəʊst/
cold (adj) ★★★ /kəʊld/
confident (adj) ★★★ /'kɒnfɪdənt/
count on (v) /'kaʊnt ɒn/
curry (n) /'kʌri/
decade (n) ★★★ /'dekeɪd/
delicious (adj) ★ /dɪ'lɪʃəs/
deny (v) ★★★ /dɪ'naɪ/
descent (n) /dɪ'sent/
dish (n) ★★ /dɪʃ/
(= e.g. a Spanish dish)
downstairs (n) /ˌdaʊn'steəz/
dressing gown (n) /'dresɪŋ ˌgaʊn/
face (n) ★★★ /feɪs/
fast food (n) ★ /fɑːst 'fuːd/
feel (v) ★★★ /fiːl/
frightening (adj) ★ /'fraɪt(ə)nɪŋ/
great (adj) ★★★ /greɪt/
guess (v) ★★ /ges/
handkerchief (n) /'hæŋkəˌtʃɪf/
hope (v) ★★★ /həʊp/
horrible (adj) ★ /'hɒrəb(ə)l/
housework (n) /'haʊsˌwɜːk/
hungry (adj) ★ /'hʌŋgri/
icon (n) /'aɪkɒn/
interested in (adj) /'ɪntrəstɪd ˌɪn/

interrupt (v) ★	/ˌɪntəˈrʌpt/
item (of clothing) (n) ★★★	/ˈaɪtəm/
kind (adj) ★	/kaɪnd/
lifestyle (n)	/ˈlaɪfˌstaɪl/
look (v) ★★★	/lʊk/
look like (somebody) (v)	/ˈlʊk ˌlaɪk/
loud (adj) ★★	/laʊd/
luxury (n)	/ˈlʌkʃəri/
mad about (v)	/ˈmæd əˌbaʊt/
married (adj) ★★★	/ˈmærid/
mix (n)	/mɪks/
move (move house) (v) ★★★	/muːv/
muscular dystrophy (n)	/ˌmʌskjələ(r) ˈdɪstrəfi/
nowadays (adv) ★★	/ˈnaʊəˌdeɪz/
occasionally (adv) ★★	/əˈkeɪʒ(ə)nli/
opposite (n) (= black is the opposite of white)	/ˈɒpəzɪt/
own (v) ★★★	/əʊn/
portrait (n) ★	/ˈpɔːtrɪt/
product (n) ★★★	/ˈprɒdʌkt/
quality (n) ★★★	/ˈkwɒləti/
representation (n)	/ˌreprɪzenˈteɪʃ(ə)n/
roast beef (n)	/rəʊst ˈbiːf/
sell (v) ★★★	/sel/
show (v) ★★★	/ʃəʊ/
side (= aspect) (n) ★★★	/saɪd/
smart (= elegant) (adj) ★	/smɑːt/
smell (v) ★	/smel/
snore (v)	/snɔː/
soft (adj) ★★★	/sɒft/
soldier (n) ★★	/ˈsəʊldʒə(r)/
sort (= type) (n) ★★★	/sɔːt/
sound (v) ★★★	/saʊnd/
sound like (v)	/ˈsaʊnd ˌlaɪk/
spectacular (adj)	/spekˈtækjʊlə/
status symbol (n)	/ˈsteɪtəs ˌsɪmbəl/
struggle (v) ★	/ˈstrʌg(ə)l/
taste (v) ★★	/teɪst/
thoughtlessly (adv)	/ˈθɔːtləsli/
tie (n) ★	/taɪ/
trainers (n)	/ˈtreɪnəz/
treat (v) ★★★	/triːt/
turn (n) ★★★	/tɜːn/
ultimate (adj)	/ˈʌltɪmət/
umbrella (n)	/ʌmˈbrelə/
vote (v) ★★★	/vəʊt/
warm (adj) ★★★	/wɔːm/
wet (adj) ★★★	/wet/
whether (conj) ★★★	/ˈweðə/
wife (n) ★★★	/waɪf/

Unit 2

Travel and transport

arrivals (n)	/əˈraɪv(ə)lz/
cancel (v)	/ˈkæns(ə)l/
catch (v) ★★★	/kætʃ/
coach (n) ★	/kəʊtʃ/
delay (n) ★★	/dɪˈleɪ/
departures (n)	/dɪˈpɑː(r)tʃə(r)z/
fare (n)	/feə/
ferry (n)	/ˈferi/
hot-air balloon (n)	/hɒtˈeə bəˌluːn/
lorry (n)	/ˈlɒri/
luggage (n)	/ˈlʌgɪdʒ/
miss (v) ★★★	/mɪs/
motorbike (n)	/ˈməʊtəˌbaɪk/
platform (n) ★	/ˈplætˌfɔːm/
return (n) ★★★	/rɪˈtɜːn/
rocket (n)	/ˈrɒkɪt/
single (n)	/ˈsɪŋg(ə)l/
spaceship (n)	/ˈspeɪsˌʃɪp/
ticket office (n)	/ˈtɪkɪt ˌɒfɪs/
van (n) ★	/væn/
yacht (n)	/jɒt/

Accommodation

bed and breakfast (n)	/ˌbed ənd ˈbrekfəst/
campsite (n)	/ˈkæmpˌsaɪt/
caravan (n)	/ˈkærəˌvæn/
hotel (n) ★★★	/həʊˈtel/
motel (n)	/məʊˈtel/
tent (n)	/tent/
youth hostel (n)	/ˈjuːθ ˌhɒst(ə)l/

Phrasal verbs connected with travel

break down (v)	/ˌbreɪk ˈdaʊn/
check in (v)	/ˌtʃek ˈɪn/
get away (v)	/ˌget əˈweɪ/
get in (v)	/ˌget ˈɪn/
get into/out of (v)	/ˌget ˈɪntu/, /ˈaʊt əv/
get on/off (v)	/ˌget ˈɒn/, /ˈɒf /
set off (v)	/ˌset ˈɒf/
take off (v)	/ˌteɪk ˈɒf/

Other words and phrases

accident (n) ★★★	/ˈæksɪd(ə)nt/
against (prep) ★★★	/əˈgenst/
alternative (n) ★★	/ɔːlˈtɜːnətɪv/
at least (phrase)	/ət ˈliːst/
bill (n) ★★★	/bɪl/
bridge (n) ★★	/brɪdʒ/
cash (n) ★★★	/kæʃ/
challenge (n) ★★	/ˈtʃælɪndʒ/
choice (n) ★★★	/tʃɔɪs/
choose (v) ★★★	/tʃuːz/
connection (n) ★★★ (= travel connection)	/kəˈnekʃ(ə)n/
credit card (n) ★★	/ˈkredɪt kɑːd/
current (n)	/ˈkʌrənt/
deserted (adj)	/dɪˈzɜːtɪd/
destination (n) ★	/ˌdestɪˈneɪʃ(ə)n/
drop (v) ★★★	/drɒp/
emperor (n)	/ˈemp(ə)rə/
end up (v)	/ˌend ˈʌp/
engine (n) ★★★	/ˈendʒɪn/
entertainment (n) ★★	/ˌentəˈteɪnmənt/
exaggerate (v) ★	/ɪgˈzædʒəˌreɪt/
exceptionally (adv)	/ɪkˈsepʃ(ə)nəli/
exhausting (adj)	/ɪgˈzɔːstɪŋ/
expedition (n)	/ˌekspəˈdɪʃ(ə)n/
experience (n) ★★★	/ɪkˈspɪəriəns/
fill (v) ★★★	/fɪl/
first class (adj) ★	/fɜːst/
fortunate (adj)	/ˈfɔːtʃənət/
gold (n) ★★	/gəʊld/
ground (n) ★★★	/graʊnd/
grow up (v)	/grəʊ ˈʌp/
gun (n) ★★★	/gʌn/
hard (= difficult) (adj) ★★★	/hɑːd/
huge (adj) ★★★	/hjuːdʒ/

hurricane (n)	/'hʌrɪkən, 'hʌrɪkeɪn/
iceberg (n)	/'aɪsˌbɜːg/
immediately (adv) ★★★	/ɪ'miːdiətli/
inland (n) ★	/'ɪnlənd/
instead (adv) ★★★	/ɪn'sted/
kayak (n)	/'kaɪæk/
keep doing (something) (v)	/ˌkiːp 'duːɪŋ/
knock somebody out (v)	/ˌnɒk sʌmbədi 'aʊt/
lie (n) ★★	/laɪ/
line (= rope) (n) ★★★	/laɪn/
luckily (adv)	/'lʌkɪli/
means (of transport) (n) ★★★	/miːnz/
monsoon (n)	/mɒn'suːn/
occasion (n) ★★★	/ə'keɪʒ(ə)n/
on top of (adj)	/ˌɒn 'tɒp əv/
packet (n) ★	/'pækɪt/
pass (= an exam) (v) ★★★	/pɑːs/
pedalo (n)	/'ped(ə)ləʊ/
pedal-powered (adj)	/'ped(ə)l ˌpaʊəd/
pepper (n)	/'pepə/
pick up (v)	/pɪk 'ʌp/
postal service (n)	/'pəʊstl ˌsɜːvɪs/
pour in (v)	/ˌpɔː(r) 'ɪn/
pull (n)	/pʊl/
pull (v) ★★★	/pʊl/
push (v) ★★★	/pʊʃ/
raft (n)	/rɑːft/
realise (v) ★★★	/'rɪəˌlaɪz/
replace (v) ★★★	/rɪ'pleɪs/
rescue (n) ★	/'reskjuː/
Rollerblade (n)	/'rəʊlə(r)ˌbleɪd/
rotate (v)	/rəʊ'teɪt/
scared (adj) ★	/skeəd/
screen (n & v) ★★	/skriːn/
set fire to (v)	/ˌset 'faɪə tu/
single-handed (adj)	/ˌsɪŋg(ə)l 'hændɪd/
smoke (n) ★★	/sməʊk/
solo (adj)	/'səʊləʊ/
space (= room to move) (n) ★★★	/speɪs/
standard (adj) ★★★ (for ticket/fare)	/'stændəd/
station (n) ★★★	/'steɪʃ(ə)n/
steal, stole (v) ★★	/stiːl, stəʊl/
storm (n) ★★	/stɔːm/
strength (n) ★★★	/streŋθ/
suddenly (adv) ★★★	/'sʌd(ə)nli/
suit (n) ★★ (= costume, uniform – survival suit)	/suːt/
terrifying (adj)	/'terəˌfaɪɪŋ/
thrill (n)	/θrɪl/
throw, threw (v) ★★★	/θrəʊ, θruː/
trip (n) ★★	/trɪp/
typhoon (n)	/ˌtaɪ'fuːn/
unicorn (n)	/'juːnɪˌkɔːn/
unlock (v)	/ʌn'lɒk/
vehicle (n) ★★★	/'viːɪk(ə)l/
wave (= sea) (n) ★★	/weɪv/
wish (v) ★★★	/wɪʃ/

Gateway to exams, Units 1–2

attach (v) ★	/ə'tætʃ/
book (v) ★	/bʊk/
channel (n) ★★	/'tʃæn(ə)l/
cheap (adj) ★★★	/tʃiːp/
collect (v) ★★★	/kə'lekt/
form (n) ★★★ (a paper you fill in)	/fɔːm/
in advance (phrase)	/ˌɪn əd'vɑːns/
involve (v) ★★★	/ɪn'vɒlv/
major (adj) ★★★	/'meɪdʒə/
route (n) ★★	/ruːt/
ruin (v)	/'ruːɪn/
scenic (adj)	/'siːnɪk/
underground (n) ★	/'ʌndə(r)ˌgraʊnd/

Unit 3

Cities and houses

block of flats (n)	/ˌblɒk əv 'flæts/
bungalow (n)	/'bʌŋgəˌləʊ/
city centre (n)	/ˌsɪti 'sentə/
cottage (n) ★	/'kɒtɪdʒ/
detached house (n)	/dɪˌtætʃt 'haʊs/
factory (n) ★★★	/'fæktri/
flat (n) ★★	/flæt/
inner city (n) ★	/ˌɪnə 'sɪti/
port (n) ★★	/pɔːt/
semi-detached house (n)	/ˌsemidɪtætʃt 'haʊs/
skyscraper (n)	/'skaɪˌskreɪpə/
square (n) ★★★	/skweə/
suburbs (n)	/'sʌbɜːbz/
terraced house (n)	/ˌterəst 'haʊs/
town hall (n)	/ˌtaʊn 'hɔːl/

Adjectives describing cities

busy (adj) ★★★	/'bɪzi/
crowded (adj) ★	/'kraʊdɪd/
dirty (adj) ★★★	/'dɜːti/
historic (adj)	/hɪ'stɒrɪk/
lively (adj)	/'laɪvli/
noisy (adj) ★	/'nɔɪzi/

Extreme adjectives

ancient (adj) ★★	/'eɪnʃ(ə)nt/
boiling (adj)	/'bɔɪlɪŋ/
dreadful (adj)	/'dredf(ə)l/
enormous (adj) ★★	/ɪ'nɔːməs/
filthy (adj)	/'fɪlθi/
freezing (adj)	/'friːzɪŋ/
packed (adj)	/pækt/
silent (adj) ★★	/'saɪlənt/
stunning (adj)	/'stʌnɪŋ/
tiny (adj) ★★	/'taɪni/

Other words and phrases

aim (n) ★★★	/eɪm/
attract (v) ★★	/ə'trækt/
attraction (= place to visit) (n)	/ə'trækʃ(ə)n/
benefit from (v)	/'benəfɪt frɒm/
board (transport) (v)	/bɔːd/
bunch up (v)	/ˌbʌntʃ 'ʌp/
canal (n)	/kə'næl/
capsule (n)	/'kæpsjuːl/
castle (n) ★★	/'kɑːs(ə)l/
commuter (n)	/kə'mjuːtə/
contribute (v) ★★★	/kən'trɪbjuːt/
convenience (n)	/kən'viːniəns/
countryside (n) ★★	/'kʌntriˌsaɪd/
customer (n) ★★★	/'kʌstəmə/

dock (n) /dɒk/
due to (adj) ★★★ /'djuː tə/
(= time, due to arrive)
entry (n) ★★★ /'entri/
exhibition (n) ★★ /ˌeksɪ'bɪʃ(ə)n/
fee (n) ★★ /fiː/
flight (n) ★★★ /flaɪt/
grass (n) ★★★ /grɑːs/
have a good time (v) /ˌhæv ə gʊd 'taɪm/
hometown (n) /'həʊmtaʊn/
hurt (v) ★★★ /hɜːt/
insurance (n) ★★★ /ɪn'ʃʊərəns/
land (v) ★★ /lænd/
leaflet (n) /'liːflət/
mile (n) ★★★ /maɪl/
nearby (adj) /ˌnɪə'baɪ/
or so (adv) /ɔː 'səʊ/
(= more or less, 20 or so)
orbit (n) /'ɔː(r)bɪt/
paradise (n) /'pærədaɪs/
path (n) ★★★ /pɑːθ/
pioneer (n) /ˌpaɪə'nɪə/
price (n) ★★★ /praɪs/
property (n) ★★★ /'prɒpəti/
pull down (v) /pʊl 'daʊn/
race track (n) /'reɪs ˌtræk/
rent (v) ★ /rent/
satellite (town) (n) ★ /'sætəˌlaɪt/
save (time and money) (v) ★★★ /seɪv/
sealed (adj) ★ /siːld/
shadow (n) ★★ /'ʃædəʊ/
sightseeing (n) /'saɪtˌsiːɪŋ/
sleeve (n) /sliːv/
souvenir (n) /ˌsuːvə'nɪə/
stadium (n) /'steɪdiəm/
stranger (n) ★ /'streɪndʒə/
switch off (v) /ˌswɪtʃ 'ɒf/
telephone box (n) /'telɪfəʊn ˌbɒks/
theme park (n) /'θiːm pɑːk/
track (v) /træk/
unique (adj) ★ /juː'niːk/
usage (n) /'juːsɪdʒ/
valid (adj) ★ /'vælɪd/
value (n) ★★★ /'væljuː/
vanish (v) ★ /'vænɪʃ/
village (n) ★★★ /'vɪlɪdʒ/
wave (v) ★★ /weɪv/
wheel (n) ★★★ /wiːl/
without (prep) ★★★ /wɪð'aʊt/

Unit 4

Food

bakery products (n) /'beɪkəri ˌprɒdʌkts/
bread (n) ★★★ /bred/
chewing gum (n) /'tʃuːɪŋ ˌgʌm/
chicken (n) ★★ /'tʃɪkɪn/
chips (n) ★★ /tʃɪps/
corn (n) /kɔːn/
dairy products (n) /'deəri ˌprɒdʌkts/
dessert (n) ★ /dɪ'zɜːt/
doughnut (n) /'dəʊˌnʌt/
fish (n) ★★★ /fɪʃ/
fruit (n) ★★★ /fruːt/
main course (n) /meɪn 'kɔːs/
meat (n) ★★★ /miːt/
oil (n) ★★★ /ɔɪl/
pea (n) /piː/
pie (n) /paɪ/
plum (n) /plʌm/
seafood (n) /'siːˌfuːd/
semi-skimmed milk (n) /ˌsemi skɪmd 'mɪlk/
snack (n) /snæk/
starter (n) /'stɑːtə/
strawberry (n) /'strɔːb(ə)ri/
sweets (n) /swiːts/
tuna (n) /'tjuːnə/
turkey (n) /'tɜːki/
vegetables (n) ★★★ /'vedʒtəb(ə)lz/

Describing food

fresh (adj) ★★★ /freʃ/
fried (adj) /fraɪd/
frozen (adj) ★ /'frəʊz(ə)n/
healthy (adj) ★★ /'helθi/
junk (adj) ★ /dʒʌŋk/
raw (adj) ★ /rɔː/
spicy (adj) /'spaɪsi/
stale (adj) /steɪl/
sweet (adj) ★★ /swiːt/
tasty (adj) /'teɪsti/
vegetarian (adj) /ˌvedʒə'teəriən/

Prefixes

cooperate (v) /kəʊ'ɒpəˌreɪt/
disadvantage (n) ★ /ˌdɪsəd'vɑːntɪdʒ/
international (adj) ★★★ /ˌɪntə'næʃ(ə)nəl/
misunderstand (v) /ˌmɪsʌndə'stænd/
overbook (v) /ˌəʊvə(r)'bʊk/
overcooked (adj) /ˌəʊvə(r)'kʊkt/
precooked (adj) /ˌpriː'kʊkt/
recooked (adj) /ˌriː'kʊkt/
redo (v) /ˌriː'duː/
undercooked (adj) /ˌʌndə(r)'kʊkt/
underestimate (v) /ˌʌndər'estɪmeɪt/

Other words and phrases

activate (v) /'æktɪˌveɪt/
astronaut (n) /'æstrəˌnɔːt/
atmosphere (n) ★★ /'ætməsˌfɪə/
burn (v) ★★★ /bɜːn/
canteen (n) /kæn'tiːn/
century (n) ★★★ /'sentʃəri/
ceremony (n) ★ /'serəməni/
channel (TV) (n) ★★ /'tʃæn(ə)l/
crop (n) ★ /krɒp/
cure (n) ★ /kjʊə/
custom (n) ★★ /'kʌstəm/
department store (n) ★★ /dɪ'pɑːtmənt stɔː/
dry (adj) ★★★ /draɪ/
economic growth (n) /'iːkənɒmɪk 'grəʊθ/
election (n) ★★★ /ɪ'lekʃ(ə)n/
fancy (v) /'fænsi/
(= do you fancy coming?)
flavour (n) ★ /'fleɪvə/
harvest (n) /'hɑːvɪst/
illness (n) ★★★ /'ɪlnəs/
improve (v) ★★★ /ɪm'pruːv/
innocent (adj) ★ /'ɪnəs(ə)nt/
manage (v) ★★★ /'mænɪdʒ/
(to do something)

matter (n) ★★★ /'mætə/
microwave (n) /'maɪkrəˌweɪv/
molecular (adj) /mə'lekjʊlə/
multinational (adj) /ˌmʌlti'næʃ(ə)nəl/
nanotechnology (n) /'nænəʊtekˌnɒlədʒi/
nutrient (n) /'nju:triənt/
obese (adj) /əʊ'bi:s/
optimistic (adj) /ˌɒptɪ'mɪstɪk/
order (food) (v) ★★★ /'ɔ:də/
oven (n) ★ /'ʌv(ə)n/
parade (n) /pə'reɪd/
pessimistic (adj) /ˌpesə'mɪstɪk/
pick (fruit) (v) ★★★ /pɪk/
powder (n) ★ /'paʊdə/
present (adj) ★★★ /'prez(ə)nt/
present (gift) (n) ★★★ /'prez(ə)nt/
preserved (adj) /ˌprɪ'zɜ:vd/
pumpkin (n) /'pʌmpkɪn/
reception (n) ★ /rɪ'sepʃ(ə)n/
risk (n) ★★★ /rɪsk/
role (n) ★★★ /rəʊl/
scale (n) ★★★ /skeɪl/
share (v) ★★★ /ʃeə/
stripe (n) /straɪp/
substance (n) ★★★ /'sʌbstəns/
taste (n) ★★★ /teɪst/
tiny (adj) ★★ /'taɪni/
transmitter (n) /trænz'mɪtə/
transparent (adj) /træns'pærənt/
waiter (n) /'weɪtə/
wedding (n) ★★ /'wedɪŋ/
width (n) /wɪdθ/

Gateway to exams, Units 3–4

absurd (adj) /əb'sɜ:d/
alpine (adj) /'ælpaɪn/
biotech (n) /'baɪəʊtek/
cancer (n) ★ /'kænsə/
fragile (adj) /'frædʒaɪl/
gene (n) /dʒi:n/
genetic engineering (n) /dʒəˌnetɪk endzɪ'nɪərɪŋ/
genetically-modified (adj) /dʒəˌnetɪkli 'mɒdɪfaɪd/
inhuman (adj) /ɪn'hju:mən/
jumper (n) /'dʒʌmpə/
organic (adj) ★ /ɔ:'gænɪk/
organism (n) /'ɔ:gəˌnɪz(ə)m/
species (n) ★★ /'spi:ʃi:z/
stick (v) ★★★ /stɪk/
underwear (n) /'ʌndəˌweə/

Unit 5

School and university subjects

art (n) ★★★ /ɑ:t/
biology (n) /baɪ'ɒlədʒi/
business studies (n) /'bɪznɪs stʌdiz/
chemistry (n) /'kemɪstri/
drama (n) ★ /'drɑ:mə/
engineering (n) ★ /ˌendʒɪ'nɪərɪŋ/
English (n) /'ɪŋglɪʃ/
geography (n) /dʒi:'ɒgrəfi/
history (n) ★★★ /'hɪst(ə)ri/
information and communication technology (ICT) (n) /ˌaɪ si: 'ti:/
law (n) ★★★ /lɔ:/
literature (n) ★★ /'lɪtrətʃə/
maths (n) /mæθs/
media studies (n) /'mi:diə ˌstʌdiz/
medicine (n) ★★ /'med(ə)s(ə)n/
music (n) ★★★ /'mju:zɪk/
physical education (PE) (n) /ˌpi: 'i:/
physics (n) ★ /'fɪzɪks/
psychology (n) ★ /saɪ'kɒlədʒi/

Words connected with school and university

certificate (n) ★★ /sə'tɪfɪkət/
cheat (v) ★ /tʃi:t/
coursework (n) /'kɔ:sˌwɜ:k/
essay (n) ★ /'eseɪ/
fail (v) ★★★ /feɪl/
grade (n) ★ /greɪd/
mark (n) ★★★ /mɑ:k/
pass (v) ★★★ /pɑ:s/
resit (v) /ˌri:'sɪt/
term (n) ★★★ /tɜ:m/
timetable (n) /'taɪmˌteɪb(ə)l/

Noun suffixes *-er, -or, -ist, -ian, -ee*

director (n) ★★★ /də'rektə, daɪ'rektə/
electrician (n) /ɪˌlek'trɪʃ(ə)n/
employee (n) ★★ /ɪm'plɔɪi:, ˌemplɔɪ'i:/
employer (n) ★★ /ɪm'plɔɪə/
historian (n) /hɪ'stɔ:riən/
instructor (n) /ɪn'strʌktə/
journalist (n) ★★ /'dʒɜ:nəlɪst/
lecturer (n) /'lektʃərə/
photographer (n) /fə'tɒgrəfə/
physicist (n) /'fɪzɪsɪst/
professor (n) ★ /prə'fesə/
scientist (n) ★★ /'saɪəntɪst/
technician (n) /tek'nɪʃ(ə)n/
trainee (n) /ˌtreɪ'ni:/

Other words and phrases

according to (prep) ★★★ /ə'kɔ:dɪŋ ˌtu:/
applicant (n) /'æplɪkənt/
application (n) ★★ /ˌæplɪ'keɪʃ(ə)n/
assessment (n) ★★ /ə'sesmənt/
attend (v) ★★ /ə'tend/
available (adj) ★★ /ə'veɪləb(ə)l/
average (adj) ★★ /'æv(ə)rɪdʒ/
candidate (n) ★ /'kændɪˌdeɪt, 'kændɪdət/
career (n) ★★ /kə'rɪə/
childcare (n) /'tʃaɪldˌkeə/
choir (n) /kwaɪə/
come up (= arise) (v) /ˌkʌm 'ʌp/
course (n) ★★★ /kɔ:s/
dedicated to (adj) /'dedɪkeɪtɪd tə/
disability (n) /ˌdɪsə'bɪləti/
discrimination (n) ★ /dɪˌskrɪmɪ'neɪʃ(ə)n/
emphasis (n) ★★ /'emfəsɪs/
empty (adj) ★★★ /'empti/
evaluate (v) /ɪ'væljuˌeɪt/
extracurricular activities (n) /ˌekstrəkərɪkjələ(r) æk'tɪvətiz/
finances (n) /'faɪnænsɪz/
foreground (n) /'fɔ:ˌgraʊnd/
freedom (n) ★★★ /'fri:dəm/
graduation (n) /ˌgrædʒu'eɪʃ(ə)n/
grateful (adj) ★ /'greɪtf(ə)l/
hand in (v) /ˌhænd 'ɪn/
health care (n) /'helθ ˌkeə(r)/

ID (n) /ˌaɪ'diː/
increase (v) ★★★ /'ɪŋkriːs/
independence (n) ★★ /ˌɪndɪ'pendəns/
leader (n) ★★★ /'liːdə/
lesson (n) ★★★ /'les(ə)n/
look after (v) /ˌlʊk 'ɑːftə/
make-up (n) ★ /'meɪkʌp/
Martian (n) /'mɑːʃ(ə)n/
maturity (n) /mə'tʃʊərəti/
moped (n) /'məʊˌped/
nervous (adj) ★★ /'nɜːvəs/
nursery school (n) /'nɜːs(ə)ri ˌskuːl/
participate (v) /pɑː'tɪsɪˌpeɪt/
previous (adj) ★★★ /'priːviəs/
primary school (n) ★ /praɪ'məri ˌskuːl/
priority (n) ★★ /praɪ'ɒrəti/
psychological (adj) ★ /ˌsaɪkə'lɒdʒɪk(ə)l/
raise (= money) (v) /reɪz/
reasonable (adj) ★★ /'riːz(ə)nəb(ə)l/
regulation (n) ★★ /ˌregjʊ'leɪʃ(ə)n/
responsibility (n) ★★★ /rɪˌspɒnsə'bɪləti/
scholarship (n) /'skɒləʃɪp/
seat belt (n) /'siːtbelt/
secondary school (n) /'sekənd(ə)ri ˌskuːl/
self-motivation (n) /ˌselfməʊtə'veɪʃ(ə)n/
sensible (adj) ★ /'sensəb(ə)l/
spare time (n) ★ /ˌspeə(r) 'taɪm/
speed limit (n) /'spiːd ˌlɪmɪt/
staff (n) ★★★ /stɑːf/
stand on your own two feet (v) /ˌstænd ɒn jɔː(r) əʊn tuː 'fiːt/
starting point (n) /'stɑːtɪŋ ˌpɔɪnt/
successfully (adv) /ˌsək'sesfʊli/
time management (n) /'taɪm ˌmænɪdʒmənt/
unfair (adj) ★ /ʌn'feə/
unfit (adj) /ʌn'fɪt/
uniform (n) ★★ /'juːnɪˌfɔːm/
visually impaired (adj) /ˌvɪʒʊəli im'peəd/

Unit 6

Everyday inventions

camcorder (n) /'kæmˌkɔːdə/
digital camera (n) /ˌdɪdʒɪtl 'kæmrə/
dishwasher (n) /'dɪʃˌwɒʃə/
DVD player (n) /ˌdiːviː'diː pleɪə/
home cinema system (n) /həʊm 'sɪnəmə ˌsɪstəm/
laptop (n) /'læpˌtɒp/
microwave oven (n) /'maɪkrəˌweɪv ʌvən/
mobile phone (n) ★★ /ˌməʊbaɪl 'fəʊn/
MP3 player (n) /ˌem piː 'θriː pleɪə/
remote control (n) ★ /rɪˌməʊt kən'trəʊl/
satnav (n) /'sætˌnæv/
vacuum cleaner (n) /'vækjuːm ˌkliːnə/
washing machine (n) ★ /'wɒʃɪŋ məˌʃiːn/

Operating technology

charge/recharge (a battery) (v) /tʃɑːdʒ, riː'tʃɑːdʒ/
connect (v) ★★★ /kə'nekt/
insert (v) /ɪn'sɜːt/
plug in (v) /plʌg 'ɪn/
press (a button) (v) ★★★ /pres/
select (v) ★ /sɪ'lekt/
(a programme/a track/a function)
switch/turn on (v) /swɪtʃ, tɜːn 'ɒn/
switch/turn off (v) /swɪtʃ, tɜːn 'ɒf/

Prepositional phrases with adjectives

afraid of (adj) /ə'freɪd əv/
aware of (adj) /ə'weə(r) əv/
bored with (adj) /'bɔːd wɪð/
different from (adj) /'dɪfrənt frəm/
good at (adj) /'gʊd ət/
interested in (adj) /'ɪntrəstɪd ɪn/
pleased with (adj) /'pliːzd wɪð/
ready for (adj) /'redi fə/
responsible for (adj) /rɪs'pɒnsəbl fə/
similar to (adj) /'sɪmɪlə tə/
tired of (adj) /'taɪəd əv/
worried about (adj) /'wʌrɪd əˌbaʊt/

Other words and phrases

acquire (v) /ə'kwaɪə/
addicted to (adj) /ə'dɪktɪd tu/
amateur (n) /'æmətə, 'æmətʃʊə/
antibiotics (n) /ˌæntibaɪ'ɒtɪks/
argue (v) ★★★ /'ɑːgjuː/
backwards (adv) ★★ /'bækwə(r)dz/
bin (n) /bɪn/
bowl (n) ★★ /bəʊl/
bug (= computer) (n) /bʌg/
carpet (n) ★★ /'kɑːpɪt/
correction fluid/tape (n) /kə'rekʃ(ə)n ˌfluːɪd, ˌteɪp/
cosmetics (n) /kɒz'metɪks/
crash (= of a computer) (v) ★ /kræʃ/
decorate (v) ★ /'dekəˌreɪt/
dynamite (n) /'daɪnəˌmaɪt/
error (n) ★★★ /'erə/
excrement (n) /'ekskrɪmənt/
eyesight (n) /'aɪsaɪt/
fatal (adj) ★ /'feɪt(ə)l/
file (= of a computer) (n) ★★★ /faɪl/
fingernail (n) /'fɪŋgəˌneɪl/
fragrance (n) /'freɪgrəns/
frown (v) /fraʊn/
get rid of (v) /ˌget 'rɪd əv/
global warming (n) /gləʊb(ə)l 'wɔːmɪŋ/
gossip (v) /'gɒsɪp/
guy (n) ★★ /gaɪ/
hairdresser's (n) /'heəˌdresəz/
heavy (adj) ★★★ /'hevi/
impatiently (adv) /ɪm'peɪʃ(ə)ntli/
input (n & v) /'ɪnpʊt/
journalist (n) ★★ /'dʒɜːnəlɪst/
launch (v) ★★ /lɔːntʃ/
malfunction (v) /mæl'fʌŋkʃ(ə)n/
messy (adj) /'mesi/
miracle (n) /'mɪrək(ə)l/
never-ending (adj) /'nevə(r)ˌendɪŋ/
nuclear reactor (n) /ˌnjuːkliːə ri'æktə/
oil tanker (n) /'ɔɪl ˌtæŋkə/
operating system (n) ★ /'ɒpəreɪtɪŋ ˌsɪstəm/
orbit (v) /'ɔːbɪt/
pigment (n) /'pɪgmənt/
play (n) ★★★ /pleɪ/
portable stereo (n) /ˌpɔːtəb(ə)l 'steriəʊ/
process (n) ★★★ /'prəʊses/
publish (v) ★★★ /'pʌblɪʃ/
rage (n) /reɪdʒ/
reckon (v) ★ /'rekən/
reinstall (v) /ˌriːɪn'stɔːl/
scientific (adj) ★★ /ˌsaɪən'tɪfɪk/
service (v) /'sɜːvɪs/

shape (n) ★★★ /ʃeɪp/
sore throat (n) /ˌsɔː 'θrəʊt/
swallow (v) ★ /'swɒləʊ/
sword (n) /sɔːd/
take care of (v) /ˌteɪk 'keə(r) əv/
X-ray machine (n) /'eksreɪ məˌsiːn/

Gateway to exams, Units 5–6

affairs (= global affairs) (n) /ə'feəz/
bionics (n) /baɪ'ɒnɪks/
blouse (n) /blaʊz/
bow tie (n) /ˌbəʊ 'taɪ/
dark (adj) ★★★ /dɑːk/
electrode (n) /ɪ'lektrəʊd/
explode (v) ★ /ɪk'spləʊd/
firework (n) /'faɪəwɜːk/
fit (v) ★★★ /fɪt/
(= fit something to something else)
Geiger counter (n) /'gaɪgə(r) ˌkaʊntə(r)/
gown (n) /gaʊn/
industrial (adj) ★★★ /ɪn'dʌstriəl/
mortarboard (n) /'mɔː(r)tə(r)ˌbɔː(r)d/
nerve (n) ★ /nɜːv/
radioactivity (n) /ˌreɪdiəʊæk'tɪvəti/
rebuild (v) /ˌriː'bɪld/
signal (n) ★★★ /'sɪgn(ə)l/
succeed (v) ★★★ /sək'siːd/
superhuman (adj) /ˌsuːpə'hjuːmən/
vibrant (adj) /'vaɪbrənt/

Unit 7

Sports

athletics (n) /æθ'letɪks/
basketball (n) /'bɑːskɪtˌbɔːl/
boxing (n) /'bɒksɪŋ/
diving (n) /'daɪvɪŋ/
football (n) ★★ /'fʊtbɔːl/
golf (n) ★ /gɒlf/
gymnastics (n) /dʒɪm'næstɪks/
ice hockey (n) /'aɪs ˌhɒki/
judo (n) /'dʒuːdəʊ/
sailing (n) /'seɪlɪŋ/
skiing (n) /'skiːɪŋ/
snowboarding (n) /'snəʊˌbɔːdɪŋ/
swimming (n) ★ /'swɪmɪŋ/
table tennis (n) /'teɪbl ˌtenɪs/
volleyball (n) /'vɒliˌbɔːl/
weightlifting (n) /'weɪtˌlɪftɪŋ/

Sports venues and equipment

boots (n) /buːts/
club (n) ★★★ /klʌb/
course (n) ★★★ /kɔːs/
court (n) ★★★ /kɔːt/
goal (n) ★★★ /gəʊl/
goggles (n) /'gɒg(ə)lz/
gym (n) /dʒɪm/
net (n) ★★ /net/
pitch (n) ★ /pɪtʃ/
pool (n) ★★ /puːl/
racket (n) /'rækɪt/
rink (n) /rɪŋk/
skates (n) /skeɪts/
skis (n) /skiːz/
slope (n) ★ /sləʊp/
track (n) ★★★ /træk/
trainers (n) /'treɪnəz/

Phrasal verbs connected with sport

give in (v) /ˌgɪv 'ɪn/
go for (v) /'gəʊ fə/
join in (v) /ˌdʒɔɪn 'ɪn/
knock out (v) /ˌnɒk 'aʊt/
take up (v) /ˌteɪk 'ʌp/
warm up (v) /ˌwɔːm 'ʌp/
work out (v) /ˌwɜːk 'aʊt/

Other words and phrases

acting (n) /'æktɪŋ/
amputate (v) /'æmpjʊˌteɪt/
artificial (adj) ★ /ˌɑːtɪ'fɪʃ(ə)l/
baggy (adj) /'bægi/
battle (n) ★★ /'bæt(ə)l/
bone (n) ★★ /bəʊn/
capture (v) ★★ /'kæptʃə/
championship (n) ★ /'tʃæmpiənʃɪp/
civilisation (n) /ˌsɪvəlaɪ'zeɪʃ(ə)n/
classify (v) /'klæsɪˌfaɪ/
clown (n) /klaʊn/
collapse (v) ★ /kə'læps/
congenital (adj) /kən'dʒenɪt(ə)l/
dehydration (n) /ˌdiːhaɪ'dreɪʃ(ə)n/
eliminate (v) /ɪ'lɪmɪˌneɪt/
emotional (adj) ★★ /ɪ'məʊʃ(ə)nəl/
enormous (adj) ★★ /ɪ'nɔːməs/
fit (adj) ★ /fɪt/
glove (n) /glʌv/
goalkeeper (n) /'gəʊlˌkiːpə/
goaltender (n) /'gəʊlˌtendə/
guilty (adj) ★★ /'gɪltɪ/
happy ending (n) /ˌhæpi 'endɪŋ/
heart (n) ★★★ /hɑːt/
hilarious (adj) /hɪ'leəriəs/
immense (adj) /ɪ'mens/
impact (n) ★★★ /'ɪmpækt/
impact (v) /ɪm'pækt/
incidentally (adv) /ˌɪnsɪ'dent(ə)li/
injury (n) ★★★ /'ɪndʒəri/
jockey (n) /'dʒɒki/
knee (n) ★★★ /niː/
label (n) ★★ /'leɪb(ə)l/
likeable (adj) /'laɪkəb(ə)l/
love (= 0 in tennis) (n) ★★★ /lʌv/
lucky mascot (n) /ˌlʌki 'mæskɒt/
main character (n) /ˌmeɪn 'kærɪktə/
martial arts (n) /ˌmɑːʃ(ə)l 'ɑːts/
massive (adj) ★ /'mæsɪv/
muscle (n) ★★ /'mʌs(ə)l/
nickname (n) /'nɪkˌneɪm/
plain (= flat land) (n) /pleɪn/
play the role of (v) /ˌpleɪ ðə 'rəʊl əv/
plot (n) ★ /plɒt/
puck (n) /pʌk/
referee (n) /ˌrefə'riː/
resistant (adj) /rɪ'zɪst(ə)nt/
ritual (n) /'rɪtʃuəl/
round (n) ★★ /raʊnd/
(= in a boxing match)

scene (n) ★★★ /siːn/
screenplay (n) /'skriːnˌpleɪ/
servant (n) /'sɜːv(ə)nt/
serve (= in tennis) (v) ★★★ /sɜːv/
slave (n) /sleɪv/
soundtrack (n) /'saʊn(d)ˌtræk/
special effects (n) /ˌspeʃ(ə)l ɪ'fekts/
spectator (n) /spek'teɪtə/
star (v) ★★ /stɑː/
straight away (adv) /streɪt ə'weɪ/
superstition (n) /ˌsuːpə'stɪʃ(ə)n/
surrender (v) /sə'rendə/
synchronised swimming (n) /ˌsɪŋkrənaɪzd 'swɪmɪŋ/
teddy bear (n) /'tedi beə/
unconscious (adj) /ʌn'kɒnʃəs/
uninspiring (adj) /ˌʌnɪn'spaɪərɪŋ/
visibility (n) /ˌvɪzə'bɪləti/
visualise (v) /'vɪʒʊəˌlaɪz/
wheelchair (n) /'wiːlˌtʃeə/
whenever (conj) ★★ /wen'evə(r)/
wonder (v) ★★★ /'wʌndə/

Unit 8

Theatre, art, music

abstract painting (n) /ˌæbstrækt 'peɪntɪŋ/
audience (n) ★★★ /'ɔːdiəns/
cast (n) /kɑːst/
cast (v) ★ /kɑːst/
drawing (n) ★★ /'drɔːɪŋ/
exhibition (n) ★★ /ˌeksɪ'bɪʃ(ə)n/
gallery (n) /'gæləri/
gig (n) /gɪg/
landscape (n) /'læn(d)ˌskeɪp/
lighting (n) /'laɪtɪŋ/
lyrics (n) /'lɪrɪks/
masterpiece (n) /'mɑːstəˌpiːs/
orchestra (n) ★ /'ɔːkɪstrə/
performance (n) ★★★ /pə'fɔːməns/
play (n & v) ★★★ /pleɪ/
sculpture (n) /'skʌlptʃə/
(self-)portrait (n) ★ /'pɔːtrɪt/
sketch (n & v) /sketʃ/
stage (n & v) ★★★ /steɪdʒ/
still life (n) /ˌstɪl 'laɪf/
studio (n) ★★ /'stjuːdiəʊ/

Artists

actor (n) ★★★ /'æktə/
artist (n) ★★ /'ɑːtɪst/
composer (n) /kəm'pəʊzə/
conductor (n) /kən'dʌktə/
dancer (n) ★★ /'dɑːnsə(r)/
musician (n) ★ /mju'zɪʃ(ə)n/
painter (n) /'peɪntə/
performer (n) /pər'fɔːmə/
sculptor (n) /'skʌlptə/
singer-songwriter (n) /ˌsɪŋə'sɒŋraɪtə/

Adjectives ending in *-ing* and *-ed*

amazed (adj) /ə'meɪzd/
amazing (adj) ★ /ə'meɪzɪŋ/
bored (adj) ★★ /bɔːd/
boring (adj) ★★ /'bɔːrɪŋ/
confused (adj) ★ /kən'fjuːzd/
confusing (adj) ★ /kən'fjuːzɪŋ/
disappointed (adj) ★ /ˌdɪsə'pɔɪntɪd/
disappointing (adj) /ˌdɪsə'pɔɪntɪŋ/
disgusted (adj) /dɪs'gʌstɪd/
disgusting (adj) /dɪs'gʌstɪŋ/
embarrassed (adj) /ɪm'bærəst/
embarrassing (adj) ★ /ɪm'bærəsɪŋ/
excited (adj) ★★ /ɪk'saɪtɪd/
exciting (adj) ★★ /ɪk'saɪtɪŋ/
frightened (adj) ★ /'fraɪt(ə)nd/
frightening (adj) ★ /'fraɪt(ə)nɪŋ/
inspired (adj) /ɪn'spaɪəd/
inspiring (adj) /ɪn'spaɪərɪŋ/
interested (adj) ★★★ /'ɪntrəstɪd/
interesting (adj) ★★★ /'ɪntrəstɪŋ/
relaxed (adj) ★ /rɪ'lækst/
relaxing (adj) /rɪ'læksɪŋ/
surprised (adj) ★★ /sə'praɪzd/
surprising (adj) ★★ /sə'praɪzɪŋ/
tired (adj) ★★★ /'taɪəd/
tiring (adj) /'taɪərɪŋ/
uninspired (adj) /ˌʌnɪn'spaɪəd/
uninspiring (adj) /ˌʌnɪn'spaɪərɪŋ/

Other words and phrases

bagpipes (n) /'bægˌpaɪps/
balcony (n) /'bælkəni/
behave (v) ★★ /bɪ'heɪv/
Bodhran (n) /'bɒdrən/
bottomless (adj) /'bɒtəmləs/
brush (n) ★★ /brʌʃ/
burst into life (v) /'bɜːst ɪntə 'laɪf/
candy (n) /'kændi/
chieftain (n) /'tʃiːftən/
coin (n) ★★ /kɔɪn/
crack (n) ★ /kræk/
creep, crept (v) /kriːp, krept/
deep (n) ★★★ /diːp/
delicate (adj) /'delɪkət/
diameter (n) /daɪ'æmɪtə/
drum (n) ★ /drʌm/
emerald (n) /'em(ə)rəld/
emigrate (v) /'emɪgreɪt/
fiddle (= violin) (n) /'fɪd(ə)l/
harp (n) /hɑːp/
installation (n) /ˌɪnstə'leɪʃ(ə)n/
intricate (adj) /'ɪntrɪkət/
isle (n) /aɪl/
panic (v) /'pænɪk/
pile (n) ★ /paɪl/
plague (n) /pleɪg/
record (n) ★★★ /'rekɔː(r)d/
record (v) ★★★ /rɪ'kɔː(r)d/
renew (v) /rɪ'njuː/
restore (v) ★★ /rɪ'stɔː/
rhythm (n) ★ /'rɪðəm/
rubbish (n) ★ /'rʌbɪʃ/
scream (n) /skriːm/
single (= just one) (adj) ★★★ /'sɪŋg(ə)l/
slight (adj) ★★ /slaɪt/
slogan (n) /'sləʊgən/
splendid (adj) /'splendɪd/
stab (v) /stæb/
tap (n) ★ /tæp/
throw away (v) /ˌθrəʊ ə'weɪ/
Uilleann pipes (n) /wiːlən 'paɪps/

valuable (adj) ★★ /'væljub(ə)l/
voice (n) ★★★ /vɔɪs/
waste (n) ★★ /weɪst/
watercolour (n) /'wɔːtəˌkʌlə/
whisper (n) /'wɪspə/
wide (adj) ★★★ /waɪd/
worth (adj) ★★★ /wɜːθ/
(= it's worth X pounds)

Gateway to exams, Units 7–8

message (n) ★★★ /'mesɪdʒ/

Unit 9

Nations

capital city (n) /ˌkæpɪt(ə)l 'sɪti/
currency (n) ★★ /'kʌrənsi/
flag (n) /flæg/
king (n) ★★★ /kɪŋ/
national anthem (n) /ˌnæʃ(ə)nl 'ænθəm/
president (n) ★★★ /'prezɪdənt/
prime minister (n) ★★★ /ˌpraɪm 'mɪnɪstə/
prince (n) /prɪns/
princess (n) /ˌprɪn'ses/
queen (n) ★★★ /kwiːn/

State and politics

constitutional monarchy (n) /kɒnstɪˌtjuːʃən(ə)l 'mɒnəki/
democracy (n) ★★ /dɪ'mɒkrəsi/
foreign affairs (n) /ˌfɒrən ə'feəz/
general election (n) /ˌdʒenr(ə)l ɪ'lekʃən/
in the centre (adj) /ˌɪn ðə 'sentə/
left-wing (adj) ★ /'left ˌwɪŋ/
member (n) ★★★ /'membə/
minister (n) ★★ /'mɪnɪstə/
monarchy (n) /'mɒnəki/
political party (n) /pə'lɪtɪk(ə)l ˌpɑːti/
republic (n) ★ /rɪ'pʌblɪk/
right-wing (adj) ★ /'raɪt ˌwɪŋ/
run a country (v) /ˌrʌn ə 'kʌntri/

Adjective suffixes *-er, -or, -ist, -ian, -ee*

aristocratic (adj) /ˌærɪstə'krætɪk/
careful (adj) ★★★ /'keəf(ə)l/
careless (adj) ★ /'keələs/
comfortable (ad) ★★★ /'kʌmftəb(ə)l/
dangerous (adj) ★★★ /'deɪndʒərəs/
enjoyable (adj) /ɪn'dʒɔɪəb(ə)l/
famous (adj) ★★★ /'feɪməs/
helpful (adj) ★ /'helpf(ə)l/
helpless (adj) /'helpləs/
hungry (adj) ★ /'hʌŋgri/
mysterious (adj) /mɪ'stɪəriəs/
natural (adj) ★★★ /'nætʃ(ə)rəl/
official (adj) ★★★ /ə'fɪʃ(ə)l/
sensible (adj) ★ /'sensəb(ə)l/
terrible (adj) ★★ /'terəb(ə)l/
thirsty (adj) ★ /'θɜːsti/
uncomfortable (adj) ★ /ʌn'kʌmftəb(ə)l/
useful (adj) ★★★ /'juːsf(ə)l/
useless (adj) /'juːsləs/

Other words and phrases

assassin (n) /ə'sæsɪn/
assassination (n) /əˌsæsɪ'neɪʃ(ə)n/
asteroid (n) /'æstəˌrɔɪd/
bell (n) ★★ /bel/
belong to (adj) /bɪ'lɒŋ tə/
bullet (n) ★ /'bʊlɪt/
captor (n) /'kæptə/
caress (v) /kə'res/
clockmaker (n) /'klɒkmeɪkə/
colonise (v) /'kɒləˌnaɪz/
colony (n) /'kɒləni/
commonwealth (n) /'kɒmənˌwelθ/
conspiracy (n) /kən'spɪrəsi/
constellation (n) /ˌkɒnstə'leɪʃ(ə)n/
convince (v) ★★ /kən'vɪns/
dare (v) ★★ /deə/
descendant (n) /dɪ'sendənt/
elaborate (adj) /ɪ'læb(ə)rət/
empire (n) ★ /'empaɪə/
equal (adj, n & v) ★★★ /'iːkwəl/
escape (v) ★★ /ɪ'skeɪp/
evidence (n) ★★★ /'evɪd(ə)ns/
evolve (v) /ɪ'vɒlv/
federation (n) /ˌfedə'reɪʃ(ə)n/
fixed (adj) ★ /fɪkst/
force (n) ★★★ /fɔːs/
friendship (n) ★ /'fren(d)ʃɪp/
gain (v) ★★★ /geɪn/
govern (v) ★ /'gʌv(ə)n/
gradually (adv) ★★ /'grædʒuəli/
gravity (n) /'grævəti/
guard (n) ★★ /gɑːd/
head of state (n) /ˌhed əv 'steɪt/
hip (n) /hɪp/
hire (v) ★ /'haɪə/
hit (v) ★★★ /hɪt/
human rights (n) ★ /ˌhjuːmən 'raɪts/
hunger (n) /'hʌŋgə/
imprison (v) /ɪm'prɪz(ə)n/
in charge of (phrase) /ɪn 'tʃɑːdʒ əv/
infant (n) /'ɪnfənt/
influential (adj) /ˌɪnflu'enʃ(ə)l/
insult (v) ★ /ɪn'sʌlt/
lifeboat (n) /'laɪfˌbəʊt/
mansion (n) /'mænʃ(ə)n/
mass (= land mass) (n) ★★ /mæs/
narrator (n) /nə'reɪtə/
nightmare (n) /'naɪtˌmeə/
nod (v) ★ /nɒd/
operation (n) ★★★ /ˌɒpə'reɪʃ(ə)n/
ornate (adj) /ɔː'neɪt/
passenger (n) ★★ /'pæsɪndʒə/
pillar (n) /'pɪlə//
power (n) ★★★ /'paʊə/
powerful (adj) ★★★ /'paʊəf(ə)l/
preserve (v) ★ /prɪ'zɜːv/
principle (n) ★★★ /'prɪnsəp(ə)l/
profitable (adj) /'prɒfɪtəb(ə)l/
relative (n) ★ /'relətɪv/
roast (v) /rəʊst/
rule (v) ★★ /ruːl/
rumour (n) /'ruːmə/
scream (v) ★ /skriːm/
senior (adj) ★ /'siːniə/
set (= a set of rules) (n) ★★★ /set/
settle (v) ★★★ /'set(ə)l/
shabby (adj) /'ʃæbi/
sign (= road sign) (n) ★★★ /saɪn/

sink, sank (v) ★★ /sɪŋk, sæŋk/
stained (= of glass) (adj) /steɪnd/
strip (of tape) (n) ★ /strɪp/
sway (v) /sweɪ/
tape (n) ★★ /teɪp/
theory (n) ★★ /'θɪəri/
torture (v) /'tɔːtʃə/
trade (n) ★★★ /treɪd/
trunk (= suitcase) (n) /trʌŋk/
tuberculosis (n) /tjuːˌbɜːkjʊ'ləʊsɪs/
twist (v) ★ /twɪst/
uncrowned (adj) /ʌn'kraʊnd/
union (n) ★★ /'juːnjən/
unity (n) /'juːnəti/

Unit 10

Shops

bakery (n) /'beɪkəri/
bank (n) /bæŋk/
butcher's (n) /'bʊtʃəz/
chemist's (n) /'kemɪsts/
clothes shop (n) /'kləʊðz ˌʃɒp/
department store (n) ★★ /dɪ'pɑːtmənt ˌstɔː/
electrical goods store (n) /ɪ'lektrɪkl gudz ˌstɔː/
greengrocer's (n) /'griːngrəʊsəz/
jeweller's (n) /'dʒuːələz/
music and DVD store (n) /'mjuːzɪk ən diː viː 'diː stɔː/
newsagent's (n) /'njuːzeɪdʒənts/
post office (n) ★★ /'pəʊst ˌɒfɪs/
shoe shop (n) /'ʃuː ˌʃɒp/
sports shop (n) /'spɔːts ˌʃɒp/
stationery shop (n) /'steɪʃən(ə)ri ˌʃɒp/
supermarket (n) ★ /'suːpəˌmɑːkɪt/

Shopping

afford (v) ★★★ /ə'fɔːd/
bargain (n) /'bɑːgɪn/
cashier (n) /kæ'ʃɪə/
changing room (n) /'tʃeɪndʒɪŋ ˌruːm/
checkout (n) /'tʃekaʊt/
credit card (n) ★★ /'kredɪt ˌkɑːd/
debit card (n) /'debɪt ˌkɑːd/
discount (n) /'dɪsˌkaʊnt/
gift (n) ★★ /gɪft/
queue (n) ★ /kjuː/
receipt (n) ★ /rɪ'siːt/
refund (n) /'riːfʌnd/
shelf (n) ★★ /ʃelf/
trolley (n) /'trɒli/

Collocations with *money*

borrow (v) ★★ /'bɒrəʊ/
donate (v) /dəʊ'neɪt/
earn (v) ★★ /ɜːn/
lend (v) ★★★ /lend/
make (v) ★★★ /meɪk/
save (v) ★★★ /seɪv/
spend (v) ★★★ /spend/
waste (v) ★★ /weɪst/
win (v) ★★★ /wɪn/

Other words and phrases

accuse (v) ★★ /ə'kjuːz/
acre (n) /'eɪkə/
advertising campaign (n) /'ædvətaɪzɪŋ kæmˌpeɪn/
apologise (v) ★★ /ə'pɒləˌdʒaɪz/
apology (n) /ə'pɒlədʒi/
bake (v) ★ /beɪk/
balance (n) ★★ /'bæləns/
blame (v) ★★ /bleɪm/
blank (n) /blæŋk/
blockbuster (n) /'blɒkˌbʌstə/
charity (n) ★★ /'tʃærəti/
circumstances (n) ★★ /'sɜːkəmstənsɪz/
colleague (n) ★★ /'kɒliːg/
complain (v) ★★★ /kəm'pleɪn/
complaint (n) ★★ /kəm'pleɪnt/
container (n) ★★ /kən'teɪnə/
demand (n) ★★★ /dɪ'mɑːnd/
dye (n & v) /daɪ/
estate agent (n) /ɪ'steɪt ˌeɪdʒ(ə)nt/
explorer (n) /ɪk'splɔːrə(r)/
faulty (adj) /'fɔːlti/
fit (v) ★★★ /fɪt/
fort (n) /fɔːt/
fur coat (n) /ˌfɜː 'kəʊt/
further (adv & v) ★★★ /'fɜːðə/
go-kart (n) /'gəʊ ˌkɑːt/
hoodie (n) /'hʊdi/
instantaneously (adv) /ɪnstən'teɪniəsli/
invest (v) ★ /ɪn'vest/
lake (n) ★★ /leɪk/
leisure facilities (n) /'leʒə fəˌsɪlətɪz/
let (= a flat) (v) ★★★ /let/
loud (adj) ★★ /laʊd/
meanwhile (adv) ★ /'miːnˌwaɪl/
packaging (n) /'pækɪdʒɪŋ/
perfume (n) /'pɜːfjuːm/
pre-wrapped (adj) /priː'ræpt/
reduction (n) ★★ /rɪ'dʌkʃ(ə)n/
remains (n) /rɪ'meɪnz/
remove (v) ★★★ /rɪ'muːv/
rude (adj) ★ /ruːd/
scent (n) /sent/
shopper (n) /'ʃɒpə/
size (n) ★★★ /saɪz/
smell (n) ★★ /smel/
spray (v) /spreɪ/
subconsciously (adv) /sʌb'kɒnʃəsli/
tandem (= bike) (n) /'tændəm/
transaction (n) /træn'zækʃ(ə)n/
unfurnished (adj) /ʌn'fɜːnɪʃt/
yard (n) ★★ /jɑːd/

Gateway to exams, Units 9–10

amnesia (n) /æm'niːziə/
arrest (v) ★★ /ə'rest/
canoe (n) /kə'nuː/
canoeist (n) /kə'nuːɪst/
drop (= of water) (n) ★ /drɒp/
expire (v) /ɪk'spaɪə/
grow a beard (v) /ˌgrəʊ ə 'bɪəd/
holiday resort (n) /'hɒlɪdeɪ rɪˌzɔːt/
insurance (n) ★★★ /ɪn'ʃʊərəns/
insurance policy (n) /ɪn'ʃʊərəns ˌpɒləsi/
limbo (n) /'lɪmbəʊ/
pretend (v) ★ /prɪ'tend/
reappearance (n) /riːə'pɪərəns/
shock (n) ★★ /ʃɒk/

Study skills

Unit 1

GRAMMAR: Grammatical structures

When we study grammar we need to think about two basic things:

- Firstly, we need to know the meaning and when to use the structure. For example, with the present simple we need to know that we use it to talk about regular habits and routines, permanent situations and scientific facts.
- Secondly, we need to know the form (including spelling). For example, we need to know that we add *-s* to form the third person singular.
- When you have problems with grammar, use reference material to find help. Here are some suggestions:
  - In Gateway, there are grammar explanations in the Grammar reference section at the end of each unit. These explanations help you to understand the correct use of the grammar (when and why to use the grammatical structure) and also the form (how to use the grammatical structure).
  - After reading about the grammar, you can check that you understand it by doing the Grammar revision exercises on the page opposite the explanation. You could try to do the practice exercises first and only look at the explanations when you have a problem.
  - Look at the grammar help on www.macmillanenglish.com/gateway. Other Internet websites can also provide help with typical grammar problems.

Taking active responsibility for your own learning

Each person has strong and weak points when learning a language. These are usually different for each person.

- When you finish an activity, think about the activity type and how well you did. Was the activity easy or difficult? Did you do it well or not? This can help you to identify your own weak points. Once you know what your weak points are, you can look for help to improve in those areas.

Unit 2

VOCABULARY: Learning new vocabulary

- Write down the meaning of new words. You can write a synonym, a definition, an example sentence, a translation, or you could draw a picture.
- Some words are similar in meaning to other words but have significant differences (e.g. *pretty* and *handsome* have similar meanings but *pretty* is usually for girls and women and *handsome* is for men). It is important to make a note of these differences.
- It is also important to write down the type of word (noun, verb, adjective, adverb, preposition, pronoun, etc.) and any other special information (e.g. pronunciation, irregular forms, etc.)
- It is a good idea to learn words in groups. Write down vocabulary in the same groups that appear in this book, e.g. 'Personality', 'Accommodation', 'Transport and travel', etc. One word in a group can help you remember other words in the same group.
- Some people write down new vocabulary using diagrams like this:

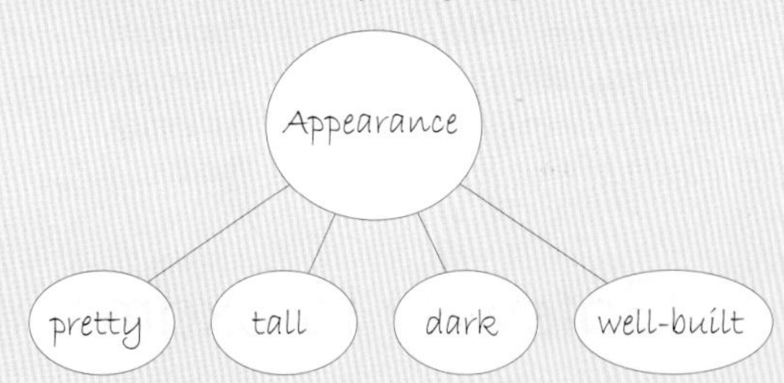

- Frequent revision is the best way to learn new words. Look at your vocabulary notebook or list every week and test yourself to see how much you remember. It is very difficult to learn vocabulary by revising just once before an exam or test.

SPEAKING: Everyday expressions

Here are some ideas for learning useful everyday expressions:

- Keep a note of new expressions in a special section of your notebook.
- Organise these expressions into groups. For example, write down expressions that we use for specific functions (e.g. *Showing understanding*, *Making suggestions*, etc.) or write down expressions that we use in different situations (e.g. *At a station* or *In a clothes shop*).
- The best way to remember everyday expressions is to speak English regularly and use the expressions as much as possible. Also, revise your notes from time to time. Short, frequent revision is the most effective way to learn.

Exercise 6b, page 26

Student A

- Destination: Oxford.
- Journey – out: Tomorrow afternoon around 5 pm
- Journey – return: Saturday

Unit 3

READING: Prediction

Before you read a text, look at the pictures or photos that go with it and read the title of the text. This can help you to think about the topic of the text and to predict some of the ideas and vocabulary in it. In this way, you will understand more when you read the text for the first time.

WRITING: Writing a text in English

Step 1: Read the title or question carefully to make sure you know what you have to write.

Step 2: Brainstorm ideas for the text and write them down as notes.

Step 3: Decide how to organise your notes in a logical way. Group similar ideas into paragraphs.

Step 4: Write the first version of your text.

Step 5: Check and rewrite your work. Check for mistakes with punctuation, capital letters, word order, spelling, tenses, vocabulary, missing words, agreement between the subject and verb etc. Apart from these mistakes, check that you have answered the question. Also, ask yourself if the person reading will understand it easily and find it interesting.

Unit 4

GRAMMAR: Knowing which structure to use

- It is important to know the exact differences between grammatical structures. You can communicate more effectively when you know the exact difference between structures. But the choice is not always between right and wrong.
- Look at this example with different future tenses:

  a *When I'll go out, I think it'll rain.*
  Wrong. Because we use the present simple with *when* when we talk about the future.

  b *It's raining tomorrow.*
  Wrong, because we use the present continuous for confirmed plans and arrangements and this is impossible with the weather.

  c *It's going to rain tomorrow.*
  Possible. A prediction based on evidence, but this evidence may be subjective.

  d *It'll rain tomorrow.*
  Possible. A general prediction, or possibly seeing the future as fact because you are sure it will rain.

VOCABULARY: Prefixes and suffixes

- By adding prefixes to words, we change the meaning of the words (e.g. from positive (*appear*) to negative (*disappear*)). By adding suffixes to words, we can change the form of a word (e.g. from a verb (*appear*) to a noun (*appearance*)).
- Prefixes and suffixes can help us to guess the type or meaning of a word that we have never seen before (e.g. we can guess from *anti*-social that it is 'against' something and we can guess that ela*tion* is a noun). So they can help with reading and listening.
- By using prefixes and suffixes we can expand our active vocabulary very quickly. For example; from *cook*, we can make *undercook*, *overcook*, *pre-cook*, *cookery*, *cooker*, etc. So they can also help us with writing and speaking.

Unit 5

READING: General and specific information

- The first time you read a text, read it quickly. Do not stop if there are words you do not understand. Just try to understand the general meaning. To help, give yourself a time limit the first time you read. It can help you to get a general understanding and not look at details. The first task will usually help you to do this.
- The next task usually checks that you understand specific information. When you read for specific information, read the question carefully and then find the exact place where you think the answer comes from. Read this section again in more detail.

SPEAKING: Spoken and written language

- Spoken language is different from written language. With writing we have more time to plan and prepare what we want to say. We have to be more precise because we cannot see or speak to the person we are writing to. If they do not understand us, we cannot help them.
- When we speak we have less time to prepare and so we sometimes make mistakes. Sometimes we begin a sentence, stop and change or clarify what we are saying. We use expressions like *mmm*, *errr*, *erm*, *the thing is*, *what I mean is*. We use these expressions to give us time to think of what we want to say. Normally, we repeat ourselves more in speaking than in writing.
- When we speak in English we should not worry excessively about making mistakes. We can go back and correct ourselves or clarify what we mean. We should use fillers because they give us thinking-time. We should not worry about repeating ourselves occasionally. All these things are normal elements of speaking, if we are native or non-native speakers.

Unit 6

SPEAKING: Accuracy and fluency

When we talk about speaking, we often use the terms *accuracy* and *fluency*.

- *Accuracy* is used to talk about how correct our use of grammar is when we speak. If we speak quickly in English but we make lots and lots of mistakes it will be difficult for people to understand us.
- *Fluency* is used to talk about how continuously we can speak without stopping to think about what we want to say next. If our use of grammar is perfect but we have to stop frequently to think of what we want to say, then people will get tired of listening to us.
- To speak English well we need to have a balance between accuracy and fluency. To do this we need to practise speaking as much as possible and try to correct any frequent mistakes.

WRITING: Paragraphs

- A paragraph is made up of several sentences which are grouped together. They are grouped together because they talk about, and develop, one main topic.
- Paragraphs help to make your writing more organised and structured. This makes your writing easier to understand. When there are no paragraphs, writing can become confusing and repetitive.
- When you have brainstormed the content of what you are going to write, stop and organise the content into logical paragraphs. You should do this before you start to write, not while you are writing.

Unit 7

PRONUNCIATION: The importance of word stress

- Our main objective when we work on pronunciation is that other people can understand us easily.
- Word stress is an important factor because people usually find it very difficult to understand the word when the stress is not in the correct place.
- Sometimes, word stress changes a word completely e.g. desert – dessert, refuse (= say no) – refuse (= rubbish).
- In English, we do not use accents to show the stress. However, in your vocabulary list/notebook, you can mark the stress to remember where it comes (e.g. basketball).
- In dictionaries word stress is usually marked like this:

  basketball /ˈbɑːskɪtˌbɔːl/ noun **1** [U] a game played by two teams of five players who get points by throwing a ball through a net **2** [C] the ball used in the game of basketball

GRAMMAR: Learning from your mistakes

Mistakes are a natural part of learning but we must work constructively on the mistakes we make in order to improve. Here are some suggestions:

- When you make a lot of mistakes with a structure, check to see if the mistakes are generally with the form, spelling or meaning of the new structure. Find out exactly what the problem is.
- If you don't understand something, ask your teacher for help, use your notes or use the Grammar Reference section in this book.
- When you think you understand better, look for more exercises in your Workbook (or on www.macmillanenglish.com/gateway or on the CD ROM) and see if you do better the second time.

Unit 8

READING: Deducing the meaning of new words

- In reading exams you cannot usually use dictionaries. When there are new words in a text, you can often find out something about the words by looking at the context.
- Look at the words that come just before or after. They will probably tell you if the word is a noun, verb, adjective, etc.
- By looking at the words and sentences around the new word, you can probably deduce something about the meaning (e.g. if it is a positive thing or a negative thing, if it is a word connected with a particular topic, etc.)
- Sometimes, you may not understand the exact meaning, but the context often gives you at least an approximate idea.
- Another strategy is to look for any prefixes or suffixes. Prefixes can help you guess the meaning of the word (e.g. *re* tells you it is doing an activity *again*). Suffixes can tell you the type of word (e.g. a word ending in *-ion* will be a noun).
- Is the word a compound (a word made up of two or more words)? If it is, do you know the meaning of one of the words?
- Look at the word and think if there is a similar word in your language.

LISTENING: Staying calm and positive

- When you are listening to English and there is a section you do not understand, stay positive. If you stop listening or if you get nervous and panic, you won't understand anything more.
- Remember that, usually, it is not necessary to understand every word in order to do a task well. When you get lost, look at the next question or two and listen out for words or ideas associated with the question(s).
- Usually in exams you can listen to the text twice. If there are things you do not understand the first time, stay calm and listen for them in the second listening.

Unit 9

VOCABULARY: Remembering words

Our memory usually works better if:

- we remember words in groups.
- we use or revise them frequently.
- we use them in a personal context – spoken or written.
- words look or sound similar to other words.
- the words are unusual for some reason.
- we are interested in the topic that the words are connected to.

Remember to:

- write down new words in groups.
- revise frequently.
- use the new words when you speak or write.

SPEAKING: Thinking of what to say

If it's your turn to speak and you can't think of what to say, use this advice:

- Use fillers to give yourself time to think of what you are going to say next (e.g. *Err, The thing is, Well, You know…*).
- Use language of speculation (*It might be, I'm not sure, I think,* etc.)
- Use the questions *What? Who? Where? Why? When?* etc. to think of ideas for something to say.
- If you are worried because you don't know a word, think of similar words, more basic or general words, or explain the word.

Unit 10

Reflection and forward-planning

At the end of the year, it is useful to reflect on what you have studied, learnt and practised during the year. Identify the things that you can now do very well, quite well, or not very well. Decide how you can work in the future on the things you don't know or can't do very well. Think of people or materials that can help. Make a plan of action for the holidays or next year.

WRITING: Improving your writing

Here are some ways that you can improve your writing:

- Make a note of your mistakes when you get corrected essays or reports back from your teacher. Look at these notes just before you write your next essay or report.
- Always have a plan before you write. Know what you are going to write before you start.
- Remember to group ideas into paragraphs.
- If you aren't sure how to write something, simplify it. Clarity is one of the most important criteria when writing.
- Make sure you know what style (e.g. formal, informal) you should be using.
- Use appropriate tenses.
- Check your writing carefully when you finish. Have you answered the question? Are there any obvious mistakes? Have you made any basic spelling mistakes? Is it easy to understand the ideas and information in your text? Is your handwriting clear?
- Remember – practice makes perfect!

Exercise 6b, page 26

Student B

Oakham

- Tomorrow: 5.30 pm
- Change at London St Pancras and Leicester, arrive 8.45 pm
- Single fare: 52.60
- Return fare: 55.60
- Cash or credit card possible
- Platform 4

Oxford

- Tomorrow: 4.15 pm
- Change at London Victoria, underground from London Victoria to London Paddington, train from London Paddington to Oxford, arrive 6.40 pm
- Single fare: 27.30
- Return fare: 30
- Cash or credit card possible
- Platform 4

Oxford

- Tomorrow: 5.25 pm
- Change at London Victoria, underground from London Victoria to London Paddington, train from London Paddington to Oxford, arrive 7.50 pm
- Single fare: 25.30
- Return fare: 28
- Cash or credit card possible
- Platform 7

Exam success

Unit 1

READING: True/false

In this type of activity you decide if statements are true or false depending on the information in the text.

Step 1: Read the text quickly to get a general understanding.

Step 2: Read the statements that you need to prove true or false.

Step 3: Find the parts of the text where you think the information comes from. Read them again in more detail.

Step 4: If there is no information to say if a sentence is true, mark the statement false.

Step 5: When you finish, check that you have an answer for each question. Never leave answers blank in an exam.

LISTENING: Identifying the speaker

In this type of activity, you match different speakers with the things they say.

Before you listen:

- think about the topic of what you are going to listen to. Think of words that could appear in the listening text.
- read the questions. This can help you to know how many speakers there are and what they may say. It also helps you to concentrate more while you listen.

While you listen:

- remember that what the speakers say may have the meaning as in the questions, but use different words or expressions.
- don't worry if you don't understand everything the first time you listen. Usually you listen twice. Use the second listening to find the answers you didn't hear the first time and to check the answers you already have.

After you listen:

- check that you have an answer for each question. Never leave answers blank in an exam.

Unit 2

SPEAKING: Conversation

- Make sure you know what the situation is. Check that you know the specific information that you need to ask for and give. Your mark usually depends on how well you give or ask for the information in the task.
- If you don't understand what the examiner or your partner says, ask them in English to repeat or to speak more slowly. Use expressions like: *Sorry, can you say that again?* or *Sorry, could you speak more slowly?*
- Listen to your partner and to the examiner. In a conversation we speak and listen.
- Show that you're interested in what the other person is saying. Use expressions like: *Really? That's interesting. Do you? Me too.*
- Use *Well, Hmm* or *Let me think* to give you time to think of what you want to say next.
- Use basic question words like *Who? What? When? Where? How? Why?* to help you think of more questions to keep the conversation going.

WRITING: Checking your work

It is normal to make mistakes when you write. That is why it is so important to read your work carefully when you finish. Check for mistakes with:

- punctuation
- capital letters
- word order
- spelling
- tenses
- vocabulary
- missing words
- agreement between the subject and verb

Apart from these mistakes, check that you answer the question and that you include all of the information that is asked for. Make sure that the style is appropriate and the content is relevant and interesting. The checking stage is almost as important as the writing stage.

Page 100 Exercise 3 The Ireland Quiz

1 What is a common name for Ireland?
The Emerald Isle

2 Which is part of the United Kingdom?
Northern Ireland

3 What is the capital of Northern Ireland?
Dublin

4 What appears on the Irish Euro coins?
A harp

5 What colour is the Republic of Ireland flag?
Green, white and orange

6 Why did so many Irish people emigrate in the nineteenth century?
Because there was not enough food.

7 Which famous rock band is from Ireland?
U2

8 What is another name for traditional Irish dancing?
Step dancing

Unit 3

READING: Missing sentences

In this type of exercise, you have to find the best place to put different sentences taken from a text. The sentences are often the first in each paragraph and there are sometimes more sentences than spaces.

Step 1: Read the text to get a general idea of the overall meaning. To do this type of exercise it is not usually necessary to understand every word, so do not panic if you don't understand everything.

Step 2: Read the missing sentences and identify the key information. What is the sentence about? Do you remember anything connected with this topic when you read the text for the first time? Look again at this part of the text in more detail.

Step 3: Try each sentence in the most probable space and read again. Is the meaning logical? Do words like *this* or *it* make sense?

Step 4: When you finish, check that you have an answer for each question. Never leave answers blank in an exam.

USE OF ENGLISH: Multiple-choice cloze

In this type of exercise, you have to complete a text by choosing which answer best fits a space.

Step 1: Read the text to get a general idea of the overall meaning. Do not worry about the gaps at first.

Step 2: Read the text more carefully and try to predict which word is missing from each gap.

Step 3: Look at the alternatives. Is one of them the same as the word you predicted?

Step 4: Look very carefully at the words which come just before and just after the space. Do they help you to decide?

Step 5: If you aren't sure which answer is right, think about why other answers are definitely wrong and eliminate them.

Step 6: When you finish, check that you have an answer for each question. Never leave answers blank in an exam.

Unit 4

SPEAKING: Negotiating

In negotiating activities, you usually work with another person. The examiner explains a situation where you and the other speaker need to come to a decision.

- It is important that neither of you dominates the conversation or is silent. The examiner will usually help you to do this. But remember to take turns and help your partner to speak if you think you are speaking too much or if your partner is not speaking enough.
- In this type of exercise, remember that there isn't usually a right or wrong answer. However, you should make sure that you come to some type of decision by the end of the activity. Above all, the examiner wants to hear you speaking English.

WRITING: Transactional tasks

- Transactional writing tasks are ones where the instructions tell you who you are writing to and what information to include. When a question asks you to put specific information in your text, you lose marks if you do not include the information. You can use your imagination but you must remember to include all the information from the instructions.
- When you write letters, invitations, messages and notes it is essential to write in the correct style. When you write to a friend, use contractions and informal expressions. When you write a formal or semi-formal letter, invitation, message or note, do not use contractions or informal language. If your letter is grammatically correct but not in the correct style, you lose marks.

Unit 5

USE OF ENGLISH: Cloze activities

In this type of activity, you have a text with gaps. You must fill each gap by thinking of a word which is grammatically correct and is logical.

Step 1: Read the complete text without thinking about the gaps. This is to get a general understanding of the text.

Step 2: Look again at the gaps and especially the words which come just before and after the gap. Do those words need a special preposition? Is an article or auxiliary verb missing? Think about the type of word missing (noun, verb, pronoun, article, etc.) and the general meaning. The missing words in cloze activities will often be prepositions, articles, pronouns, auxiliary verbs, modal verbs, and conjunctions (*and*, *but*, *although*, etc).

Step 3: Fill in the gap with the word that you think is best. Read the sentence again with your answer in the gap. Sometimes there is more than one possible answer but you only need to put one.

Step 4: When you finish, check that you have one answer for each question. Never leave answers blank in an exam.

WRITING: Following the instructions

In writing exams, you must be careful to answer the question and follow the instructions exactly. Before you start writing, check that you know the answers to these questions:

- Who are you writing to or for?
- Is there a word limit? In some exams you may get no marks if you write too many words or not enough words.
- Do you know what information is relevant to include? For example, if you write about the plot of a film, but not your opinion, this is not a film review.
- Is there a paragraph plan to follow? Do you have to write a specific number of paragraphs? Do you have to begin or finish your composition in a specific way?

Unit 6

READING: Matching

In this type of activity, you have to say which text or part of a text contains a piece of information.

Step 1: Read all the texts or parts of the text quickly to get a general understanding.

Step 2: Read the piece(s) of information that you need to find. Are there are any special words that help you to find the text or part of the text which contains the information? Remember that, in the text, the same information will probably be expressed in different words.

Step 3: Read the specific text or part of the text where you think the information comes from again in more detail.

Step 4: If you are not sure that you have found the correct answer, read other sections again in more detail.

Step 5: When you finish, check that you have an answer for each question. Never leave answers blank in an exam.

LISTENING: Multiple-choice

In this type of activity, you choose the best answer from three or four different answers.

You usually hear the text twice. The questions are usually in the order that you hear them in the recording.

Step 1: Read the different answers before you listen. They can give you ideas about the topic of the text and the vocabulary you are going to hear in it. Remember that, sometimes, the difference between two answers is just one word.

Step 2: When you listen, remember that you may hear the correct answer but expressed in different words. You may also hear a word or words that come in one of the possible answers, but this does not mean it is the correct answer. The word(s) may be there just to distract you.

Step 3: You usually hear the recording twice. Do not worry if you do not understand information the first time. If you don't hear the answer to one question, start listening immediately for the answer to the next question.

Step 4: Use the second listening to find the answers you didn't hear the first time and to check the answers you already have.

Step 5: When you finish, check that you have an answer for each question. Never leave answers blank in an exam.

Unit 7

LISTENING: True/false

In this type of activity, you have to listen and decide if statements are true or false. You usually hear the text twice. The statements are usually in the order that you hear them in the recording.

Step 1: Read the answers before you listen. They can give you ideas about the topic of the text and the vocabulary you are going to hear in it.

Step 2: You can usually hear the recording twice. Do not worry if you do not understand information the first time. If you don't hear the answer to one question, start listening immediately for the answer to the next question.

Step 3: Use the second listening to find the answers you didn't hear the first time and to check the answers you already have.

Step 4: When you finish, check that you have an answer for each question. Never leave answers blank in an exam.

SPEAKING: Giving presentations

Look at this advice for giving good presentations:

- Make notes with the information you want to give in your presentation and use them when you are giving it; but don't just read your notes aloud.
- Look at your audience. See if they understand you and are interested.
- Don't speak too fast. If you speak too quickly, people will not be able to follow you.
- Try to speak for exactly the right amount of time. The more you practise, the easier it will become.
- Use intonation to show that you are interested and to make others interested.
- Don't worry excessively about vocabulary. When you don't know a word, explain it or use a simpler word.
- Don't let mistakes stop you from speaking. Correct your own mistakes if possible, or start the sentence again, but don't stop completely.

Unit 8

SPEAKING: Reporting past events

In some speaking exams, you have to talk about something that you did in the past.

Before the exam, make sure you know:

- as many regular and irregular past forms as possible.
- when and how to use the past simple, past continuous and past perfect.
- words and expressions to explain the order of events (e.g. *First, Then, Next, In the end …*).

During the exam, make sure you:

- understand and answer the question the examiner asks you.
- ask the examiner or your partner in English to repeat or to speak more slowly if they say something that you don't understand. Use expressions like: *Sorry, can you say that again?* or *Sorry, could you speak more slowly?*
- use fillers like *Well, Hmm* or *Let me think* to give you time to think of what you want to say next.
- use basic question words like *Who? What? When? Where? How? Why?* to help you to think of more things to say.

WRITING: Thinking about the reader

We write in different ways depending on who and how many people we are writing to. Usually in writing exams, you will get more marks if you write in an appropriate way for the task. Always read the instructions carefully and check that you know exactly who you are writing to. Write in the correct style for that reader. Ask yourself if the person reading will understand it easily. Will they find it interesting, informative, useful or exciting (depending on the task)?

Unit 9

USE OF ENGLISH: Word formation cloze

In this type of activity, you must use the word given in capitals to form a word that fits in the gap. The words can be any type: noun, adjective, adverb, verb, etc.

Step 1: Read the text once quickly to get a general understanding.

Step 2: Look at the words just before and after the gap. They can help you to decide what type of word is missing. Usually, to change the type of word, you will need a suffix (e.g. *-ion* to make a noun, *-ly* to make an adverb).

Step 3: Look at the words just before and after the gap and make sure you understand the whole sentence. This will help you to decide if you need to change the meaning of the word (e.g. making it negative). Usually, to change the meaning of the word, you will need a prefix (e.g. *im-*, *re-*).

Step 4: Read the completed sentence and check your answer. Check that you have an answer for each question. Never leave answers blank in an exam.

WRITING: Timing yourself

Some people have a problem finishing on time in writing exams. Follow this advice to stop this problem.

- Make sure you know how many pieces of writing you have to do, and how much time you have to do them.
- Keep looking at the time to check that you are following your schedule.
- Decide if you need, or have time, to write a rough version. Make sure you leave enough time to write up the final version. Don't write the final version so quickly that you make a lot of new mistakes.
- If you don't know how to write something, don't spend a long time thinking about it. Change or simplify what you were going to write.

Unit 10

GENERAL: Doing well in exams

To do well in English exams, think about these tips.

- Make sure you know what type of tasks and exercises will appear in your exams. If you are familiar with these types of exercises, they will become easier. If you have problems with a type of exercise, practise!
- In grammar and vocabulary exams, make sure you know what topics and grammar are tested so that you study the relevant structures and words.
- You should spend more time practising the things that you find difficult than the things you find easy.
- Revise frequently a long time before the exam. It is very difficult to revise English just before the exam.
- Read the instructions and questions carefully, and make sure you do what they say or ask.
- Write carefully and clearly.
- Don't leave answers blank.
- Check your exam carefully before giving it in.

SPEAKING: Doing well in oral exams

To get a good mark in a speaking exam, follow this advice:

- Make sure that what you say is relevant to the question(s) that the examiner asks you.
- If you don't understand the examiner's questions or instructions, ask them to repeat.
- Speak! If you are too nervous or shy, the examiner won't be able to give you a good mark. Relax and remember that the examiner is on your side.
- Speak loudly and clearly so that the examiner can hear you.
- Don't write complete answers before you speak. React to what the examiner or your partner(s) are saying.
- Practise speaking as much as you can before the exam.

Speaking bank

General

Showing you understand

I see.
OK.
That's great.
Right.
Really?

Checking understanding

Pardon?
Could you repeat that, please?
Sorry, I didn't catch that.
Sorry, I missed that.
Sorry, can you say that again?
Sorry, could you speak more slowly?
Sorry, did you say…?
I'm not sure I understood.

Question tags

You're Australian, ***aren't you?***
This is your book, ***isn't it?***
You play the guitar, ***don't you?***
You don't agree, ***do you?***
You can speak German, ***can't you?***

Showing interest

Really?
That's interesting.
That's incredible!
I see.
Do you?
Me too.

Filling the conversation

Errr…
Well…
The thing is…
I'm not (really/totally/completely) sure but…
Maybe…
You know…
I think…
I imagine…
It looks like…
I imagine that…
Let me think.
What do you think?

When you don't know a word

It's like/similar to…
It's the opposite of…
It's when you…

Common situations

Giving opinions

Personally, …
I think (that)…
I don't think (that)…
I'm convinced that…
I don't really know if…
In my view…
In my opinion…
As I see it…

Asking for opinions

What do you think?
What's your opinion/view?
Do you agree?
What about you?

Agreeing or partially agreeing

I (totally) agree (with you) (that…)
I agree to an extent (that…)
That's true.
You're right.
You've got a point.
I take your point.
I see what you mean.

Disagreeing or partially disagreeing

I (totally) disagree (with you) (that…)
I agree to an extent, but…
That's true, but…
You've got a point, but…
I take your point, but…
I see what you mean, but…
I'm not sure that's true.
But what about…?

Making suggestions

Do you fancy (coming)?
Why don't we (have lunch together)?
How about (going tomorrow afternoon)?
Let's (do something).

Accepting suggestions

Yes, I'd love to.
Great!
OK.
Why not?
Fine.
Yes, let's.
Good idea.

Rejecting suggestions

Sorry, I can't.
I prefer to (stay in).

Asking for help

Would you mind (helping to prepare some food)?
Could you give me a hand (buying some food)?
Could you help me to (tidy up)?

Offering to help

Would you like any help?
How can I help?
Can I help you?
Do you want me to (do the shopping)?
Shall I (clean up) for you?
How about if I (do the invitations) for you?

Accepting offers of help

Thanks!
That would be great!

In a shop: The shop assistant

Can I help you?
What size are you?
How about this/these?
What seems to be the problem?
We can replace it.
Sorry about that.

In a shop: The customer

Yes, I'm looking for…
No, thanks. I'm just looking.
Have you got anything in blue/green/medium/large?
I like it/them.
I'll take this one/these.
Can I bring it back?
I'd like to make a complaint.
It's the wrong size.
It's faulty.
Can I have a refund?

Describing a photo

Starting

In the picture I can see…
The picture shows…
This is a picture of…

Position

In the foreground
In the background
At the top of the picture
At the bottom of the picture
In the middle of the picture
On the right
On the left
In the top/bottom right/left corner

Speculation and deduction

I think
I imagine
(It) must be
(It) may/might/could be
(It) can't be
(He/She/It/They) is/are probably
(It) is probably
It seems that
(It) looks as if/like
I'm not sure but
(It) must have been
(It) may/might/could have been
(It) can't/couldn't have been

Giving a presentation

Beginning a presentation

I'd like to begin by saying…
I'm going to talk about…

Introducing arguments

Firstly,
First of all,
Secondly,
Another thing is that…
It's also true that…
Furthermore,
What's more,

Giving examples

For example,
For instance,
Look at the case of…
Concluding,
Finally,
To sum up,
Last but not least,
The point I'm trying to make is…
In short,

Talking about the past

Expressions of time and sequence

At first
First
First of all
Next
Then
Suddenly
Later
A few seconds/minutes/hours/days later
After ten minutes/half an hour/a while
After that
Finally
In the end

Pronunciation guide

Vowels

/ɑː/	arm, large
/æ/	cap, bad
/aɪ/	ride, fly
/aɪə/	diary, science
/aʊ/	how, mouth
/aʊə/	our, shower
/e/	bed, head
/eɪ/	day, grey
/eə/	hair, there
/ɪ/	give, did
/i/	happy, honeymoon
/iː/	we, heat
/ɪə/	ear, here
/ɒ/	not, watch
/əʊ/	cold, boat
/ɔː/	door, talk
/ɔɪ/	point, boy
/ʊ/	foot, could
/u/	annual
/uː/	two, food
/ʊə/	sure, tourist
/ɜː/	bird, heard
/ʌ/	fun, come
/ə/	mother, actor

Consonants

/b/	bag, rubbish
/d/	desk, cold
/f/	fill, laugh
/g/	girl, big
/h/	hand, home
/j/	yes, young
/k/	cook, back
/l/	like, fill
/m/	mean, climb
/n/	new, want
/p/	park, happy
/r/	ring, borrow
/s/	say, this
/t/	town, city
/v/	very, live
/w/	water, away
/z/	zoo, his
/ʃ/	shop, machine
/ʒ/	usually, television
/ŋ/	thank, doing
/tʃ/	cheese, picture
/θ/	thing, north
/ð/	that, clothes
/dʒ/	jeans, bridge

Writing bank

Informal emails

page 15 (Unit 1)

Start: *Hi*

Style: Use contractions and the short form of words (e.g. *Thanks*, not *Thank you*). Use interjections like *Oh* and *Well*. We can also use exclamation marks and emoticons (e.g. ☺).

Useful expressions: To begin, ask questions like *How are you? How are things? Are you doing exams/on holiday at the moment?* Use *By the way* or *Anyway* to change the subject.

End: *That's all for now, Write back soon, All the best.*

Informal letters

page 41 (Unit 3)

Start: Write your address and the date in the top right corner. Then we write *Dear* or *Hi* and the name (not surname) of the person you are writing to.

Style: Use contractions and the short form of words (e.g. *Thanks*, not *Thank you*). Use interjections like *Oh* and *Well*. Use exclamation marks.

Useful expressions: Begin *Thanks for your last letter, It was great to hear from you* or *I'm writing to tell you about....* Ask questions like *How are you?, How are things?, Are you doing exams/on holiday at the moment?*. Use *By the way* or *Anyway* to change the subject.

End: *Write back soon, That's all for now, All the best.*

Descriptions

page 15 (Unit 1)
page 41 (Unit 3)

Style: Adjectives are important to make our descriptions interesting.

Useful expressions: In descriptions, we often use the verb *look*. We can use *look + adjective* (e.g. *He looks* __________.), *look like + noun/pronoun* (e.g. *It looks like* __________.), *look like/as if + noun/pronoun + verb* (e.g. *She looks as if* __________.).

Useful vocabulary: To describe people, see the vocabulary on page 6. To describe places, see the vocabulary on page 32.

Useful grammar:

1 We use modifying adverbs to make adjectives stronger or softer in order to give more accurate descriptions. For example, we use *very, extremely* and *really* to make 'normal' adjectives (e.g. *good, bad*) stronger. We use *totally, absolutely, really* and *completely* to make 'extreme' adjectives (e.g. *fantastic, awful*) stronger. We use *quite* and *rather* to make 'normal' adjectives a little softer.

2 To make descriptions more interesting, use *so + adjective* or *such + (adjective) + noun*, e.g. *It was so beautiful, He's such a great friend.*

Postcards

page 27 (Unit 2)

Start: Write the name and address of the person you are writing to on the right. On the left, write *Dear* or *Hi* and the name (not surname) of the person you are writing to. You can also write the date if you want.

Style: Informal. Use contractions and the short form of words (e.g. *Thanks*, not *Thank you*). Use interjections like *Oh* and *Well*. Use exclamation marks.

Useful expressions: Begin *Here we are in ..., We're having a great/good/terrible time*. Use *By the way* or *Anyway* to change the subject.

Useful grammar: Here are some ways of giving emphasis to what we write, to make our writing more interesting.

1 Use *What + (adjective) + noun!* e.g. *What a place! What a beautiful day!*

2 Use *so + adjective* or *such + (adjective) + noun*, e.g. *It was so beautiful. It's such a big building.*

3 Use *do* and *did* in affirmative sentences, e.g. *We do have tickets for the plane. They did come in the end.*

End: *See you soon, Wish you were here, All the best, Best wishes, Love.*

Content: Use these questions for ideas of what to write:

- Where are you?
- Where are you staying?
- When did you get there?
- Did anything good or bad happen during your journey?
- How did you get there?
- What is the place like? Are you very happy there? Why/Why not?
- What did you do yesterday?
- What are your plans for the next few days?

Informal invitations and replies

page 53 (Unit 4)

Start: *Dear* or *Hi...*

Style: Use contractions and the short form of words (e.g. *Thanks*, not *Thank you*). Use exclamation marks.

Useful expressions: In invitations: *Please come, I'd love to see you there.* In replies: *Thanks for the invitation* and *I'm really sorry but I/we won't be able to come* (when you can't accept the invitation).

End: In invitations: *Hope to see you there! Hope you can make it!* In replies: *All the best, Best wishes*

Content: In invitations: say what the event is and why you are celebrating it. Say where and when it will take place. Say if people need to bring something or to confirm if they are coming. In replies: if you can't go, give a reason.

Formal invitations and replies

page 53 (Unit 4)

Start: *Dear Mr/Mrs/Ms*

Style: Do not use contractions.

Useful expressions: In invitations: *We request the pleasure of your company.* In replies: *Thank you very much for your kind invitation* and *We regret to say that we will be unable to attend* (when you can't accept the invitation).

End: In invitations: *RSVP* (which means that you want people to confirm if they are accepting the invitation). In replies: *Best wishes* and *We wish you all the best and will be thinking of you* (when you can't accept the invitation).

Content: In invitations: say what the event is and why you are celebrating it. Say where and when it will take place. Say if people need to bring something or confirm if they are coming. In replies: if you can't go, give a reason.

A *for* and *against* essay

page 79 (Unit 6)

Style: Formal. Do not use contractions.

Useful vocabulary: *advantage, disadvantage*

Useful linkers: Introducing and sequencing arguments: *Firstly, Secondly, Finally*. Adding arguments: *Furthermore, What's more, In addition*. Making contrasts: *On the one hand…, On the other hand…, In contrast, However, but, although, Nevertheless.* Consequence: *Therefore, and so, As a result.* Reason: *because, as, since.* Opinions: *In my opinion, Personally I think…, As far as I'm concerned.* Concluding: *In conclusion, To sum up.*

Content: Suggested paragraph plan

- Paragraph 1: State the topic of the essay using general statements
- Paragraph 2: Make points for (or against)
- Paragraph 3: Make points against (or for)
- Paragraph 4: Conclusion – restate the most important arguments and give your own opinion

Formal letters

page 67 (Unit 5) page 131 (Unit 10)

Start: Write your address and the date in the top right corner. Write the address of the person you are writing to a little lower, on the left. Then write *Dear Mr (Smith)* (for a man), *Dear Mrs (Smith)* (for a married woman), or *Dear Ms (Smith)* (when we make no distinction if a woman is married or not). When we do not know the name of the person we are writing to, we write *Dear Sir or Madam.*

Style: Do not use contractions.

Useful expressions in applications: Begin *I am writing to apply for…* or *I am writing in response to the advertisement in…* Use *I believe I would be perfect for this (scholarship/job) because…, I would be grateful to receive the chance to (study/work) in your (university/company).* Use *I believe* (instead of *I think*), *I would be very grateful* (instead of *I'd like*). End *I look forward to receiving your reply*, or *I look forward to hearing from you.*

Useful expressions in letters of complaint: Begin *I am writing to complain about…* Use *I demand (a refund/replacement/apology), If I do not hear from you (in the next two weeks), I will take my complaint to a Consumer Advice Centre.* Use *I believe* (instead of *I think*), *I would be very grateful* (instead of *I'd like*). End *I look forward to receiving your reply*, or *I look forward to hearing from you.*

Useful linkers: Consequence: *Therefore, and so, As a result.* Time and sequence: *Firstly, Next, Then, In the end.* Contrast: *but, although, However, Nevertheless.* Reason: *because, as, since.* Addition: *In addition, What is more, Furthermore.*

End: When we know the name of the person we are writing to, use *Yours sincerely.* When we don't know the name of the person we are writing to, use *Yours faithfully.*

Content in applications: Begin by saying what you are applying for. Explain why you would be good for this position. Mention any experience you have. Give details of some of your strengths that make you a good candidate.

Content in letters of complaint: Begin by explaining why you are writing. Say where and when the problem began. Give details of the complaint. Demand a solution. Say what action you will take if there is no solution.

A film review

page 93 (Unit 7)

Useful vocabulary: Films: *happy ending, main character, play the role of, plot, scene, screenplay, special effects, the acting, to star*. Positive adjectives to describe films: *amazing, exciting, funny, hilarious, great, inspiring, interesting, spectacular*. Negative adjectives to describe films: *awful, boring, stupid, uninspiring*. Types of film: *action, animated film, comedy, drama, fantasy, horror, musical, science fiction, thriller, war, western*.

Useful expressions: To give your opinions, use *Personally, I think, As far as I'm concerned, In my opinion, I agree/disagree with…* To explain and justify your opinions, use *This is because, For example*. To give recommendations: *I would/wouldn't recommend you to see this film because…* To give a conclusion, use *To sum up, In conclusion*.

Useful grammar:

1 We use modifying adverbs to make adjectives stronger or softer in order to give more accurate descriptions. For example, we use *very*, *extremely* and *really* to make 'normal' adjectives (e.g. *good, bad*) stronger. We use *totally*, *absolutely*, *really* and *completely* to make 'extreme' adjectives (e.g. *fantastic, awful*) stronger. We use *quite* and *rather* to make 'normal' adjectives a little softer.

2 To make descriptions more interesting, use *so + adjective* or *such + (adjective) + noun*, e.g. *It was so beautiful, He's such a great friend.*

Content: Suggested paragraph plan

- Paragraph 1: Basic information about the film
- Paragraph 2: A summary of the plot or story
- Paragraph 3: Your opinion of the film
- Paragraph 4: A recommendation to see the film

Stories, narratives and anecdotes

page 119 (Unit 9)

Useful expressions: To say when things happened use, for example: *Last weekend, Two weeks ago, On Friday, On Saturday night.*

Useful linkers: To explain the sequence of events use *At first, First of all, Next, Then, After that, Later, Suddenly, Finally, In the end.*

Useful grammar: Narrative tenses

1 Past simple. We use it to tell the main events and actions in the story.

2 Past continuous. We use it to describe scenes, to say what activity was in progress when another interrupted it.

3 Past perfect. We use it for the background of the story, to talk about actions that happened before other actions in the past.

4 *used to*. We use it to talk about past habits.

5 *must/may/might/can't have*. We use these to make speculations or deductions about what happened.

Content: Suggested paragraph plan:

- Paragraph 1: Explain where and when the story begins. Introduce the characters.
- Paragraphs 2 and 3: Explain the main events in the story.
- Paragraph 4: Explain how the story ended and what the consequences were.

An announcement

page 105 (Unit 8)

Style: Use short, clear sentences. Make the announcement easy, fast and interesting to read. Begin each new idea on a new line, with a bullet (•) or dash (–). Use exclamation marks.

Start: Have a slogan or a title which attracts attention.

End: Use *For more information, call/contact…*

Content: Say what the event is that you are announcing. Include all the practical information that a reader needs to know, for example:

- What the event is.
- What you want from people.
- When you want it.
- If there are any prizes.
- When the event is.
- Who can be in the event.
- What people should do if they want more information.

Checking your writing

All units

Check for mistakes with:

- punctuation
- capital letters
- word order
- spelling
- tenses
- vocabulary
- missing words
- agreement between the subject and verb (e.g. ~~He go.~~)
- style
- content

Irregular verbs

Infinitive	Past simple	Past participle
be	was/were	been
beat	beat	beaten
become	became	become
begin	began	begun
break	broke	broken
bring	brought	brought
build	built	built
burn	burnt	burnt
buy	bought	bought
catch	caught	caught
choose	chose	chosen
come	came	come
cost	cost	cost
cut	cut	cut
do	did	done
draw	drew	drawn
drink	drank	drunk
drive	drove	driven
eat	ate	eaten
fall	fell	fallen
feel	felt	felt
find	found	found
fly	flew	flown
forget	forgot	forgotten
forgive	forgave	forgiven
get	got	got
give	gave	given
go	went	gone
grow	grew	grown
hang out	hung out	hung out
have	had	had
hear	heard	heard
hide	hid	hidden
hit	hit	hit
hurt	hurt	hurt
keep	kept	kept
know	knew	known
lay	laid	laid
leave	left	left
learn	learned/learnt	learned/learnt

Infinitive	Past simple	Past participle
let	let	let
lie	lay	lain
lose	lost	lost
make	made	made
mean	meant	meant
meet	met	met
pay	paid	paid
put	put	put
read	read	read
ride	rode	ridden
ring	rang	rung
run	ran	run
say	said	said
see	saw	seen
sell	sold	sold
send	sent	sent
set up	set up	set up
shine	shone	shone
shoot	shot	shot
show	showed	shown
sing	sang	sung
sit	sat	sat
sleep	slept	slept
speak	spoke	spoken
speed	sped	sped
spell	spelt	spelt
spend	spent	spent
split up	split up	split up
stand up	stood up	stood up
steal	stole	stolen
swim	swam	swum
take	took	taken
teach	taught	taught
tell	told	told
think	thought	thought
understand	understood	understood
wake up	woke up	woken up
wear	wore	worn
win	won	won
write	wrote	written

Macmillan Education
Between Towns Road, Oxford OX4 3PP
A division of Macmillan Publishers Limited
Companies and representatives throughout the world

ISBN 978-0-230-72350-4
ISBN 978-0-230-41763-2 (plus Gateway Online)

Page make-up by right on the line limited, eMC Design Ltd
Illustrated by Fred Blunt (pp46, 129), Milivoj Ceran (p101), James Field (p25), Vince Fraser (pp8, 45, 50l), Jim Hansen (pp21, 52, 71, 133), Javier Joaquin (pp103, 104), Peter Lubach (pp17, 38, 39), Gustavo Mazali (p88), Ed McLachlan (pp98, 116r, 117), Julian Mosedale (p124), ODI (p23), right on the line limited (pp60, 84), Martin Sanders (pp35, 70, 77), and Simon Williams (pp11, 50r, 75). Illustrations (p59) from Stella Cottrell, The Study Skills Handbook, published 1999, Macmillan Publishers Limited, reproduced with permission of Palgrave Macmillan.
Cover design by Andrew Oliver.
Cover photos by Brand X, Image Source, PHOTODISC, Science Library / James King-Holmes; Science Photo Library / Mehau Kulyk.
Cover photographs by Brand X, Getty/Thomas Kelly-Mooney Photography, Image Source, Science Photo Library/Mehau Kulyl

Author's acknowledgements
I would like to thank the whole Macmillan team in Oxford for their dedication and hard work during the creation of this book. A big thanks also to all the students that I have had the pleasure of teaching at Colegio Europeo Aristos, Getafe and to my colleagues there. Finally, writing this book would not have been possible without the support of my wonderful family. All my love and thanks to Gemma, Jamie and Becky.

The publishers would like to thank all of those who reviewed or piloted Gateway: Benjamin Affolter, Evelyn Andorfer, Anna Ciereszynska, Regina Culver, Anna Dabrowska, Ondrej Dosedel, Lisa Durham, Dagmar Eder, Eva Ellederovan, H Fouad, Sabrina Funes, Luiza Gervescu, Isabel González Bueno, Jutta Habringer, Stela Halmageanu, Andrea Hutterer, Nicole Ioakimidis, Mag. Annemarie Kammerhofer, Sonja Lengauer, Gabriela Liptakova, María Cristina Maggi, Silvia Miranda Barbara Nowak, Agnieszka Orlińska, Anna Orlowska, María Paula Palou Marta Piotrowska, N Reda, Katharina Schatz, Roswitha Schwarz, Barbara Ścibor, Katarzyna Sochacka, Joanna Spoz, Marisol Suppan, Stephanie Sutter, Halina Tyliba, Prilipko, Vladyko, Pia Wimmer, Katarzyna Zadrożna-Attia, and Katarzyna Zaremba-Jaworska.

The authors and publishers would like to thank the following for permission to reproduce their photographic materials:
AKG/ North Wind Picture Archives p24(b); **Alamy/** imagebroker p12(5), Alamy/ A ROOM WITH VIEWS p18(lc), Alamy/ Roger Lee p18(ld), Alamy/ Alex Segre p18(ra), Alamy/ Peter Schneiter p18(rb), Alamy/ David Colbran p18(rc), Alamy/ Chris Howes/Wild Places Photography p18(rd), Alamy/ Charles Stirling p18(re), Alamy/ Bjanka Kadic p18(rf), Alamy/ Kumar Sriskandan p27(m), Alamy/ Paul Thompson Images p32(ta), Alamy/ David Gee 1 p32(e), Alamy/ keith morris p32(tc), Alamy/ Doug Houghton p32(tf), Alamy/ adam eastland p32(bb), Alamy/ Imagestate Media Partners Limited - Impact Photos p40(tr), Alamy/ Kuttig - People – 2 p64(a), Alamy/ Ian Shaw p64(b), Alamy/ Adrian Muttitt p66(l), Alamy/ ScottyH p122(a), Alamy/ T.M.O.Buildings p122(b and e), Alamy/ CuboImages srl p122(c), Alamy/ Julio Etchart p122(d), Alamy/ Retro Kitsch p123(bl), Alamy/ Greg Balfour Evans p126, Alamy/ david pearson p128, Alamy/ geogphotos p131(t), Alamy/ Oleksiy Maksymenko 2 p135(tr); **Ardea/** M. Watson p12(a), Ardea/ Jean-Michel Labat p12(c and e), Ardea/ Valerie Taylor p65(bl), Ardea/ Duncan Usher p117; **BANANASTOCK** p109; **BRAND X** pp10(t), 18(lb), 40(mr), 49(b), 77, 86(tl); **Camera Press/** PHOTOGRAPH BY RUKHSANA HAMID, CAMERA PRESS LONDON p115; **COMSTOCK IMAGES** pp44(c), 70(a); **Corbis/** Hoch Zwei/Juergen Tap/NewSport p6(t), Corbis/ Jim Craigmyle p12(1), Corbis/ ImageShop p12(3), Corbis/ MAPS.com p24(t), Corbis/ Martin Ruetschi/Keystone p30, Corbis/ Simon Marcus p38(b), Corbis/ RD / Dziekan / Retna Digital /Retna Ltd. p65(br), Corbis/ BBC p74(bl), Corbis/ Waltraud Grubitzsch/epa p82, Corbis/ Greg Fiume p85(l), Corbis/ Paul J. Sutton/PCN p89(t), Corbis/ Chen Xiaowei/Xinhua Press/ p91, Corbis/ Salvador Dali, Gala-Salvador Dali Foundation / Artists Rights Society (ARS), New York p99, Corbis/ René Mattes/Hemis p100(t), Corbis/ Robbie Jack p100(b), Corbis/ MOHAMED MESSARA/epa p110(c), Corbis/ BBC TV GRAB/ epa p110(r), Corbis/ Andrew Holbrooke p119, Corbis/ Turba p129(l), Corbis/ Mika p135(l); **CORBIS** pp14, 40(br), 73; **DIGITAL STOCK** p110(a); **DIGITALVISION** pp12(d), 61(b), 62; **Getty/** Ron Levine p12(2), Getty/ Image Source p12(4), Getty/ Win Initiative p15(t), Getty/ Blend Images/Dave and Les Jacobs p15(b), Getty/ Hola Images p31, Getty/ Richard Nowitz p32(bc), Getty/ Siegfried Eigstler p38(t), Getty/ Thomas Kelly - Mooney Photography p63, Getty/ Amwell p64(d), Getty/ Jen Fong p65(bm), Getty/ Philip and Karen Smith p66(br), Getty/ AFP p71, Getty/ AFP p72, Getty/ AFP p74(t), Getty/ SM/AIUEO p74(br), Getty/ Clive Brunskill p84, Getty/ Supernova p86(tr), Getty/ Jun Tsukuda / Aflo p86(br), Getty/ AFP p89(b), Getty/ Popperfoto p90(r), Getty/ ColorBlind Images p92(r), Getty/ AFP p97(a), Getty/ Barcroft Media via Getty Images p110(d), Getty/ AFP p114(b), Getty/ WireImage p118(l), Getty/ Brand X Pictures p125, Getty/ Michael Blann p129(r), Getty/ Nicole Hill p130; GETTY pp13(3, 6 and 7), 9, 23, 78(r), 96, 109, 110(b), 118(tr and br), 123(t and br); **IMAGE SOURCE** pp10(b), 13(5 and 8), 18(rg), 32(BD), 34(t), 40(l), 65(t), 66(tr), 79(b); **MACMILLAN/** Haddon Davies p70(d); **MACMILLAN/** David Tolley pp44(a), 102(b); **Mary Evans Picture Library** p116; **PHOTODISC** pp13(2), 70(c); **Photolibrary/** Christian Hütter p12(b), Photolibrary/ Steve Belkowitz p13(1), Photolibrary/ Thomas Schneider p18(ta), Photolibrary/ Mark & Audrey Gibson p27(t), Photolibrary/ Stéphane Hubert p32(ba), Photolibrary/ John Maclean p34(b), Photolibrary/ George Coppock p44(b), Photolibrary/ Alberto Paredesp64(c), Photolibrary/ Günter Flegar p79(tl), Photolibrary/ Mike Kemp p79(tr), Photolibrary/ Trevor Lush p86(bl), Photolibrary/ Keith Levit p112; **PIXTAL** p32(tb); **Reuters/** Nir Elias p33; **Rex Features/** Greg Allen p6(b), Rex/ Peter Brooker p6(m), Rex/ David Magnus p11(t), Rex/ Rory Gilder p19, Rex Features pp49(t), 51, 56, 85(r),92(l) and 134, Rex/ SHOUT p61(t), Rex/ Ray Tang p86(l), Rex/ Caters News Agency Ltd p97(b), Rex/ Nils Jorgensen p97(c), Rex/ White House/Rex Features p113(b), Rex/ WestEnd61 p114(t), Rex/ NBCUPHOTOBANK p131(b); **Robert Harding World Imagery/** Ethel Davies pp27(b) and 41; **Science Photo Library/** VOLKER STEGER p7, SPL/ JAMES KING-HOLMES p76, SPL/ MEHAU KULYK p78(l), SPL/ ARTHUS BERTRAND p78(m); **STOCKBYTE** pp13(4), 21, 32(td), 70(b); **SUPERSTOCK** pp37(b), 113(t); **The Bridgeman Art Library/** A Royal Game of Tennis in the Jeu de Paume, Versailles, published by Charles Hulpeau (engraving) (b/w photo) by French School, (16th century) Private Collection p90(l), The Bridgeman Art Library/ The Bay, 1963 (acrylic on canvas), Frankenthaler, Helen (b.1928) / Detroit Institute of Arts, USA / Founders Society Purchase, Dr & Mrs Hilbert H. DeLawter Fund p102(t), The Bridgamen Art Library/ Bibliothèque Nationale, Paris, France/ Lauros / Giraudon p111(t), The Bridgeman Art Library/ Medallion Portrait of Louis-Charles (1785-95) King Louis XVII of France (oil on canvas) by Kucharski, Alexandre (1741-1819)/ Chateau de Versailles, France/ Giraudon p111(m), The Bridgeman Art Library/ The Temple (engraving) by French School, (19th century) /Private Collection/ Ken Welsh p111(b); **The Picture Desk/** 20TH CENTURY FOX/ALLIED STARS/ENIGMA / THE KOBAL COLLECTION p93(l), The Picture Desk/ SATURN FILMS / THE KOBAL COLLECTION p93(ml), The Picture Desk/ PARAMOUNT / THE KOBAL COLLECTION p93(mr), The Picture Desk/ TOUCHSTONE / THE KOBAL COLLECTION p93(r); **TopFoto/** Topham Picturepoint p10(m).

Macmillan Readers cover image:
I, Robot, cover image by Alamy/I.Glory

The authors and publishers would like to thank the following for permission to reproduce the following copyright material:
Robbie Cooper for details about Avatars, reproduced with permission;
W.W. Norton & Company, Inc. and Stuart Krichevsky Literary Agency for an extract from *The Perfect Storm* by Sebastian Junger. Copyright © 1997 by Sebastian Junger. Reprinted by permission of W.W. Norton & Company, Inc. and Stuart Krichevsky Literary Agency, Inc.;
Penguin Books for an extract adapted from *The Rough Guide to Switzerland*, 3/ed, by Matthew Teller, Rough Guides 2000, 2006, copyright © Matthew Teller, 2006 ;
Extract from "Welcome to China's Thames Town" by Clifford Coonan copyright © The Independent 2006, first published in *The Independent* 14.08.06, reprinted by permission of the publisher;
Pollinger Limited for the poem *"This is just to say"* by William Carlos Williams, 1934. Reproduced by permission of Pollinger Limited and New Directions;
Extract from "Yakutsk: Journey to the coldest city on Earth" by Shaun Walker, copyright © The Independent 2008, first published in *The Independent* 21.01.08, reprinted by permission of the publisher;
Material and illustrations adapted from *The Study Skills Handbook* by Stella Cottrell, copyright © Third Edition 2008, by permission of the author and Palgrave Macmillan;
The Open University for an extract about *The Open University*, reproduced with permission;
Improbable Research for details about The Ig® Nobel Prizes adapted from http://improbable.com/ig, reproduced with permission;
Science Museum for details about *The British Science Museum* www.sciencemuseum.org.uk, copyright © Board of Trustees of the Science Museum;
Random House, Inc. and HarperCollins Publishers for an extract from "Robbie" from *I, Robot* by Isaac Asimov, copyright © 1950 by Isaac Asimov. Used by permission of Bantam Books, a division of Random House, Inc. and by permission of HarperCollins Publishers Ltd;
Extract from 'Teenage pupils deserve 11am lie-in' by Paul Gallagher copyright © Paul Gallagher 2009, first published in *The Guardian* 08.03.09, reprinted by permission of the publisher;
David Grossman Literary Agency Ltd for an extract from *Small Island* by Andrea Levy, published by Headline Book Publishing, reprinted by permission of David Grossman Literary Agency;
Blueco for details about *Bluewater Shopping Centre* from www.bluewater.co.uk, reproduced with permission;
Buy Nothing Day for details adapted from www.buynothingday.co.uk, reproduced with permission;
If I Had a $1,000,000 – Words and Music by Stephen Page and Ed Robertson copyright © Tret Baker Music, USA Warner/Chappell Music Limited, London W6 8BS 1993, reprinted by permission of International Music Publications Limited. All Rights Reserved;
She's Leaving Home – Words and Music by Lennon and McCartney, copyright © 1967 Northern Songs Limited, reprinted by permission of Sony/ATV Music Limited.

Dictionary extracts taken from Macmillan Essential Dictionary copyright © Macmillan Publishers Limited 2003 and Macmillan English Dictionary 2nd Edition copyright © Macmillan Publishers Limited 2007

Printed and bound in Thailand

2016 2015 2014 2013
12 11 10 9 8 7 6 5 4